TUNE

W

DEREK KIRK KIM

BOOK 1
VANISHING POINT

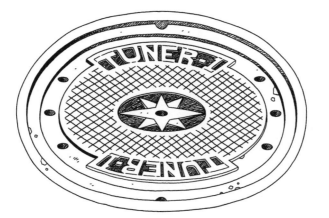

First Second

NEW YORK

First Second

Special thanks to Michael Stupin

Published by First Second
First Second is an imprint of Roaring Brook Press, a division of Holtzbrinck Publishing Holdings Limited Partnership
175 Fifth Avenue, New York, New York 10010

Library of Congress Cataloging-in-Publication Data

Kim, Derek Kirk.
Tune: vanishing point / Derek Kirk Kim – 1st ed.
p. cm.
ISBN 978-1-59643-516-2 (pbk.)
1. Graphic novels. I. Title.
PN6727.K487T86 2012
741.5'973–dc23
2012011400

First Second books are available for special promotions and premiums.
For details, contact: Director of Special Markets, Holtzbrinck Publishers.

FIRST EDITION

First Edition 2012
Book design by Ananth Panagariya
Printed in United States of America

10 9 8 7 6 5 4 3 2 1

BY ART WE LIVE

CHAPTER
01

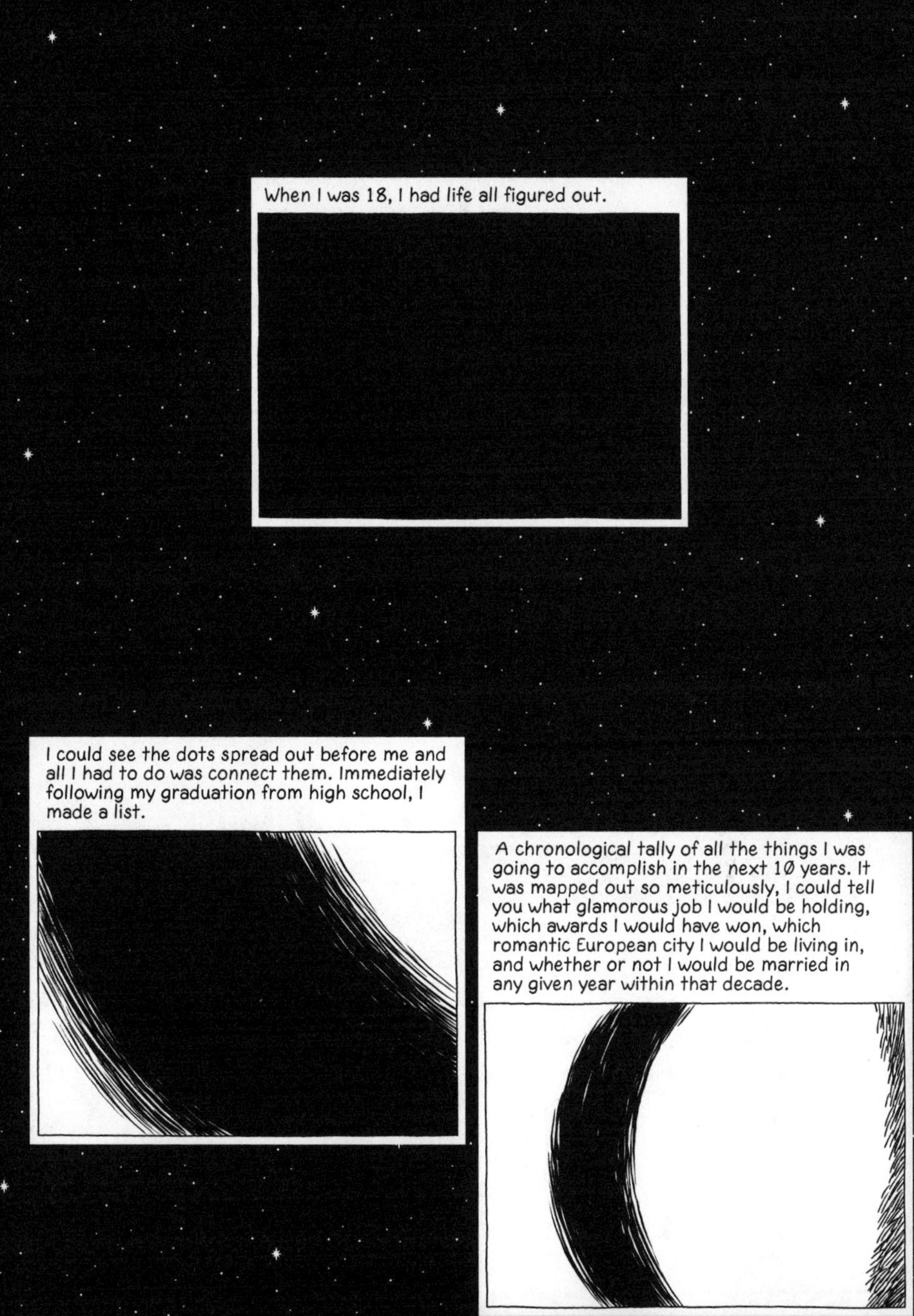
When I was 18, I had life all figured out.
I could see the dots spread out before me and all I had to do was connect them. Immediately following my graduation from high school, I made a list.
A chronological tally of all the things I was going to accomplish in the next 10 years. It was mapped out so meticulously, I could tell you what glamorous job I would be holding, which awards I would have won, which romantic European city I would be living in, and whether or not I would be married in any given year within that decade.

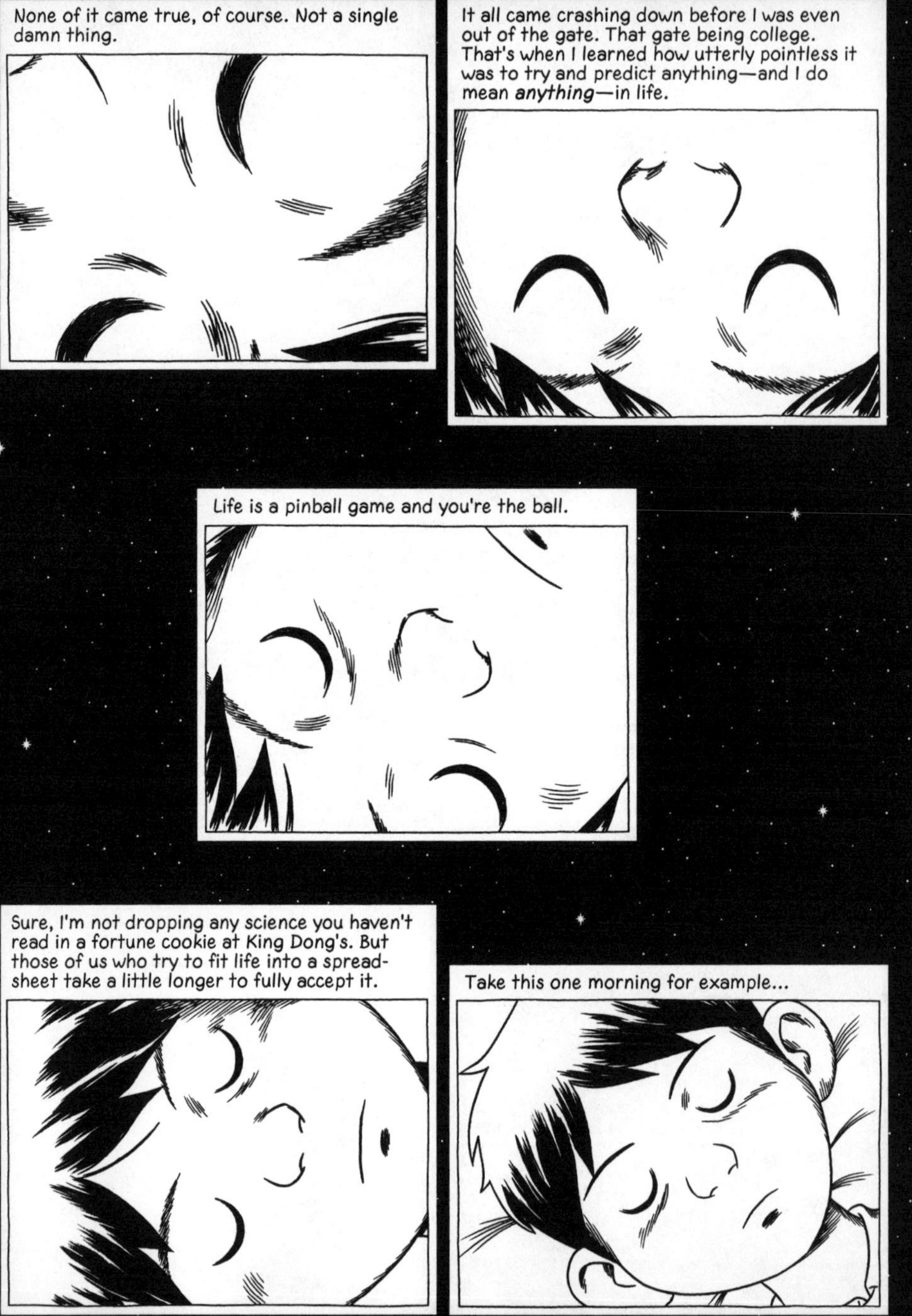
None of it came true, of course. Not a single damn thing.
It all came crashing down before I was even out of the gate. That gate being college. That's when I learned how utterly pointless it was to try and predict anything—and I do mean *anything*—in life.
Life is a pinball game and you're the ball.
Sure, I'm not dropping any science you haven't read in a fortune cookie at King Dong's. But those of us who try to fit life into a spread-sheet take a little longer to fully accept it.
Take this one morning for example...

I was in the deepest sleep of my life. I don't think I had that much trouble opening my eyes since I was born.

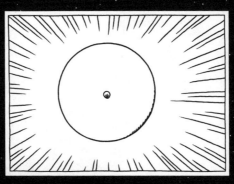

Being an OCD slave to routine, it was extremely odd for me to have fallen asleep with the light on.

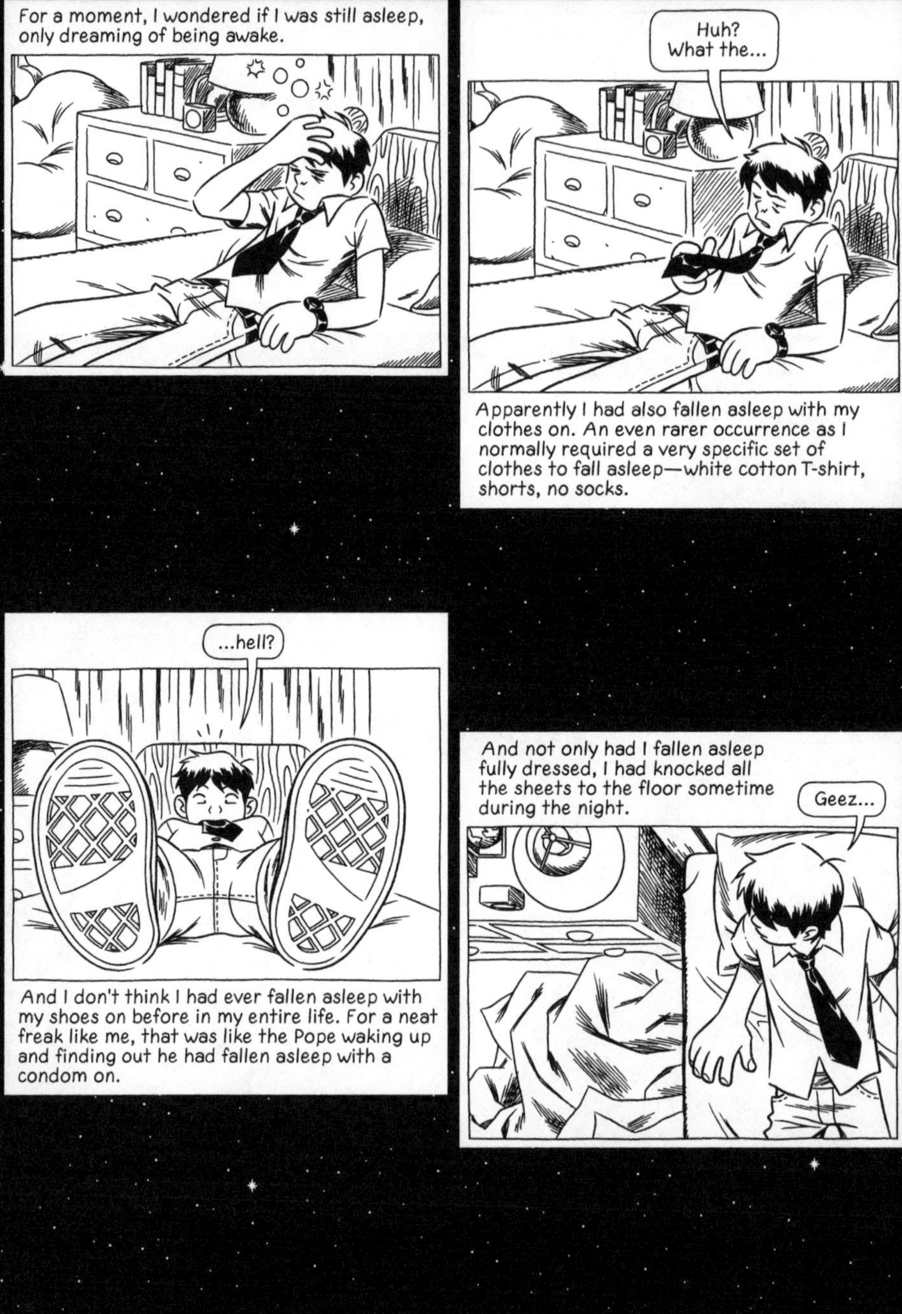
For a moment, I wondered if I was still asleep, only dreaming of being awake.
Huh? What the...
Apparently I had also fallen asleep with my clothes on. An even rarer occurrence as I normally required a very specific set of clothes to fall asleep—white cotton T-shirt, shorts, no socks.
...hell?
And I don't think I had ever fallen asleep with my shoes on before in my entire life. For a neat freak like me, that was like the Pope waking up and finding out he had fallen asleep with a condom on.
And not only had I fallen asleep fully dressed, I had knocked all the sheets to the floor sometime during the night.
Geez...

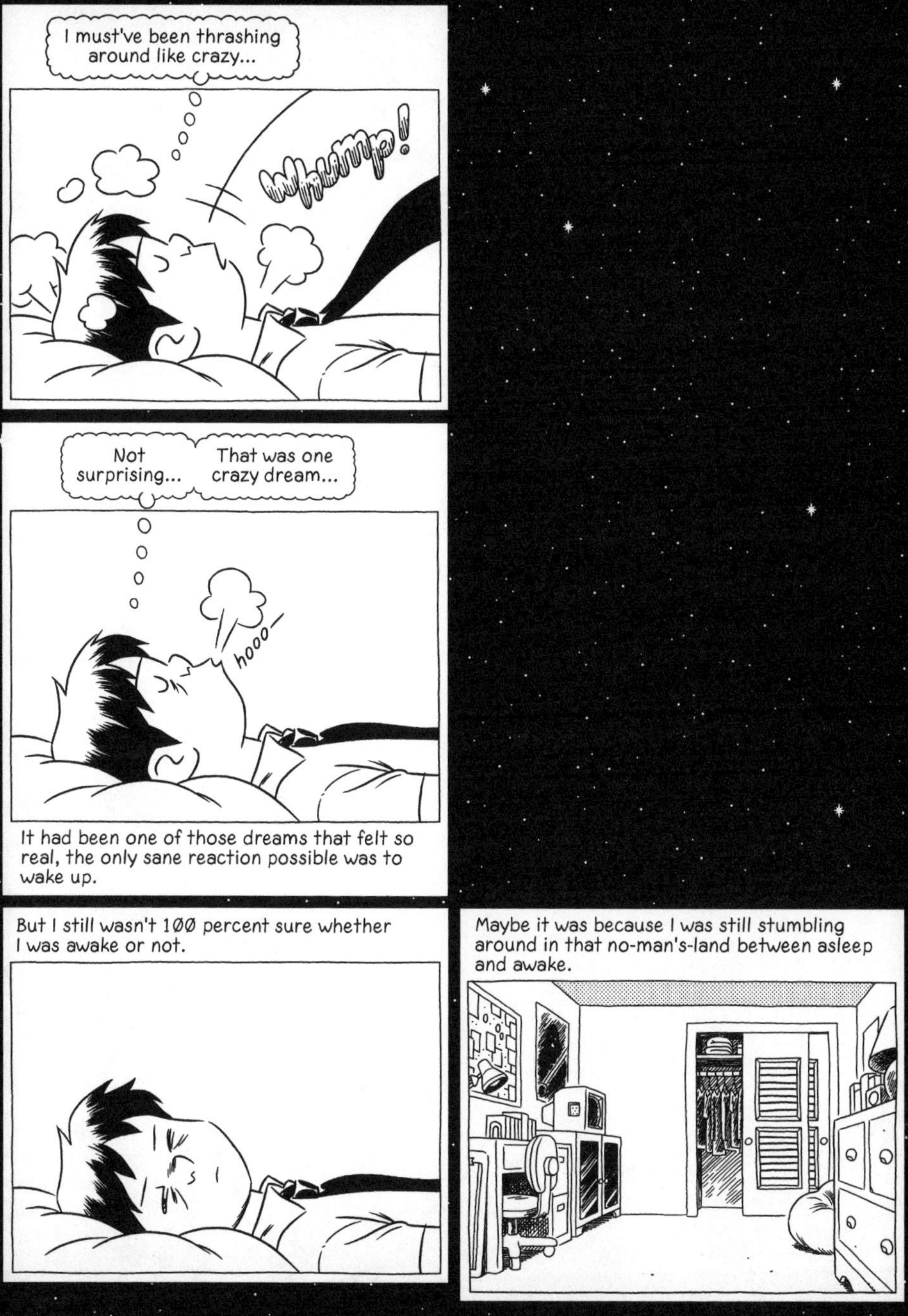
I must've been thrashing around like crazy...
Whump!
Not surprising...
That was one crazy dream...
hooo-
It had been one of those dreams that felt so real, the only sane reaction possible was to wake up.
But I still wasn't 100 percent sure whether I was awake or not.
Maybe it was because I was still stumbling around in that no-man's-land between asleep and awake.

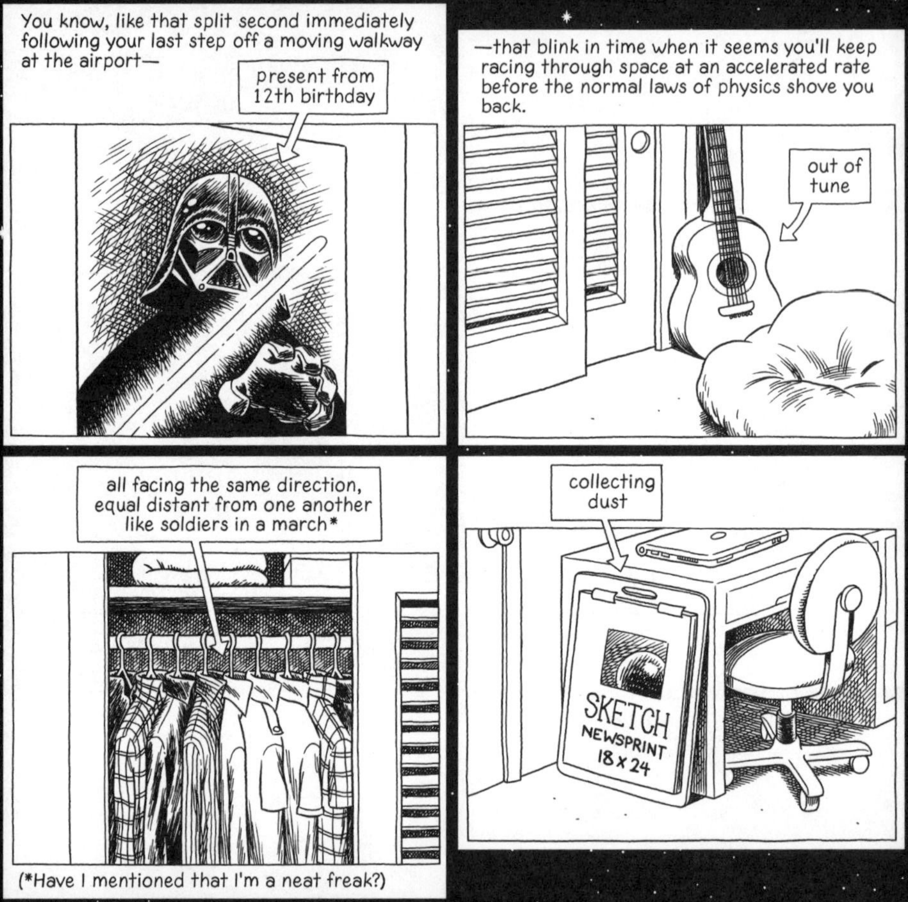
You know, like that split second immediately following your last step off a moving walkway at the airport—
present from 12th birthday
—that blink in time when it seems you'll keep racing through space at an accelerated rate before the normal laws of physics shove you back.
out of tune
all facing the same direction, equal distant from one another like soldiers in a march*
(*Have I mentioned that I'm a neat freak?)
collecting dust
SKETCH
NEWSPRINT
18 x 24

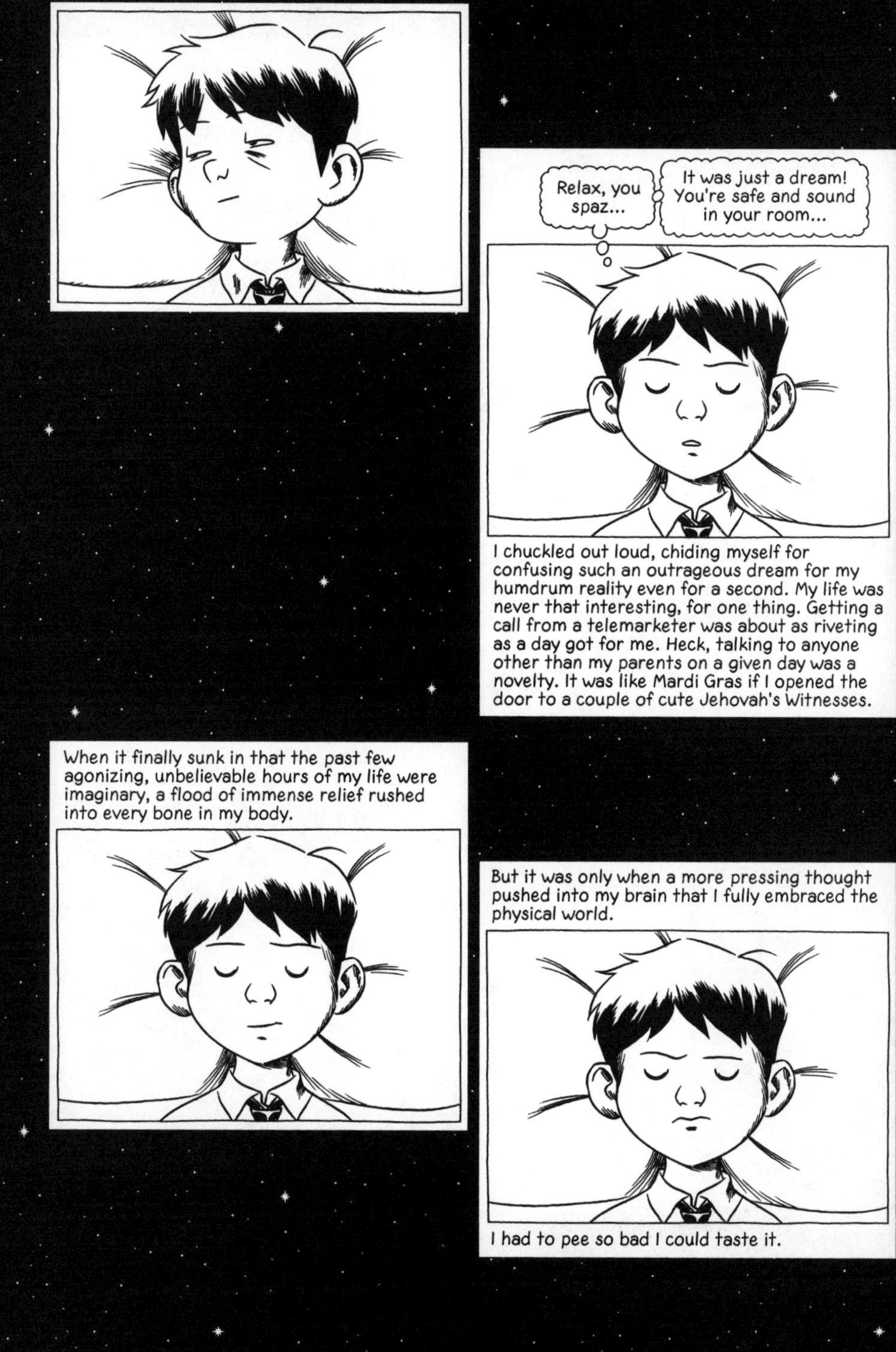
Relax, you spaz...
It was just a dream! You're safe and sound in your room...
I chuckled out loud, chiding myself for confusing such an outrageous dream for my humdrum reality even for a second. My life was never that interesting, for one thing. Getting a call from a telemarketer was about as riveting as a day got for me. Heck, talking to anyone other than my parents on a given day was a novelty. It was like Mardi Gras if I opened the door to a couple of cute Jehovah's Witnesses.
When it finally sunk in that the past few agonizing, unbelievable hours of my life were imaginary, a flood of immense relief rushed into every bone in my body.
But it was only when a more pressing thought pushed into my brain that I fully embraced the physical world.
I had to pee so bad I could taste it.

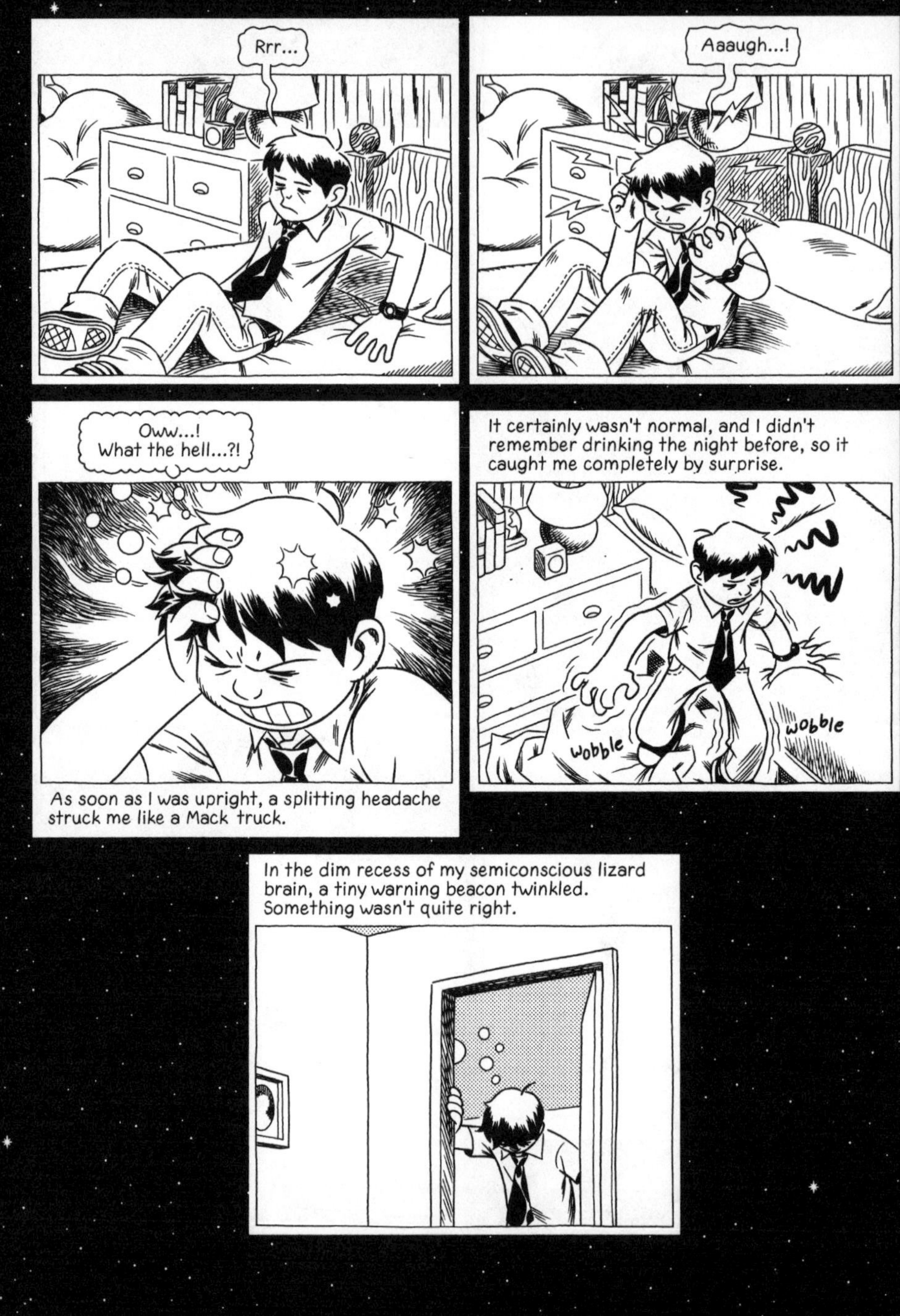
Rrr...
Aaaugh...!
Oww...! What the hell...?!
As soon as I was upright, a splitting headache struck me like a Mack truck.
It certainly wasn't normal, and I didn't remember drinking the night before, so it caught me completely by surprise.
wobble
wobble
In the dim recess of my semiconscious lizard brain, a tiny warning beacon twinkled. Something wasn't quite right.

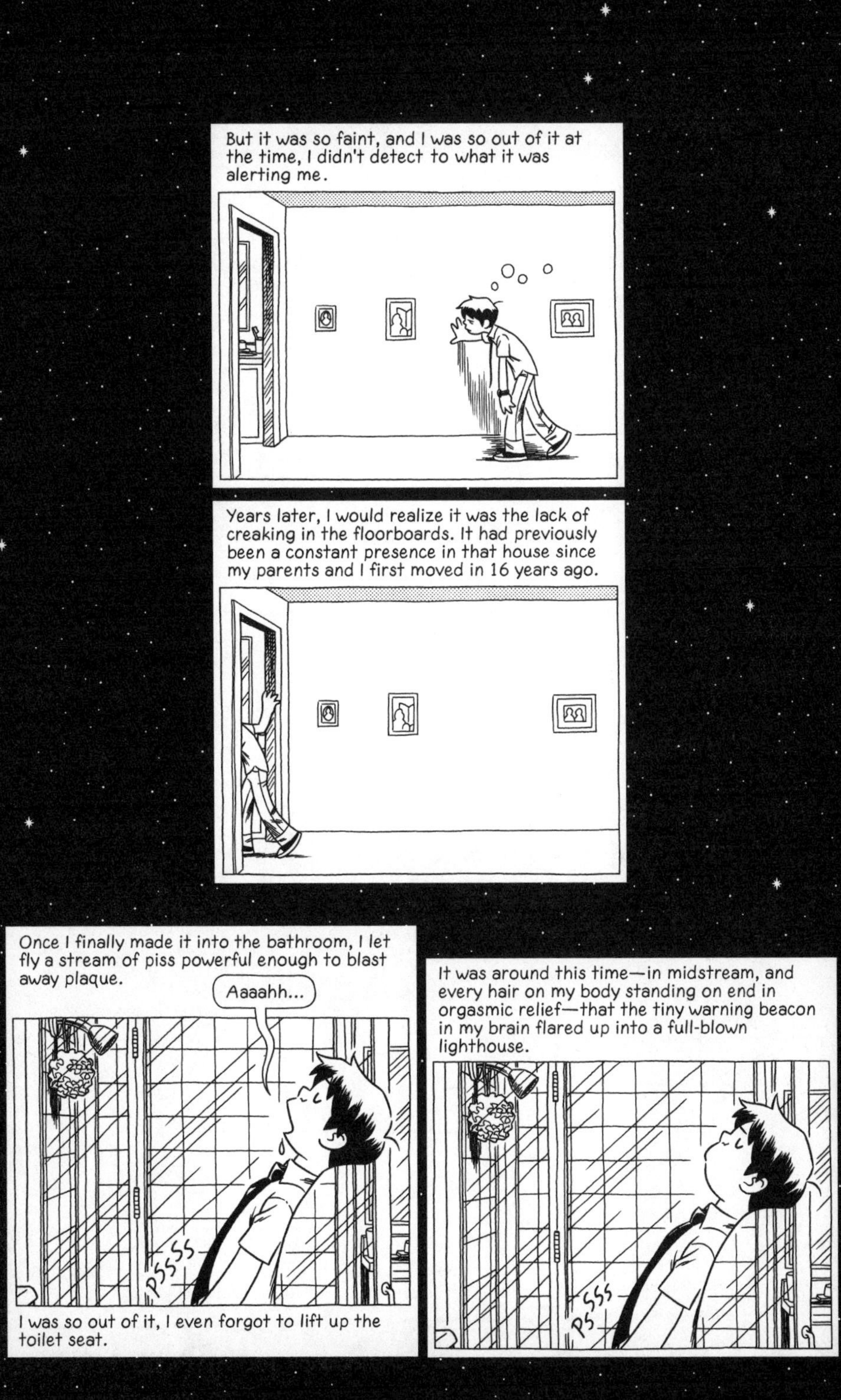

But it was so faint, and I was so out of it at the time, I didn't detect to what it was alerting me.
Years later, I would realize it was the lack of creaking in the floorboards. It had previously been a constant presence in that house since my parents and I first moved in 16 years ago.
Once I finally made it into the bathroom, I let fly a stream of piss powerful enough to blast away plaque.
Aaaahh...
PSSSS
I was so out of it, I even forgot to lift up the toilet seat.
It was around this time—in midstream, and every hair on my body standing on end in orgasmic relief—that the tiny warning beacon in my brain flared up into a full-blown lighthouse.
PSSSS

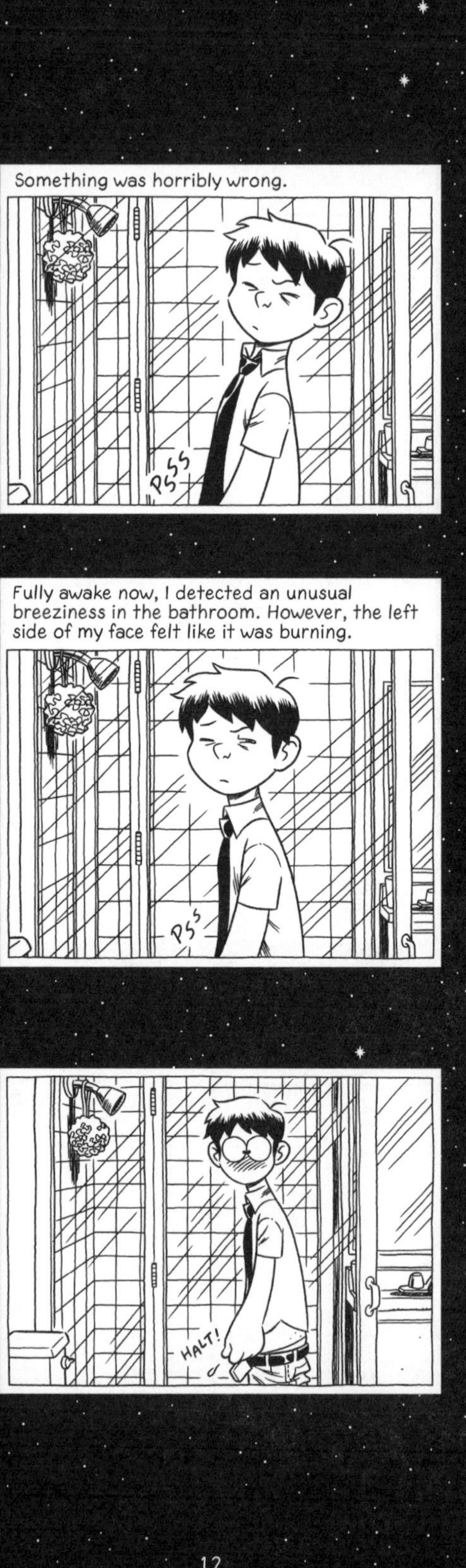
Something was horribly wrong.
PSSS
Fully awake now, I detected an unusual breeziness in the bathroom. However, the left side of my face felt like it was burning.
PSS
HALT!

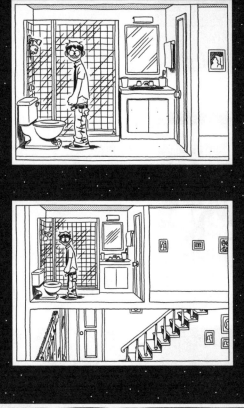

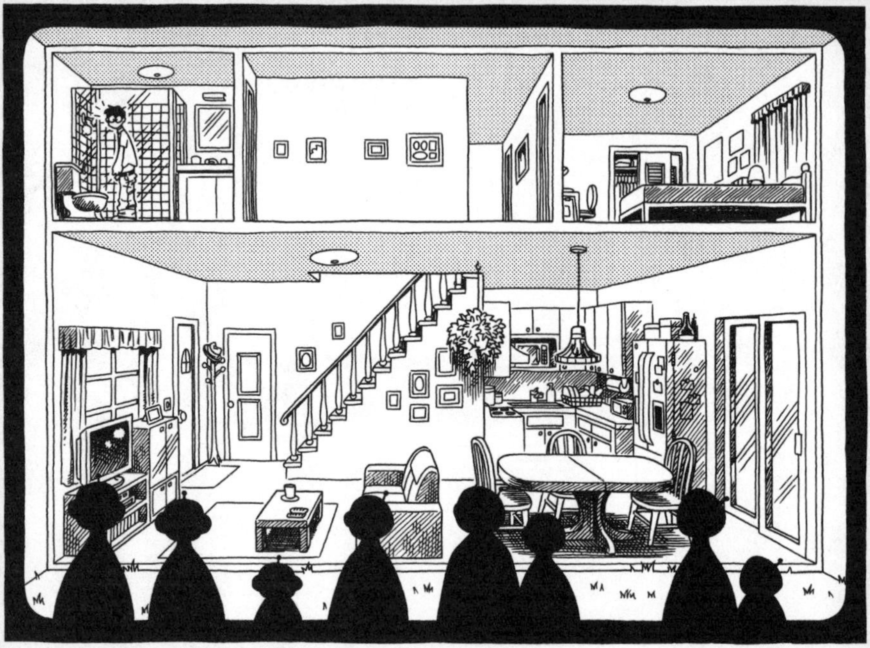

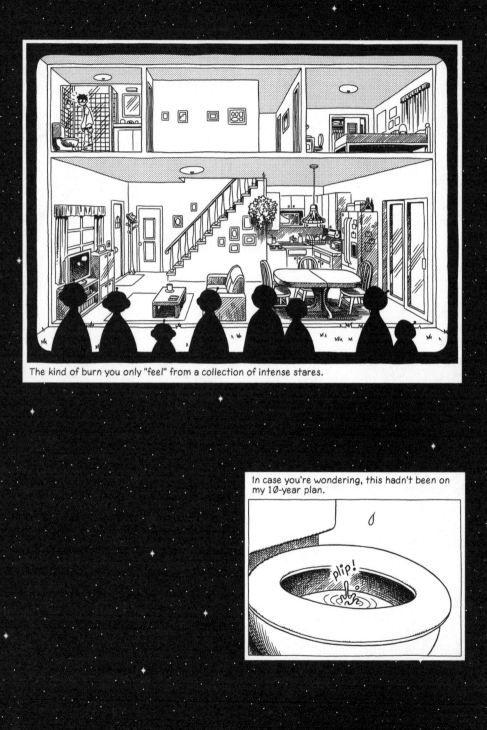

The kind of burn you only "feel" from a collection of intense stares.

In case you're wondering, this hadn't been on my 1Ø-year plan.

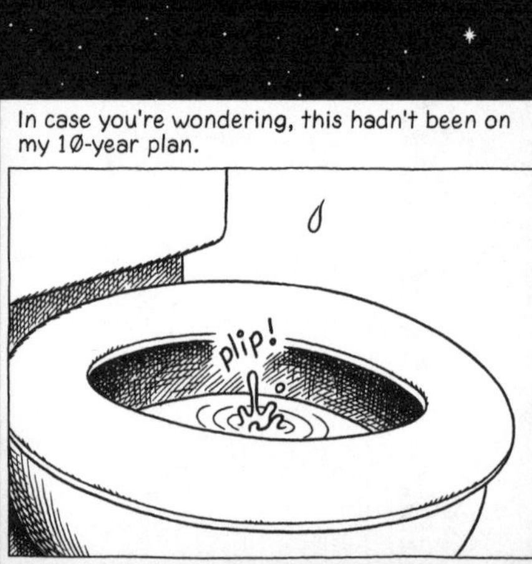
plip!

CHAPTER 02

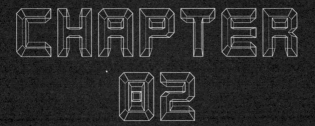

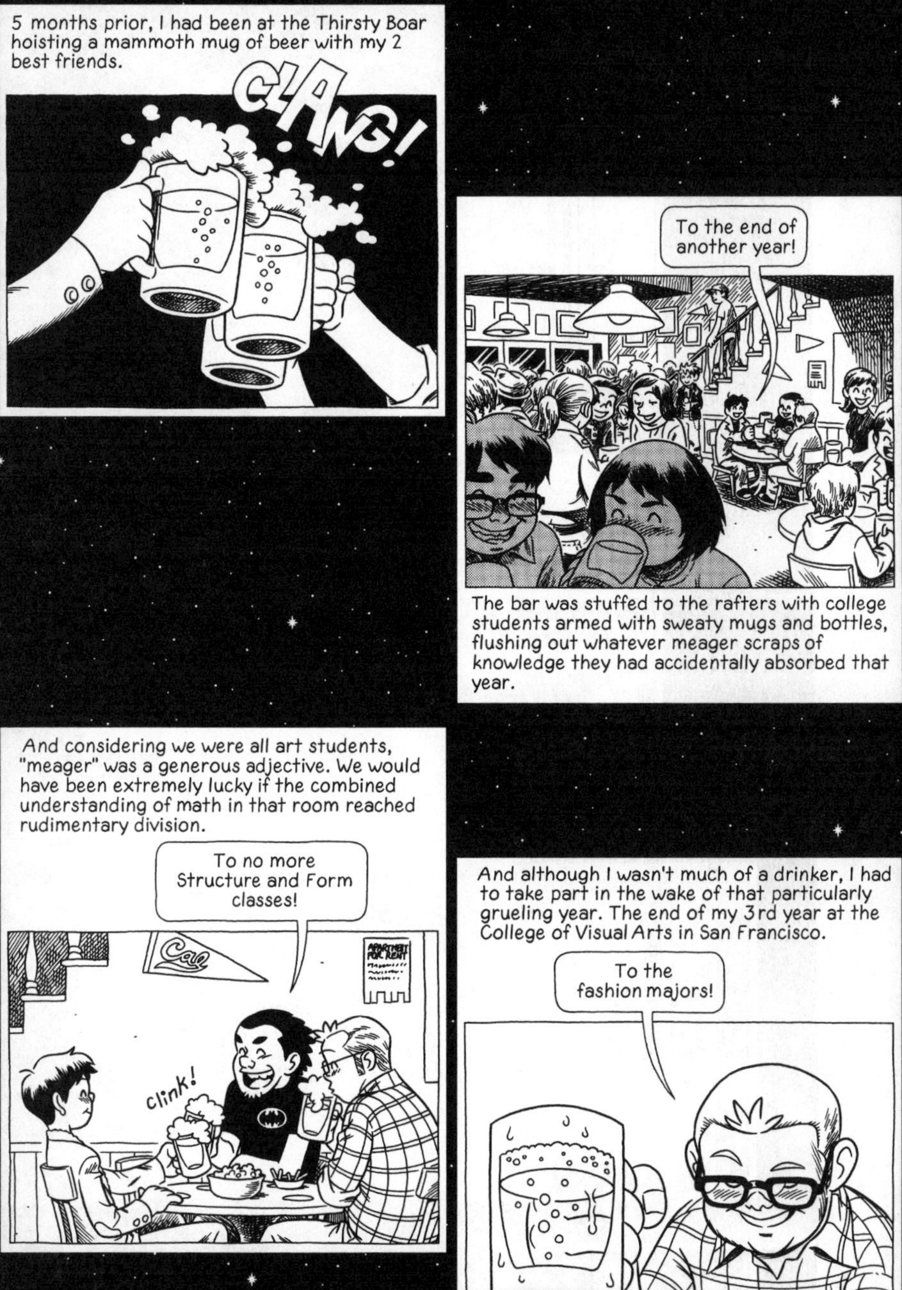

5 months prior, I had been at the Thirsty Boar hoisting a mammoth mug of beer with my 2 best friends.
CLANG!
To the end of another year!
The bar was stuffed to the rafters with college students armed with sweaty mugs and bottles, flushing out whatever meager scraps of knowledge they had accidentally absorbed that year.
And considering we were all art students, "meager" was a generous adjective. We would have been extremely lucky if the combined understanding of math in that room reached rudimentary division.
To no more Structure and Form classes!
Cal
APARTMENT FOR RENT
clink!
And although I wasn't much of a drinker, I had to take part in the wake of that particularly grueling year. The end of my 3rd year at the College of Visual Arts in San Francisco.
To the fashion majors!

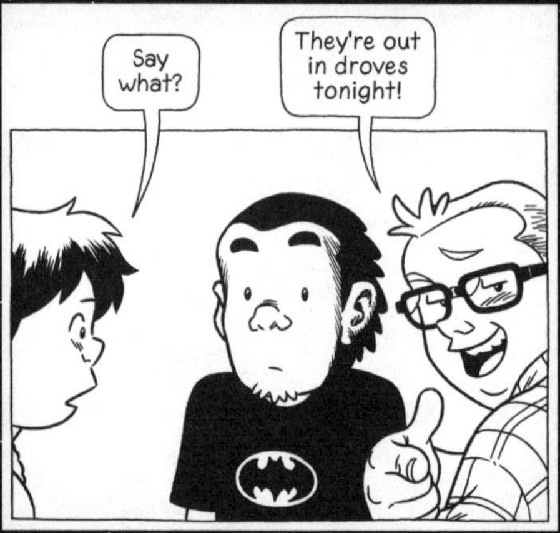
Say what?
They're out in droves tonight!

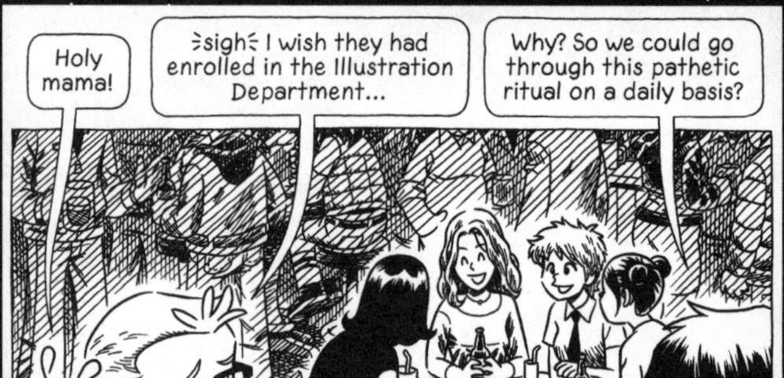
Holy mama!
≷sigh≶ I wish they had enrolled in the Illustration Department...
Why? So we could go through this pathetic ritual on a daily basis?

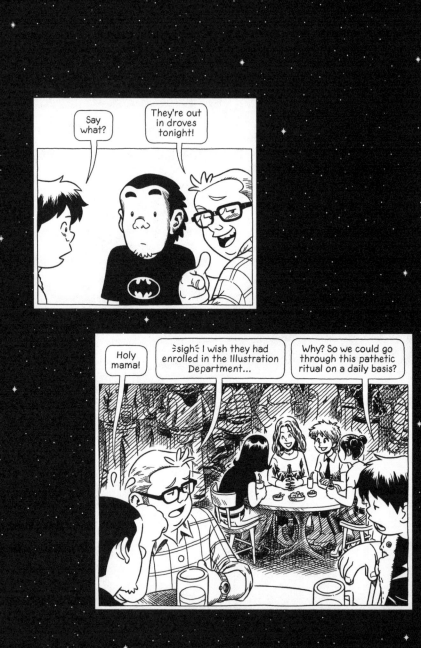

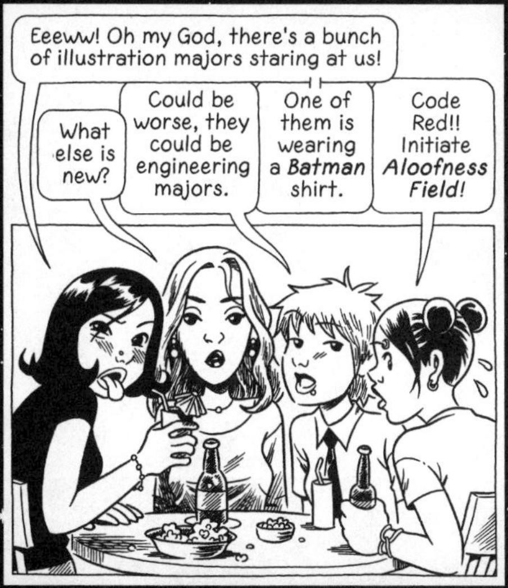
Eeeww! Oh my God, there's a bunch of illustration majors staring at us!
What else is new?
Could be worse, they could be engineering majors.
One of them is wearing a *Batman* shirt.
Code Red!! Initiate *Aloofness Field!*

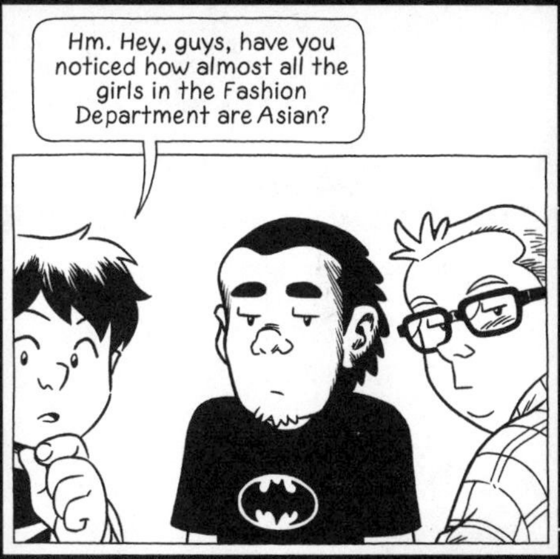
Hm. Hey, guys, have you noticed how almost all the girls in the Fashion Department are Asian?

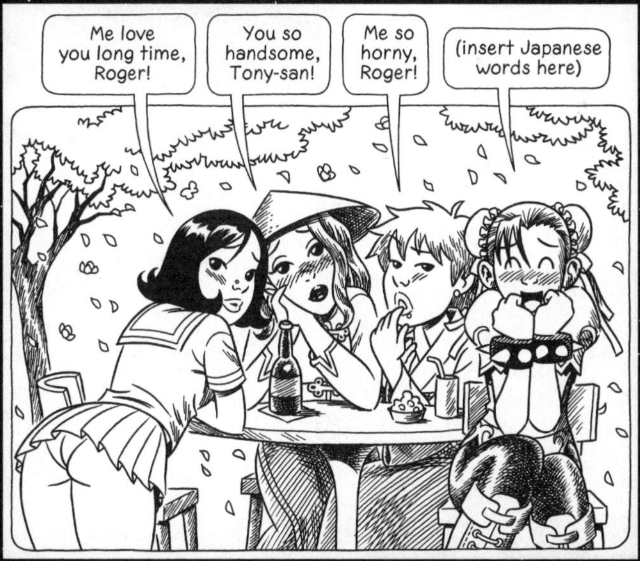
Me love you long time, Roger!
You so handsome, Tony-san!
Me so horny, Roger!
(insert Japanese words here)

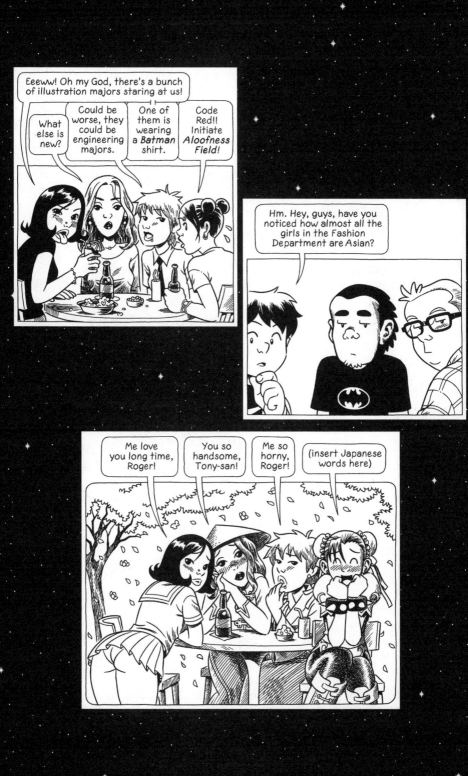

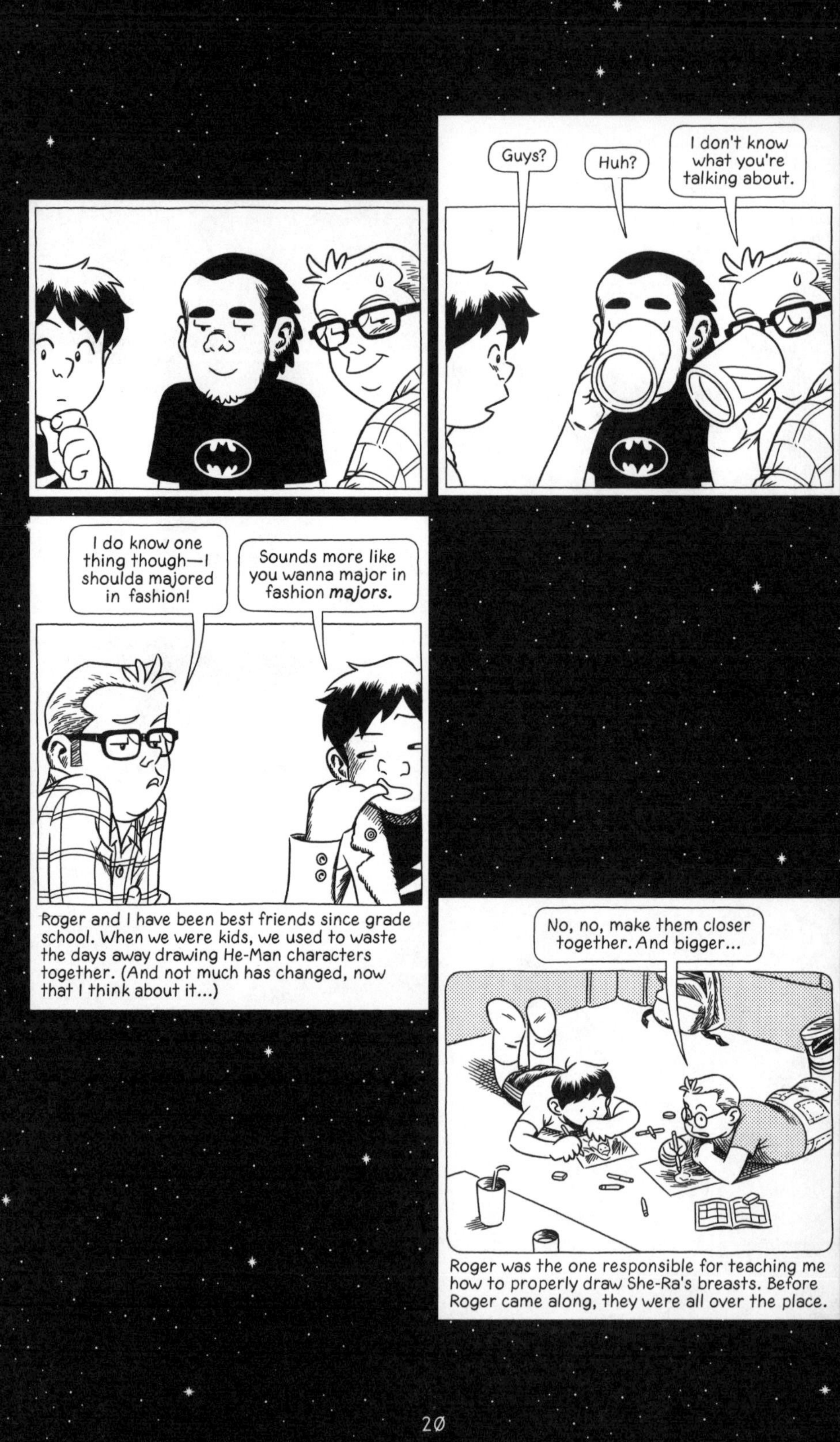
Guys?
Huh?
I don't know what you're talking about.
I do know one thing though—I shoulda majored in fashion!
Sounds more like you wanna major in fashion *majors.*
Roger and I have been best friends since grade school. When we were kids, we used to waste the days away drawing He-Man characters together. (And not much has changed, now that I think about it...)
No, no, make them closer together. And bigger...
Roger was the one responsible for teaching me how to properly draw She-Ra's breasts. Before Roger came along, they were all over the place.

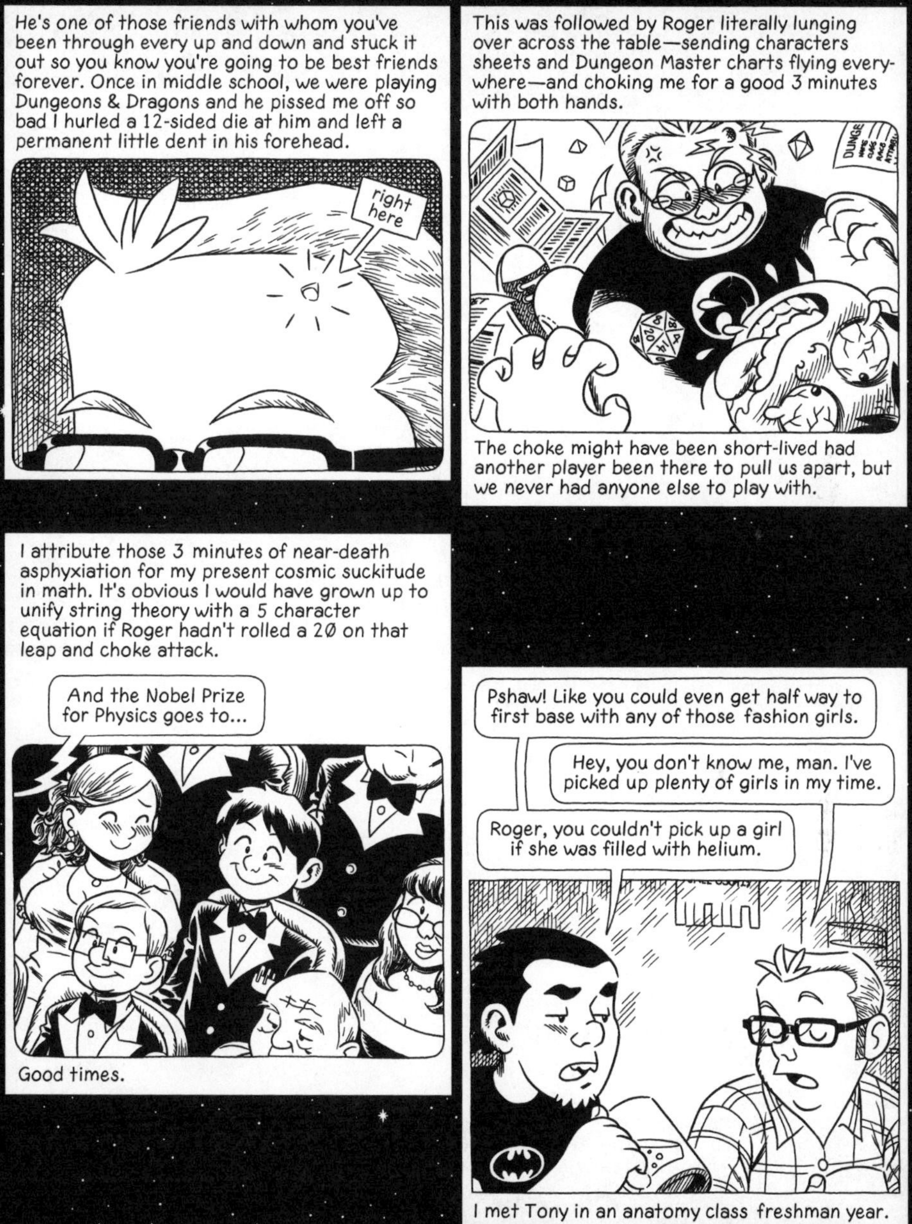
He's one of those friends with whom you've been through every up and down and stuck it out so you know you're going to be best friends forever. Once in middle school, we were playing Dungeons & Dragons and he pissed me off so bad I hurled a 12-sided die at him and left a permanent little dent in his forehead.
right here
This was followed by Roger literally lunging over across the table—sending characters sheets and Dungeon Master charts flying everywhere—and choking me for a good 3 minutes with both hands.
The choke might have been short-lived had another player been there to pull us apart, but we never had anyone else to play with.
I attribute those 3 minutes of near-death asphyxiation for my present cosmic suckitude in math. It's obvious I would have grown up to unify string theory with a 5 character equation if Roger hadn't rolled a 2Ø on that leap and choke attack.
And the Nobel Prize for Physics goes to...
Good times.
Pshaw! Like you could even get half way to first base with any of those fashion girls.
Hey, you don't know me, man. I've picked up plenty of girls in my time.
Roger, you couldn't pick up a girl if she was filled with helium.
I met Tony in an anatomy class freshman year.

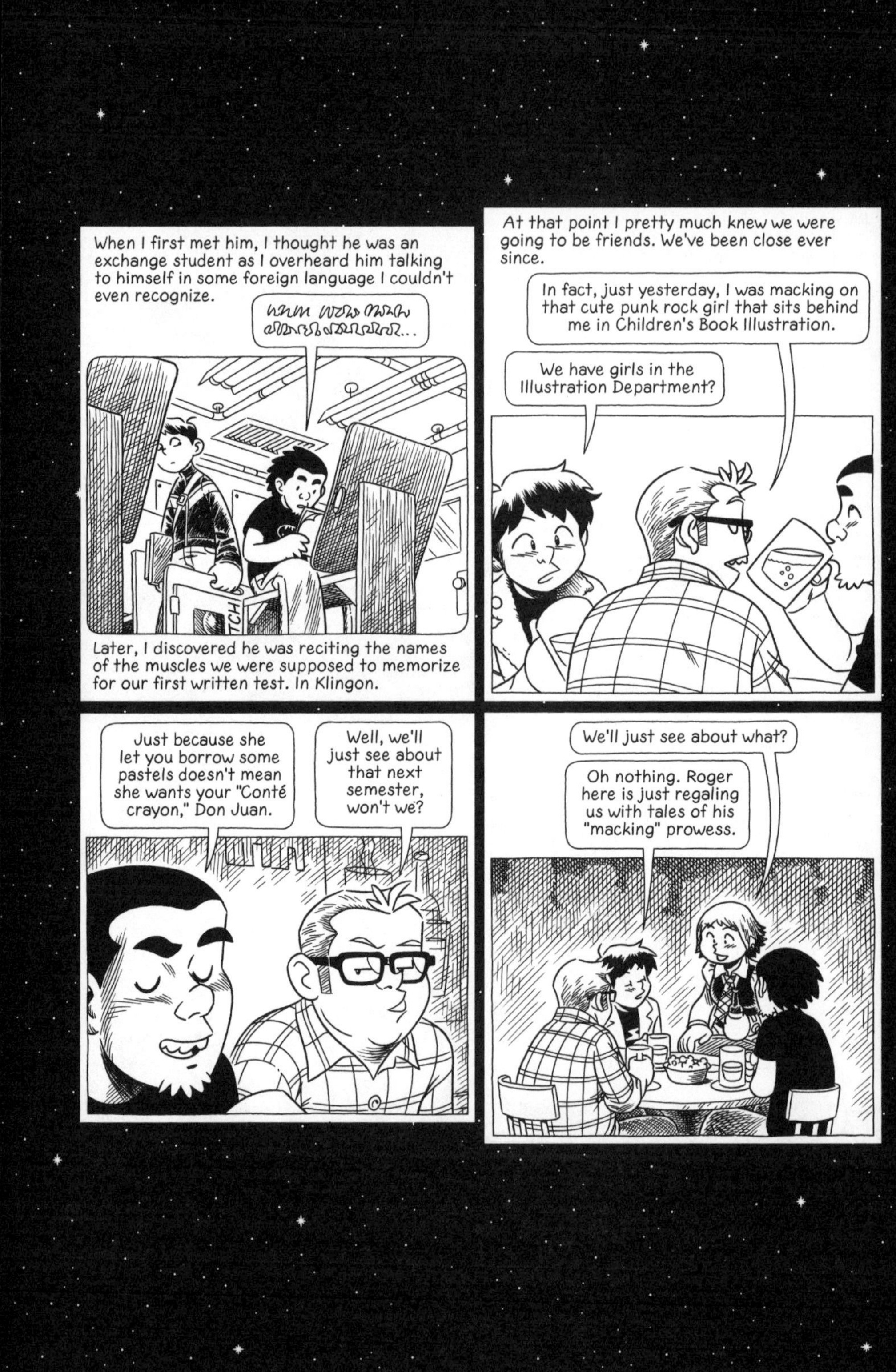
When I first met him, I thought he was an exchange student as I overheard him talking to himself in some foreign language I couldn't even recognize.
Later, I discovered he was reciting the names of the muscles we were supposed to memorize for our first written test. In Klingon.
At that point I pretty much knew we were going to be friends. We've been close ever since.
In fact, just yesterday, I was macking on that cute punk rock girl that sits behind me in Children's Book Illustration.
We have girls in the Illustration Department?
Just because she let you borrow some pastels doesn't mean she wants your "Conté crayon," Don Juan.
Well, we'll just see about that next semester, won't we?
We'll just see about what?
Oh nothing. Roger here is just regaling us with tales of his "macking" prowess.

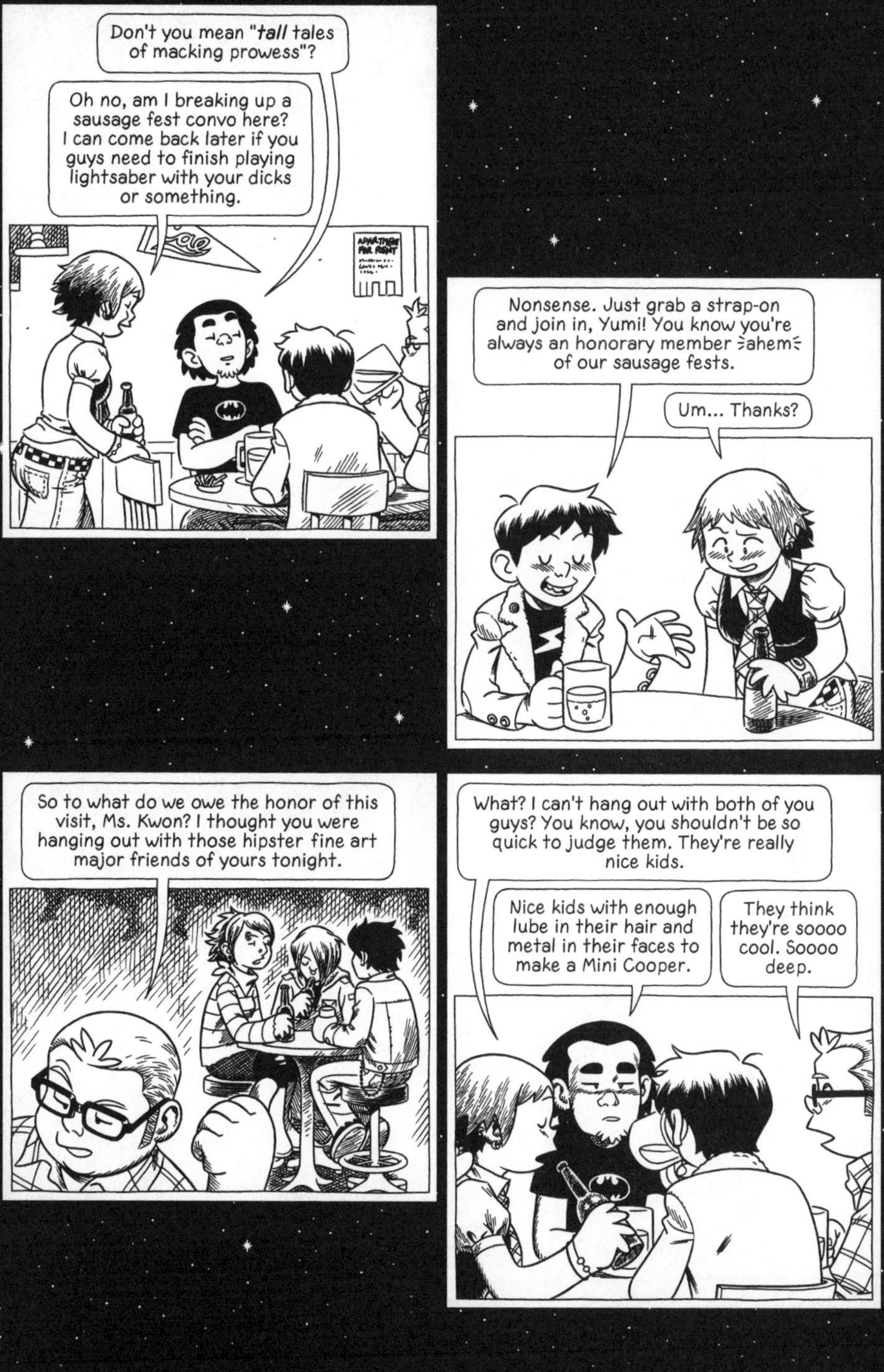
Don't you mean "*tall* tales of macking prowess"?
Oh no, am I breaking up a sausage fest convo here? I can come back later if you guys need to finish playing lightsaber with your dicks or something.
Nonsense. Just grab a strap-on and join in, Yumi! You know you're always an honorary member ≑ahem≑ of our sausage fests.
Um... Thanks?
So to what do we owe the honor of this visit, Ms. Kwon? I thought you were hanging out with those hipster fine art major friends of yours tonight.
What? I can't hang out with both of you guys? You know, you shouldn't be so quick to judge them. They're really nice kids.
Nice kids with enough lube in their hair and metal in their faces to make a Mini Cooper.
They think they're soooo cool. Soooo deep.

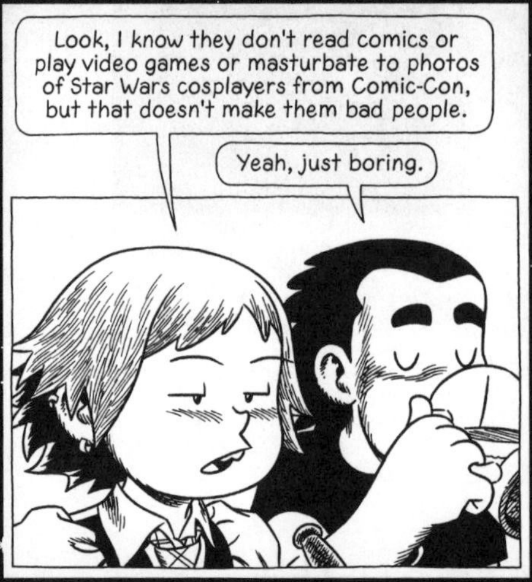
Look, I know they don't read comics or play video games or masturbate to photos of Star Wars cosplayers from Comic-Con, but that doesn't make them bad people.
Yeah, just boring.

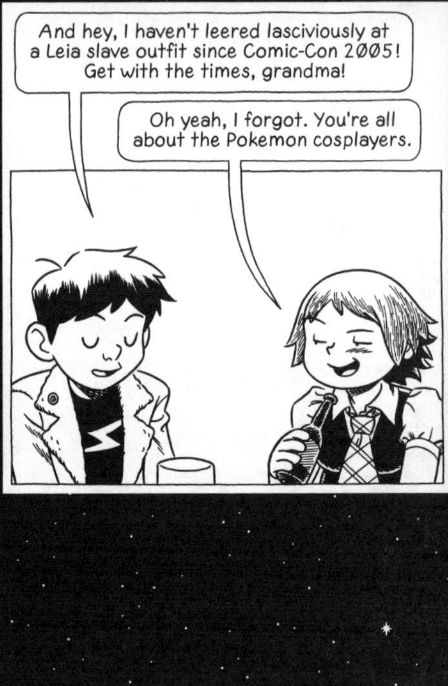
And hey, I haven't leered lasciviously at a Leia slave outfit since Comic-Con 2005! Get with the times, grandma!
Oh yeah, I forgot. You're all about the Pokemon cosplayers.

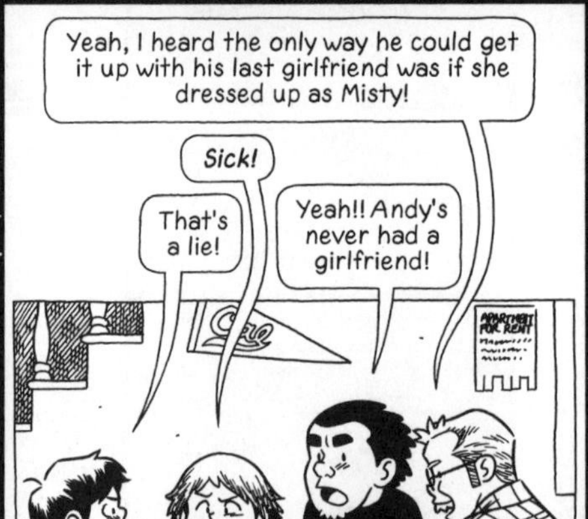
Yeah, I heard the only way he could get it up with his last girlfriend was if she dressed up as Misty!
Sick!
That's a lie!
Yeah!! Andy's never had a girlfriend!
APARTMENT FOR RENT

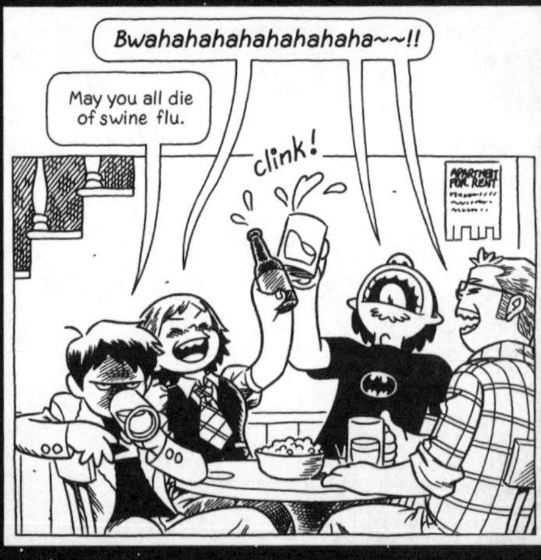
Bwahahahahahahahaha~~!!
May you all die of swine flu.
Clink!
APARTMENT FOR RENT

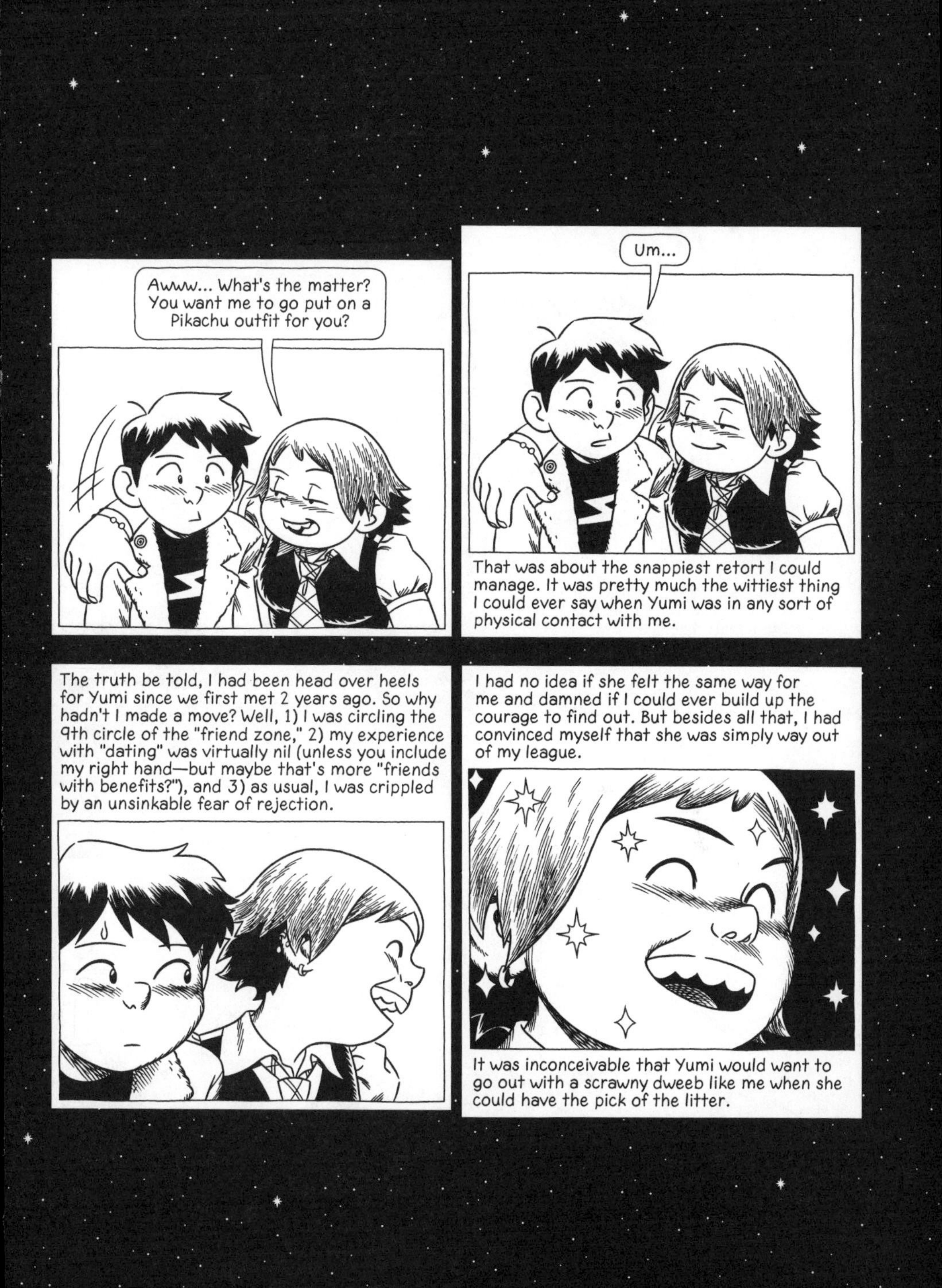
Awww... What's the matter? You want me to go put on a Pikachu outfit for you?
Um...
That was about the snappiest retort I could manage. It was pretty much the wittiest thing I could ever say when Yumi was in any sort of physical contact with me.
The truth be told, I had been head over heels for Yumi since we first met 2 years ago. So why hadn't I made a move? Well, 1) I was circling the 9th circle of the "friend zone," 2) my experience with "dating" was virtually nil (unless you include my right hand—but maybe that's more "friends with benefits?"), and 3) as usual, I was crippled by an unsinkable fear of rejection.
I had no idea if she felt the same way for me and damned if I could ever build up the courage to find out. But besides all that, I had convinced myself that she was simply way out of my league.
It was inconceivable that Yumi would want to go out with a scrawny dweeb like me when she could have the pick of the litter.

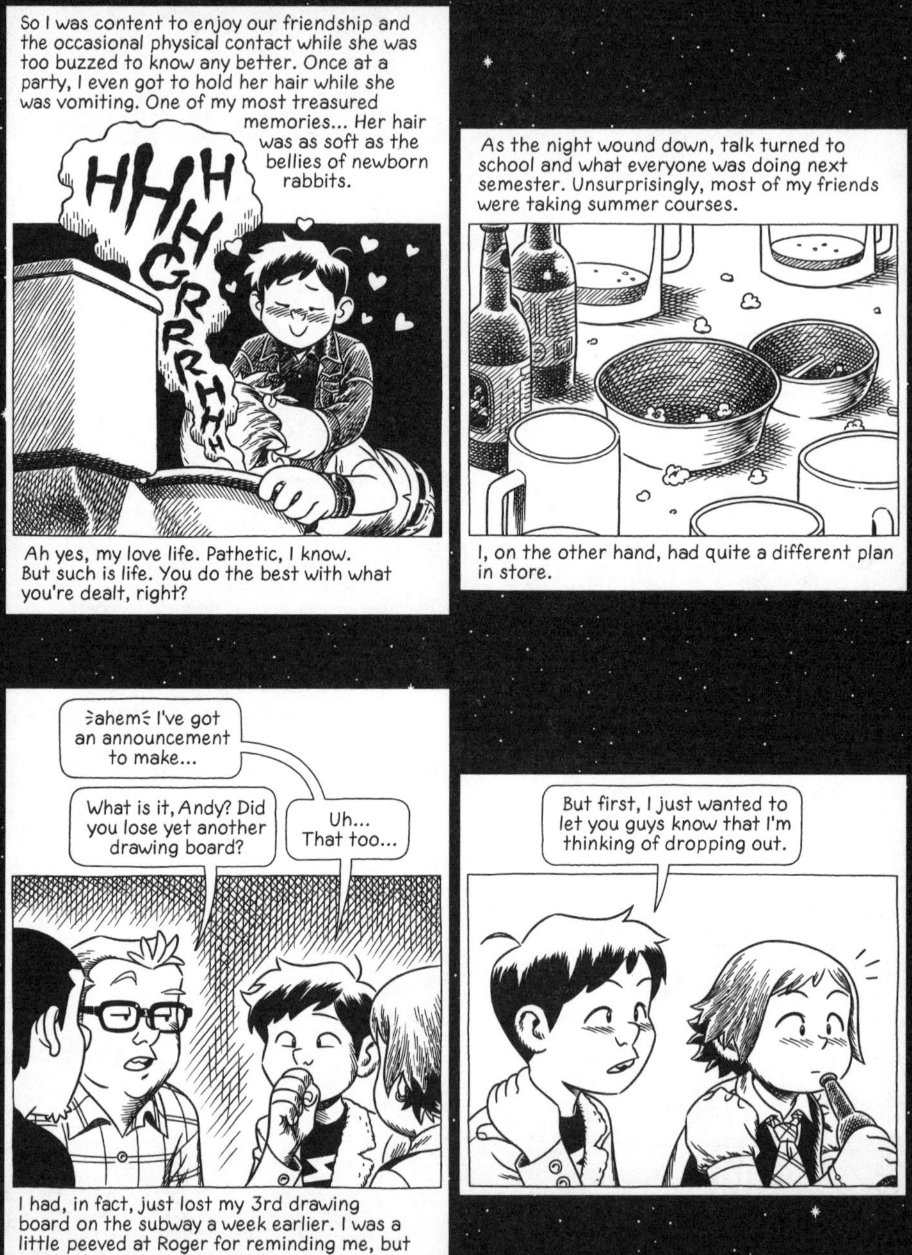

So I was content to enjoy our friendship and the occasional physical contact while she was too buzzed to know any better. Once at a party, I even got to hold her hair while she was vomiting. One of my most treasured memories... Her hair was as soft as the bellies of newborn rabbits.
HHHHGRRRRHHH
Ah yes, my love life. Pathetic, I know. But such is life. You do the best with what you're dealt, right?
As the night wound down, talk turned to school and what everyone was doing next semester. Unsurprisingly, most of my friends were taking summer courses.
I, on the other hand, had quite a different plan in store.
ahem I've got an announcement to make...
What is it, Andy? Did you lose yet another drawing board?
Uh... That too...
I had, in fact, just lost my 3rd drawing board on the subway a week earlier. I was a little peeved at Roger for reminding me, but pressed on.
But first, I just wanted to let you guys know that I'm thinking of dropping out.

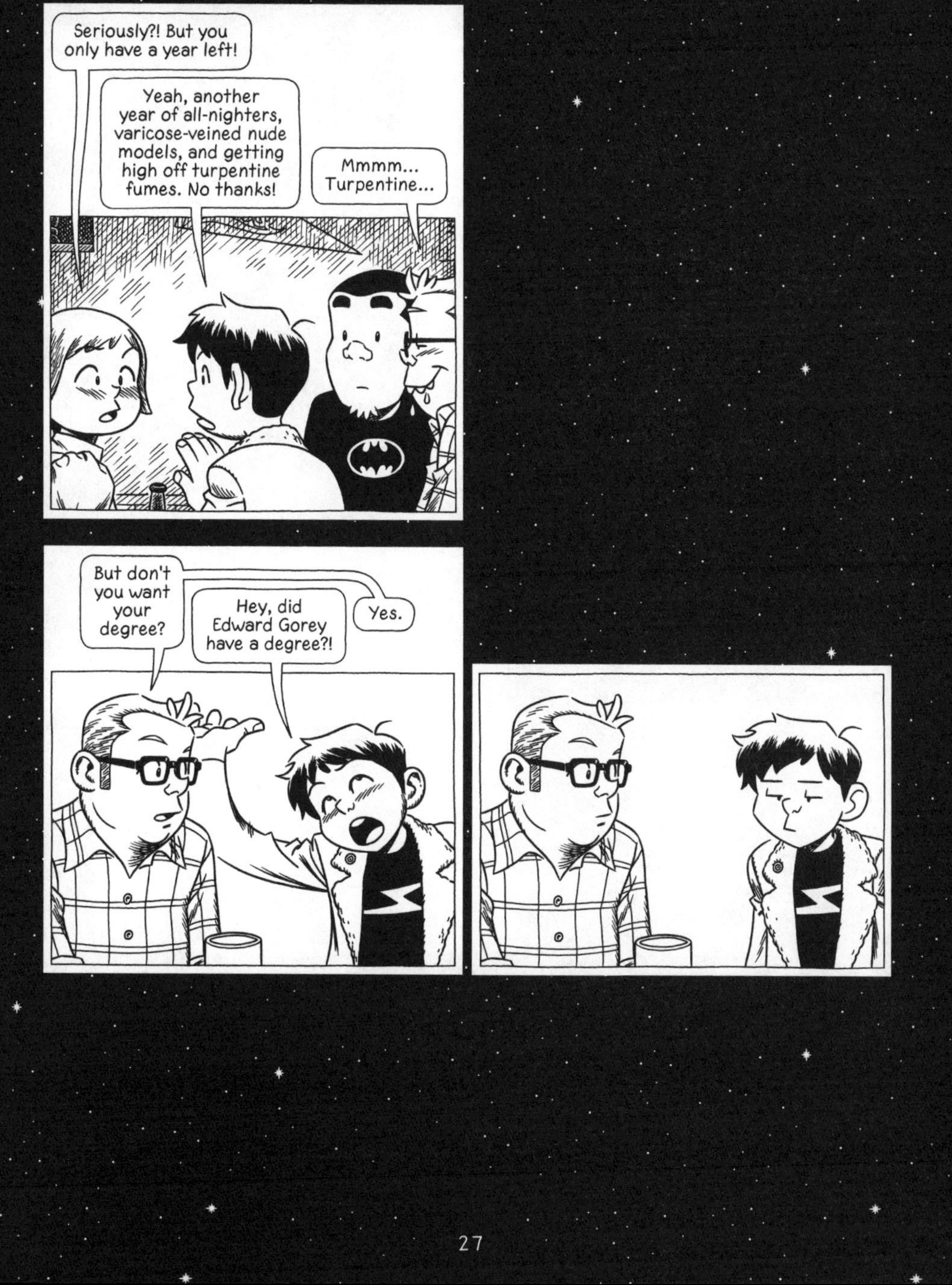
Seriously?! But you only have a year left!
Yeah, another year of all-nighters, varicose-veined nude models, and getting high off turpentine fumes. No thanks!
Mmmm... Turpentine...
But don't you want your degree?
Hey, did Edward Gorey have a degree?!
Yes.

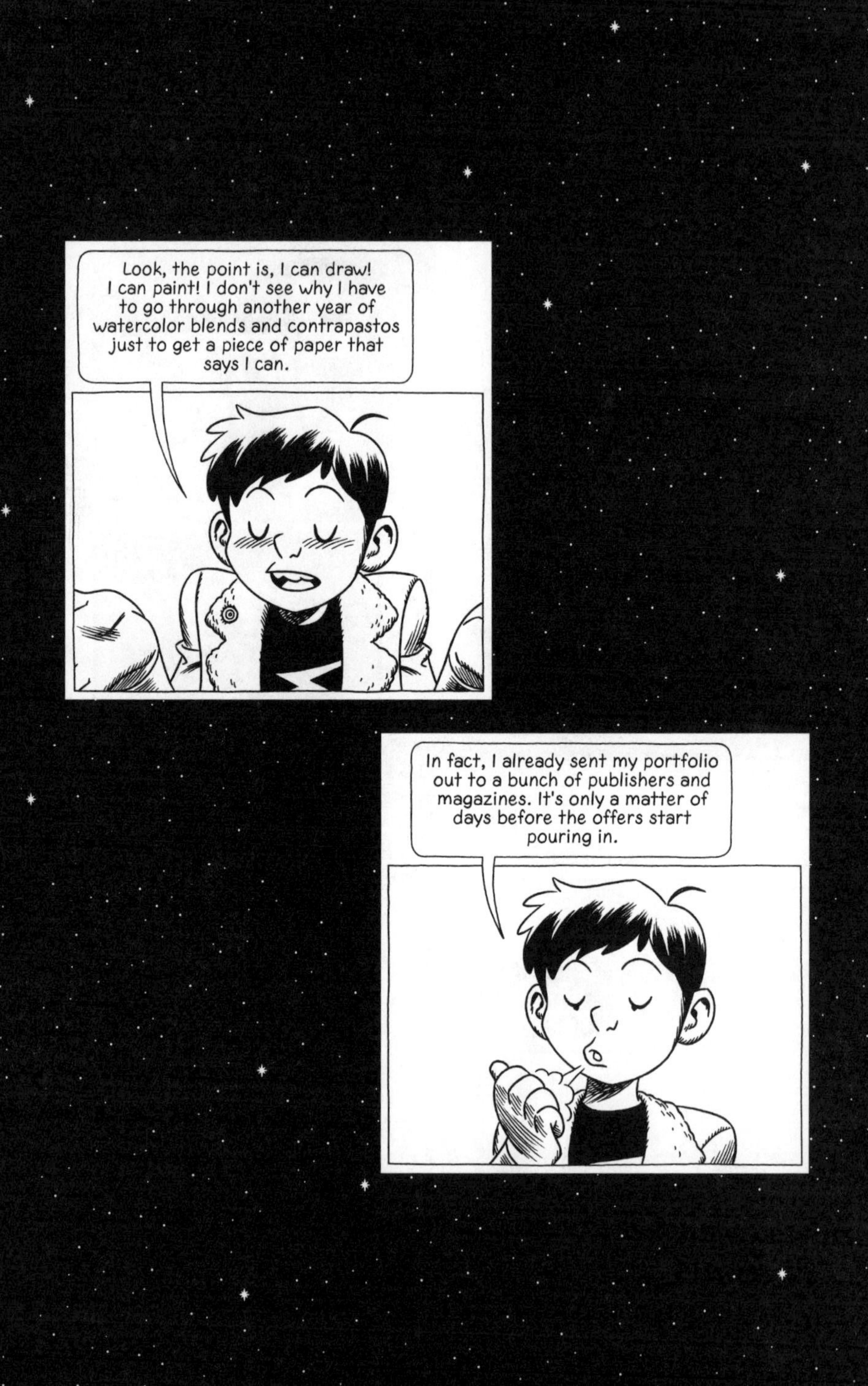
Look, the point is, I can draw! I can paint! I don't see why I have to go through another year of watercolor blends and contrapastos just to get a piece of paper that says I can.
In fact, I already sent my portfolio out to a bunch of publishers and magazines. It's only a matter of days before the offers start pouring in.

CHAPTER
03

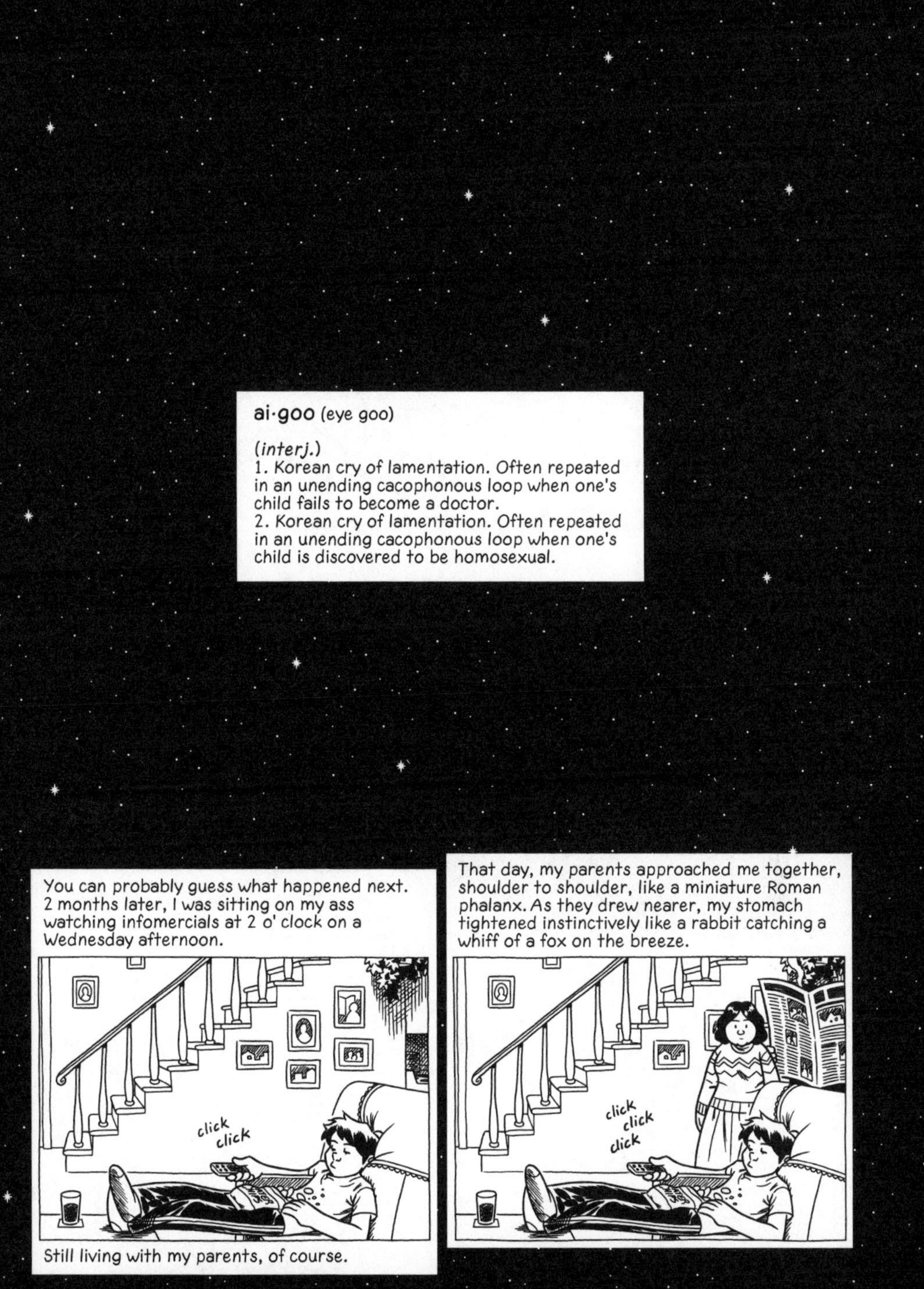
ai·goo (eye goo)
(interj.)
1. Korean cry of lamentation. Often repeated in an unending cacophonous loop when one's child fails to become a doctor.
2. Korean cry of lamentation. Often repeated in an unending cacophonous loop when one's child is discovered to be homosexual.
You can probably guess what happened next. 2 months later, I was sitting on my ass watching infomercials at 2 o' clock on a Wednesday afternoon.
click click
Still living with my parents, of course.
That day, my parents approached me together, shoulder to shoulder, like a miniature Roman phalanx. As they drew nearer, my stomach tightened instinctively like a rabbit catching a whiff of a fox on the breeze.
click click click

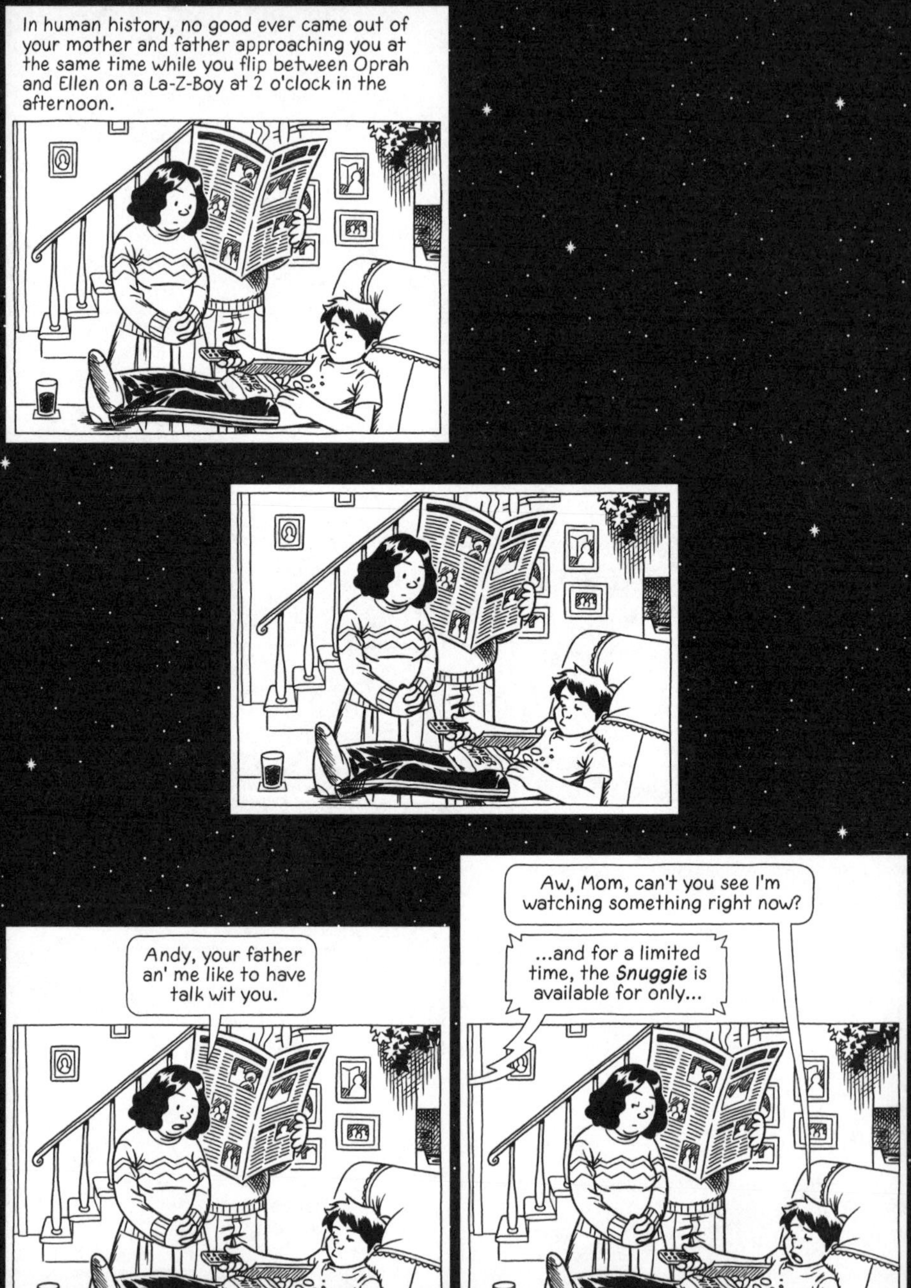
In human history, no good ever came out of your mother and father approaching you at the same time while you flip between Oprah and Ellen on a La-Z-Boy at 2 o'clock in the afternoon.
Andy, your father an' me like to have talk wit you.
Aw, Mom, can't you see I'm watching something right now?
...and for a limited time, the *Snuggie* is available for only...

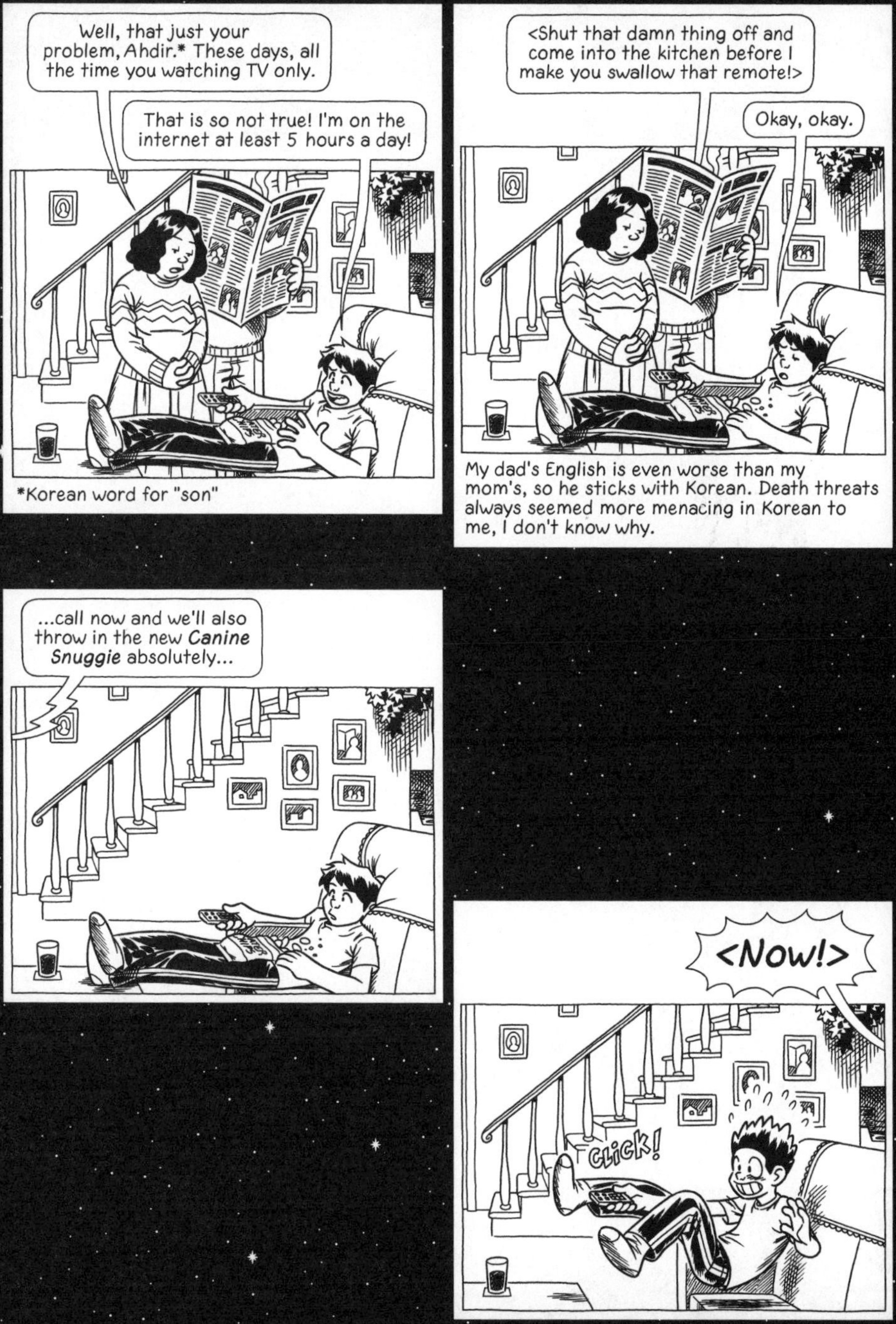
Well, that just your problem, Ahdir.* These days, all the time you watching TV only.
That is so not true! I'm on the internet at least 5 hours a day!
*Korean word for "son"
<Shut that damn thing off and come into the kitchen before I make you swallow that remote!>
Okay, okay.
My dad's English is even worse than my mom's, so he sticks with Korean. Death threats always seemed more menacing in Korean to me, I don't know why.
...call now and we'll also throw in the new *Canine Snuggie* absolutely...
<Now!>
CLICK!

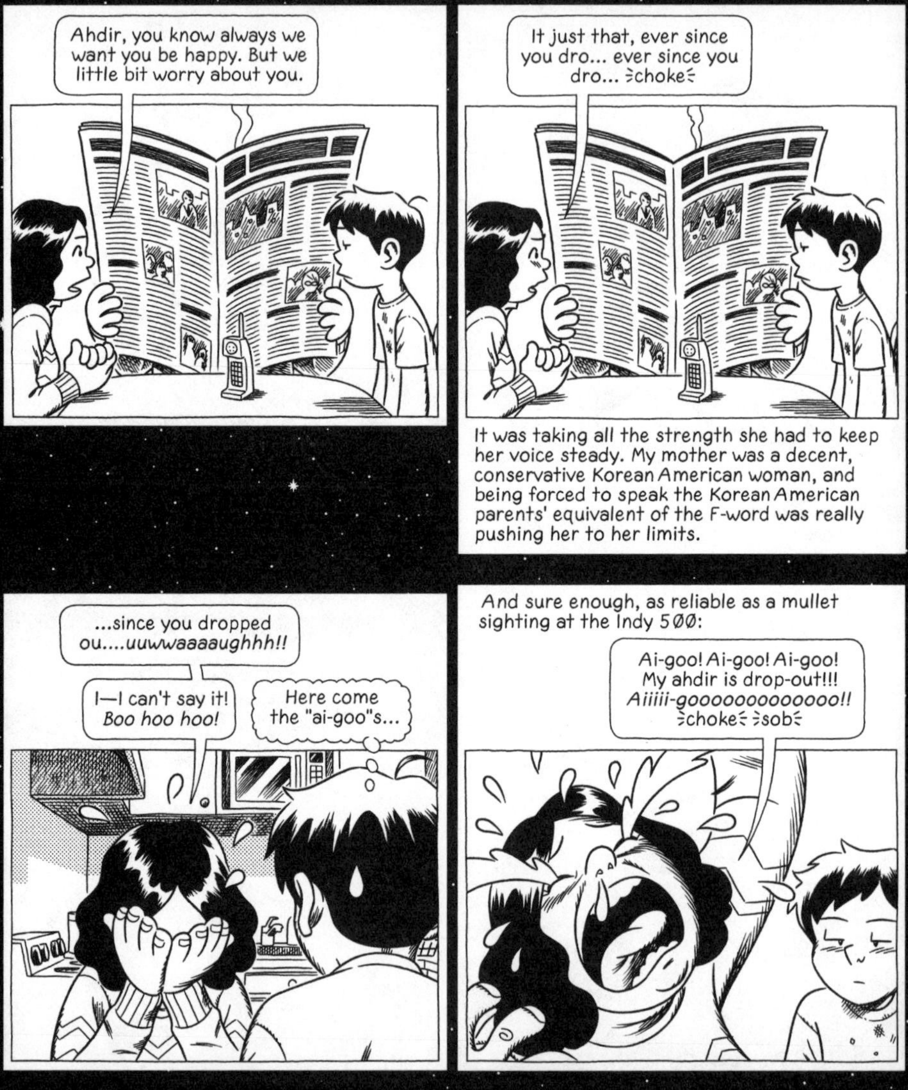
Ahdir, you know always we want you be happy. But we little bit worry about you.
It just that, ever since you dro... ever since you dro... =choke=
It was taking all the strength she had to keep her voice steady. My mother was a decent, conservative Korean American woman, and being forced to speak the Korean American parents' equivalent of the F-word was really pushing her to her limits.
...since you dropped ou....*uuwwaaaaughhh!!*
I—I can't say it! *Boo hoo hoo!*
Here come the "ai-goo"s...
And sure enough, as reliable as a mullet sighting at the Indy 5ØØ:
Ai-goo! Ai-goo! Ai-goo! My ahdir is drop-out!!! *Aiiiii-gooooooooooooo!!* =choke= =sob=

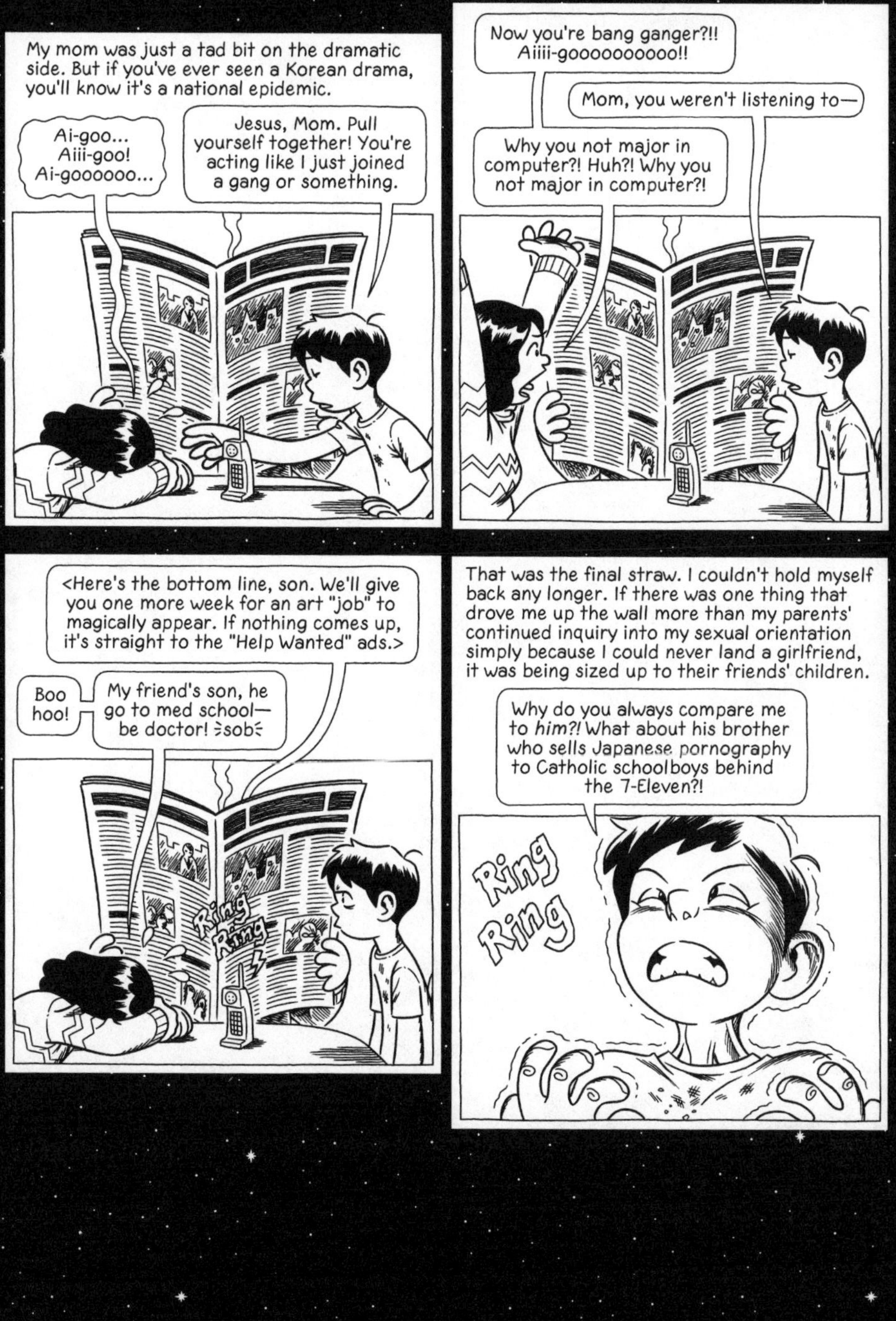

My mom was just a tad bit on the dramatic side. But if you've ever seen a Korean drama, you'll know it's a national epidemic.
Ai-goo... Aiii-goo! Ai-goooooo...
Jesus, Mom. Pull yourself together! You're acting like I just joined a gang or something.
Now you're bang ganger?!! Aiiii-gooooooooo!!
Mom, you weren't listening to—
Why you not major in computer?! Huh?! Why you not major in computer?!
<Here's the bottom line, son. We'll give you one more week for an art "job" to magically appear. If nothing comes up, it's straight to the "Help Wanted" ads.>
Boo hoo!
My friend's son, he go to med school— be doctor! ≷sob≶
Ring Ring
That was the final straw. I couldn't hold myself back any longer. If there was one thing that drove me up the wall more than my parents' continued inquiry into my sexual orientation simply because I could never land a girlfriend, it was being sized up to their friends' children.
Why do you always compare me to *him?!* What about his brother who sells Japanese pornography to Catholic schoolboys behind the 7-Eleven?!
Ring Ring

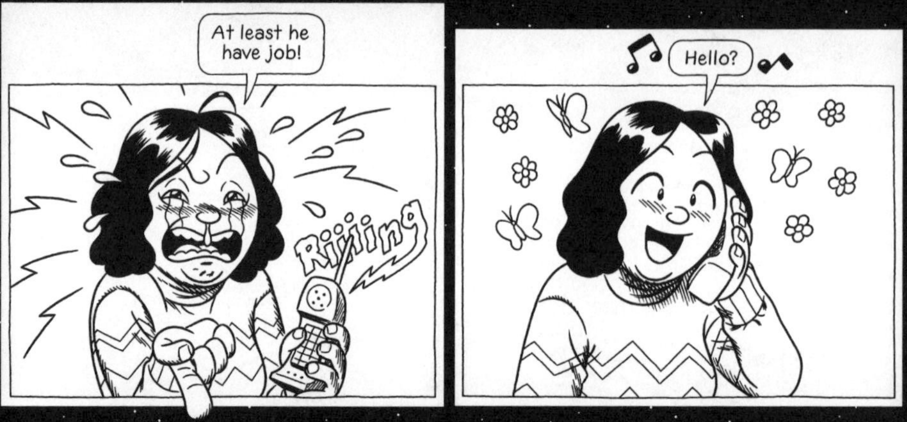
At least he have job!
Riiiing
Hello?

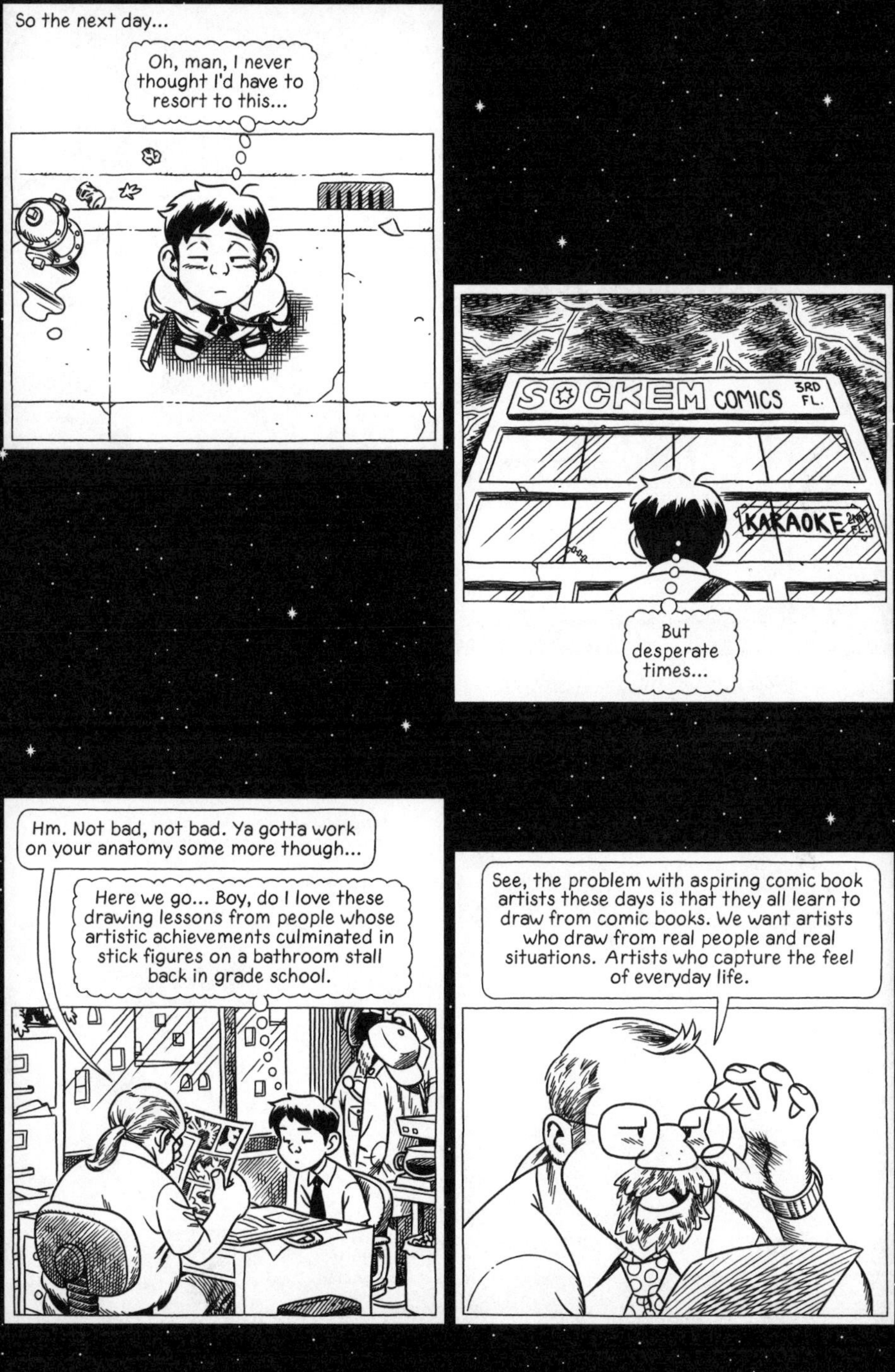
So the next day...
Oh, man, I never thought I'd have to resort to this...
SOCKEM COMICS 3RD FL.
KARAOKE 2ND FL.
But desperate times...
Hm. Not bad, not bad. Ya gotta work on your anatomy some more though...
Here we go... Boy, do I love these drawing lessons from people whose artistic achievements culminated in stick figures on a bathroom stall back in grade school.
See, the problem with aspiring comic book artists these days is that they all learn to draw from comic books. We want artists who draw from real people and real situations. Artists who capture the feel of everyday life.

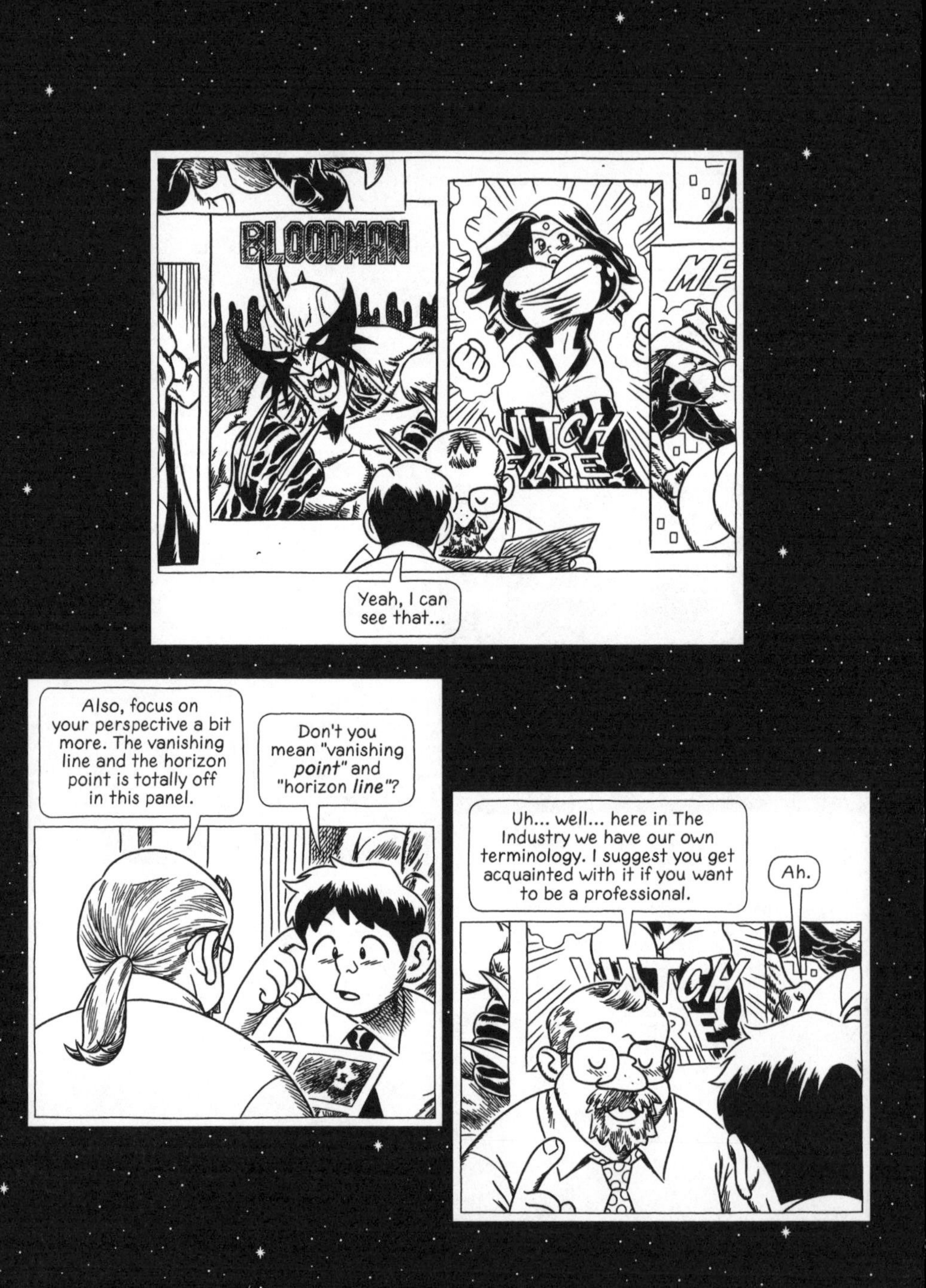
BLOODMAN
Yeah, I can see that...
Also, focus on your perspective a bit more. The vanishing line and the horizon point is totally off in this panel.
Don't you mean "vanishing *point*" and "horizon *line*"?
Uh... well... here in The Industry we have our own terminology. I suggest you get acquainted with it if you want to be a professional.
Ah.

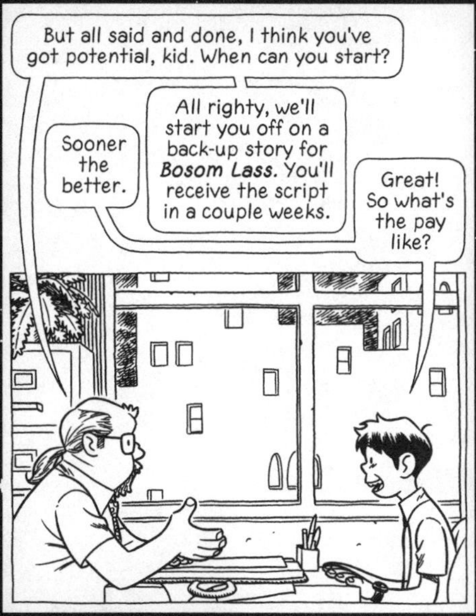
But all said and done, I think you've got potential, kid. When can you start?
Sooner the better.
All righty, we'll start you off on a back-up story for *Bosom Lass.* You'll receive the script in a couple weeks.
Great! So what's the pay like?

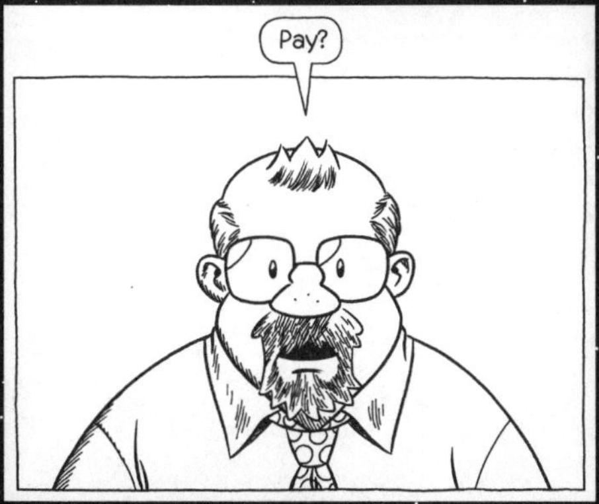
Pay?

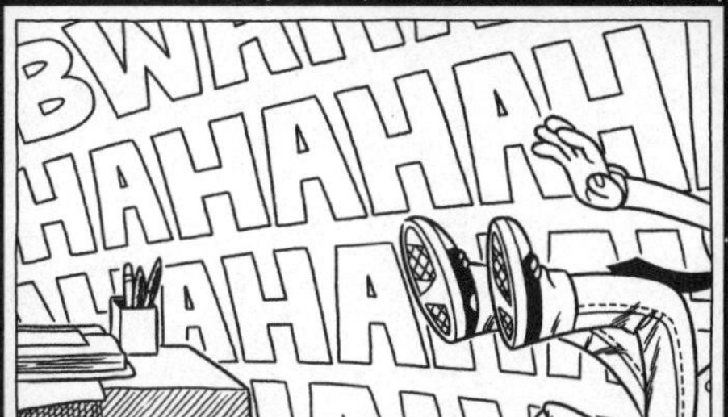

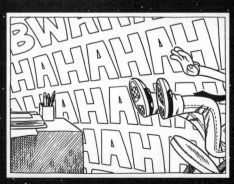

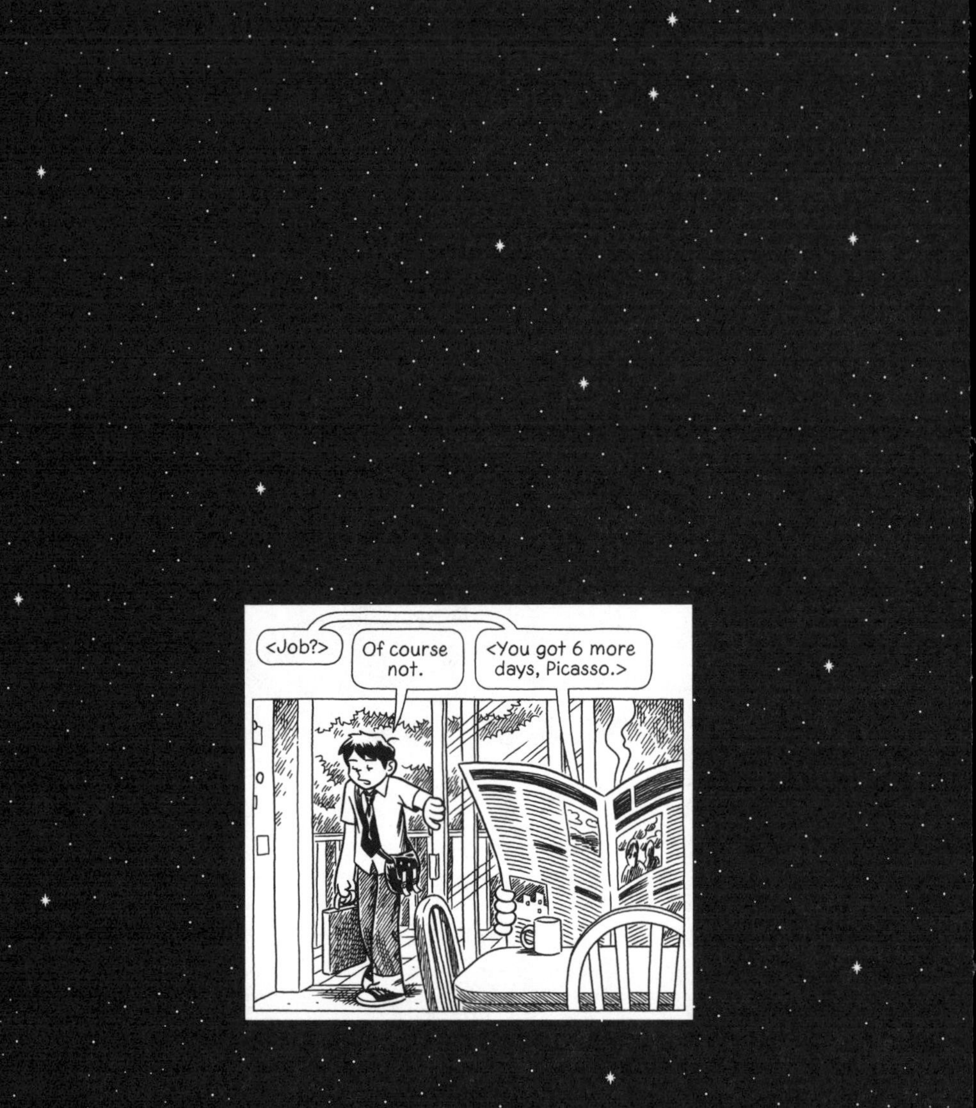
<Job?>
Of course not.
<You got 6 more days, Picasso.>

CHAPTER
04

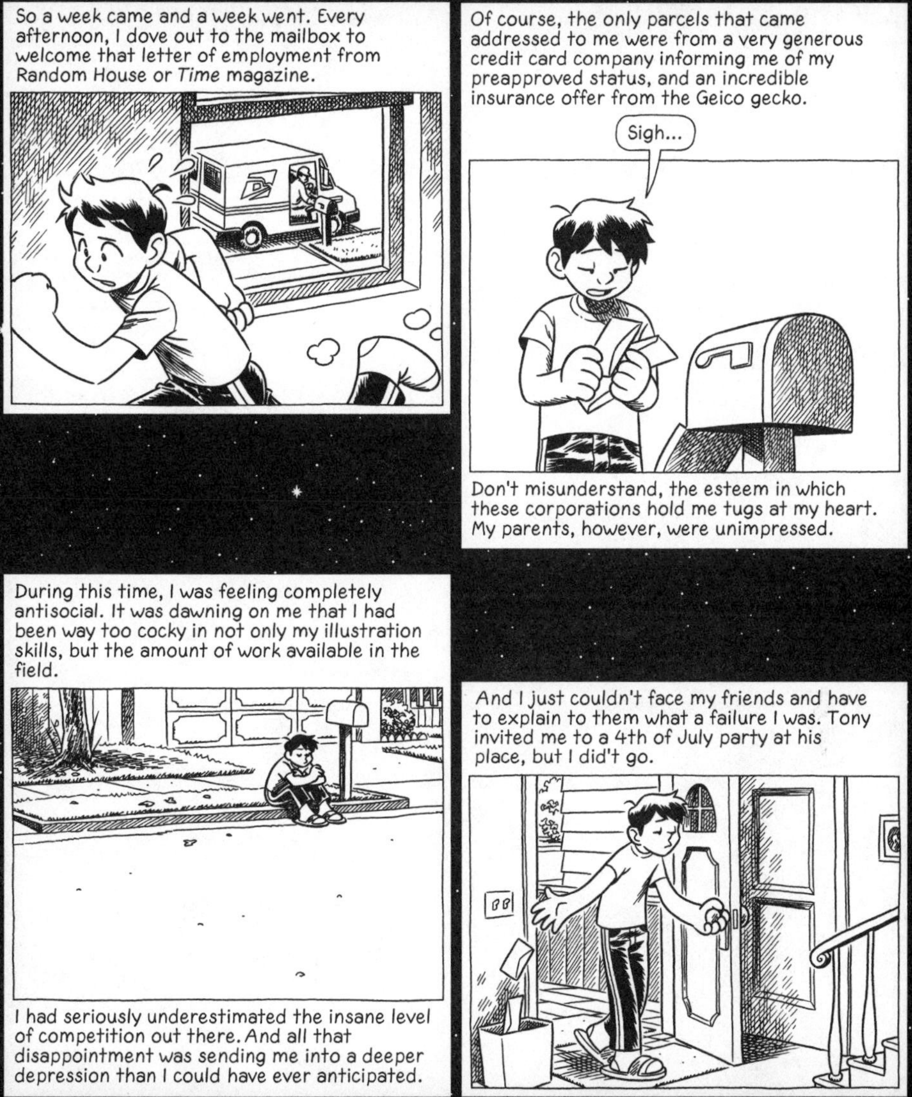
So a week came and a week went. Every afternoon, I dove out to the mailbox to welcome that letter of employment from Random House or *Time* magazine.
Of course, the only parcels that came addressed to me were from a very generous credit card company informing me of my preapproved status, and an incredible insurance offer from the Geico gecko.
Sigh...
Don't misunderstand, the esteem in which these corporations hold me tugs at my heart. My parents, however, were unimpressed.
During this time, I was feeling completely antisocial. It was dawning on me that I had been way too cocky in not only my illustration skills, but the amount of work available in the field.
I had seriously underestimated the insane level of competition out there. And all that disappointment was sending me into a deeper depression than I could have ever anticipated.
And I just couldn't face my friends and have to explain to them what a failure I was. Tony invited me to a 4th of July party at his place, but I did't go.

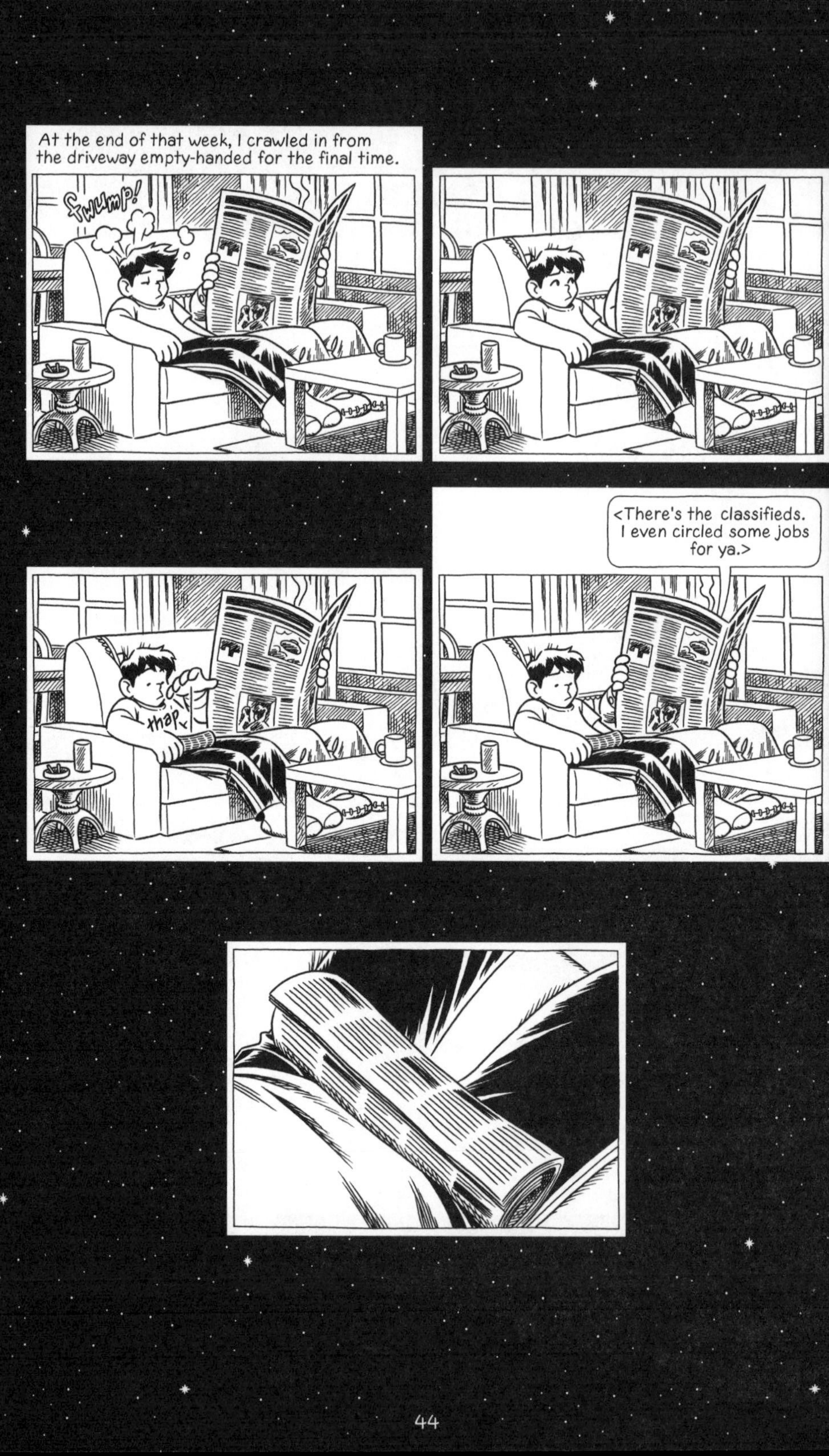
At the end of that week, I crawled in from the driveway empty-handed for the final time.
fwump!
thap
<There's the classifieds. I even circled some jobs for ya.>

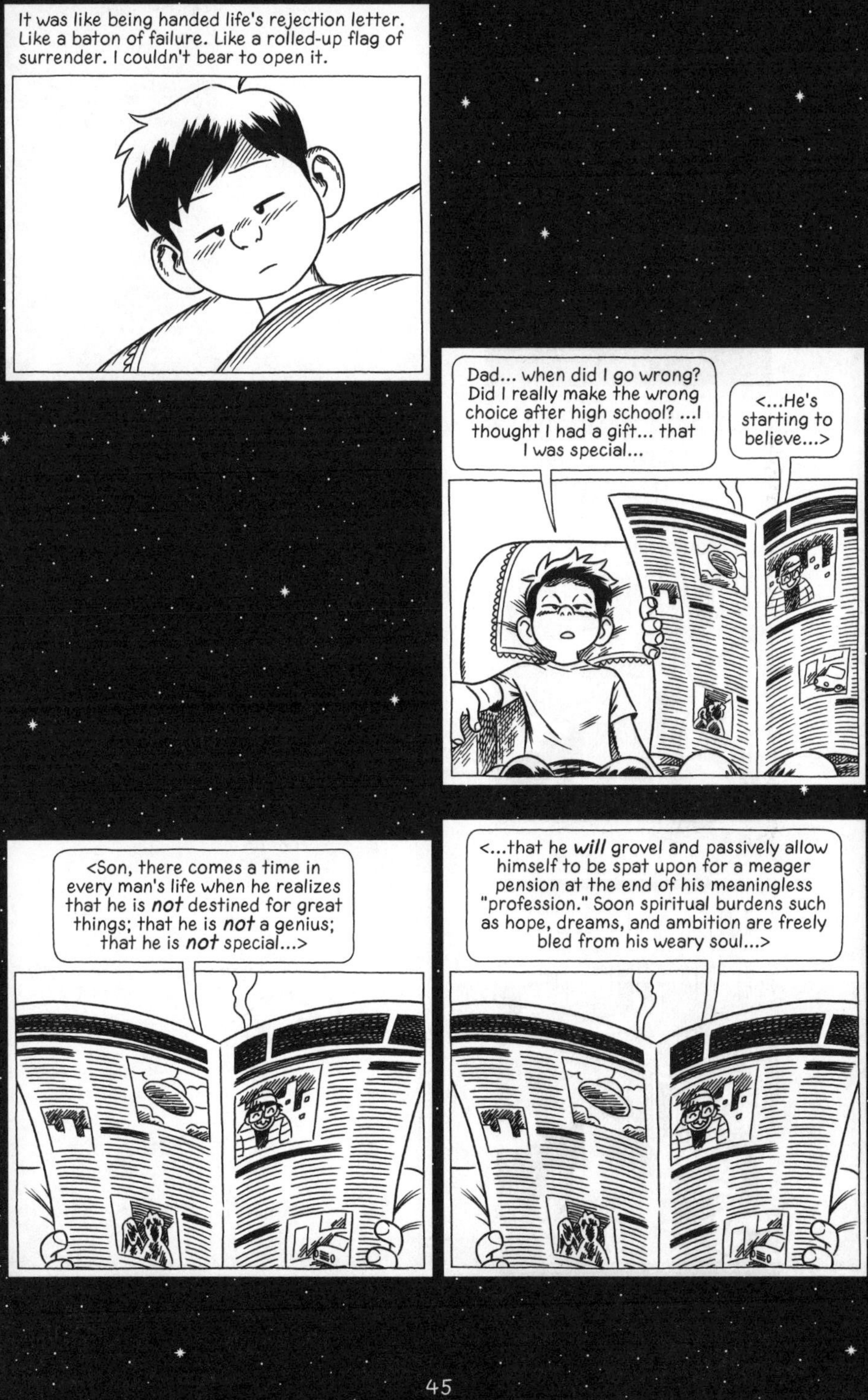
It was like being handed life's rejection letter. Like a baton of failure. Like a rolled-up flag of surrender. I couldn't bear to open it.
Dad... when did I go wrong? Did I really make the wrong choice after high school? ...I thought I had a gift... that I was special...
<...He's starting to believe...>
<Son, there comes a time in every man's life when he realizes that he is *not* destined for great things; that he is *not* a genius; that he is *not* special...>
<...that he *will* grovel and passively allow himself to be spat upon for a meager pension at the end of his meaningless "profession." Soon spiritual burdens such as hope, dreams, and ambition are freely bled from his weary soul...>

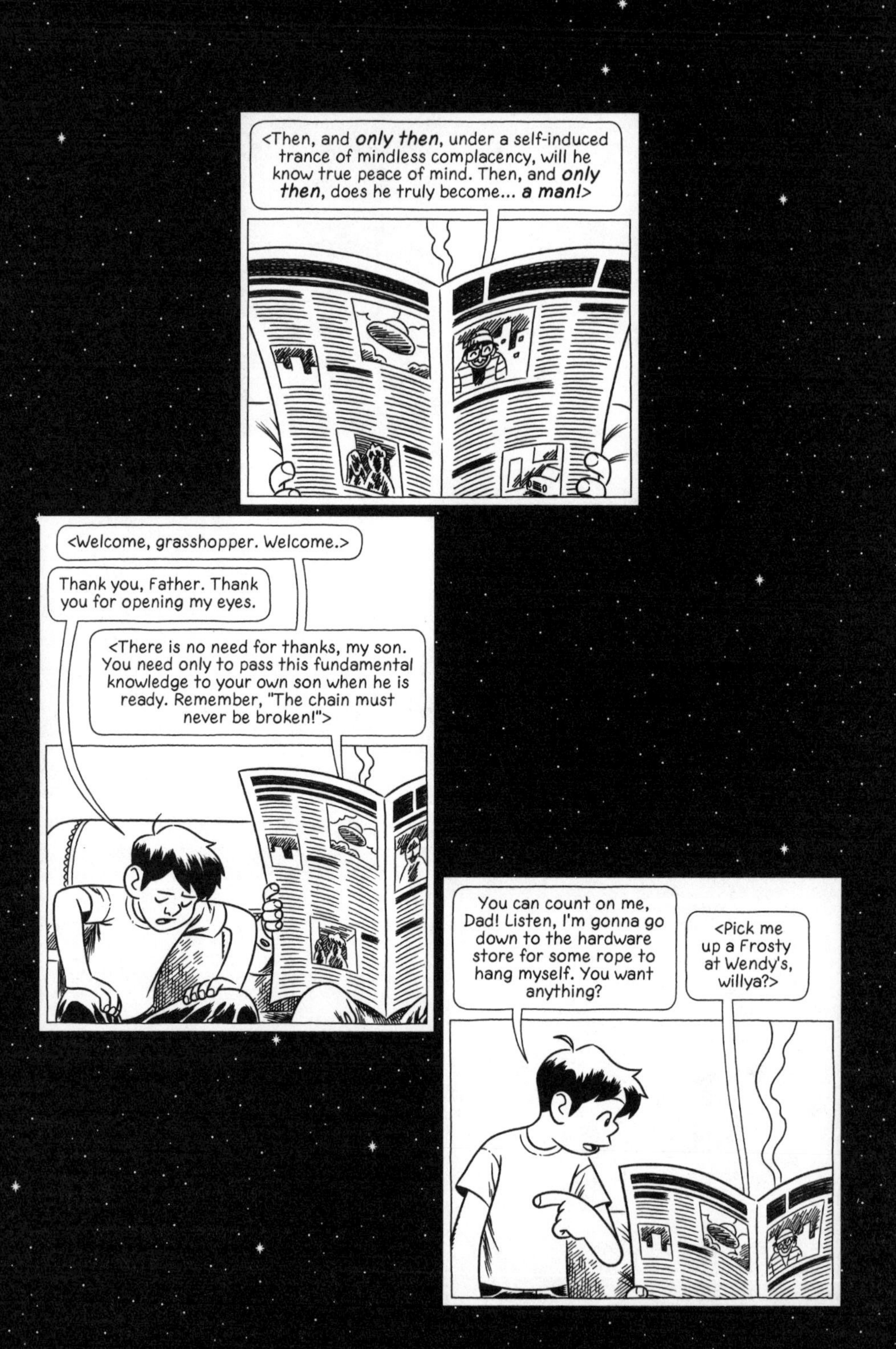

<Then, and only then, under a self-induced trance of mindless complacency, will he know true peace of mind. Then, and only then, does he truly become... a man!>
<Welcome, grasshopper. Welcome.>
Thank you, Father. Thank you for opening my eyes.
<There is no need for thanks, my son. You need only to pass this fundamental knowledge to your own son when he is ready. Remember, "The chain must never be broken!">
You can count on me, Dad! Listen, I'm gonna go down to the hardware store for some rope to hang myself. You want anything?
<Pick me up a Frosty at Wendy's, willya?>

CHAPTER 05

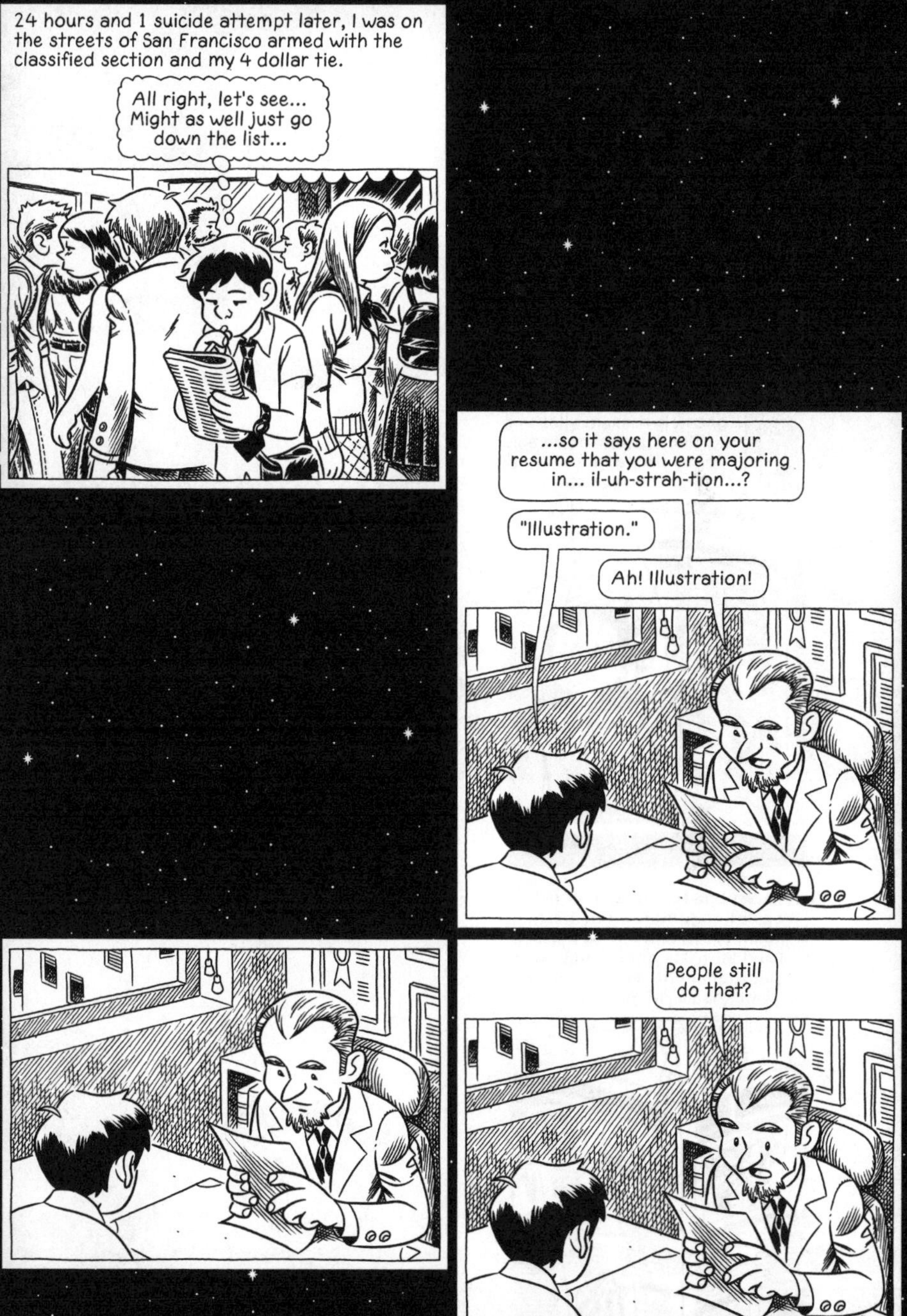

24 hours and 1 suicide attempt later, I was on the streets of San Francisco armed with the classified section and my 4 dollar tie.
All right, let's see... Might as well just go down the list...
...so it says here on your resume that you were majoring in... il-uh-strah-tion...?
"Illustration."
Ah! Illustration!
People still do that?

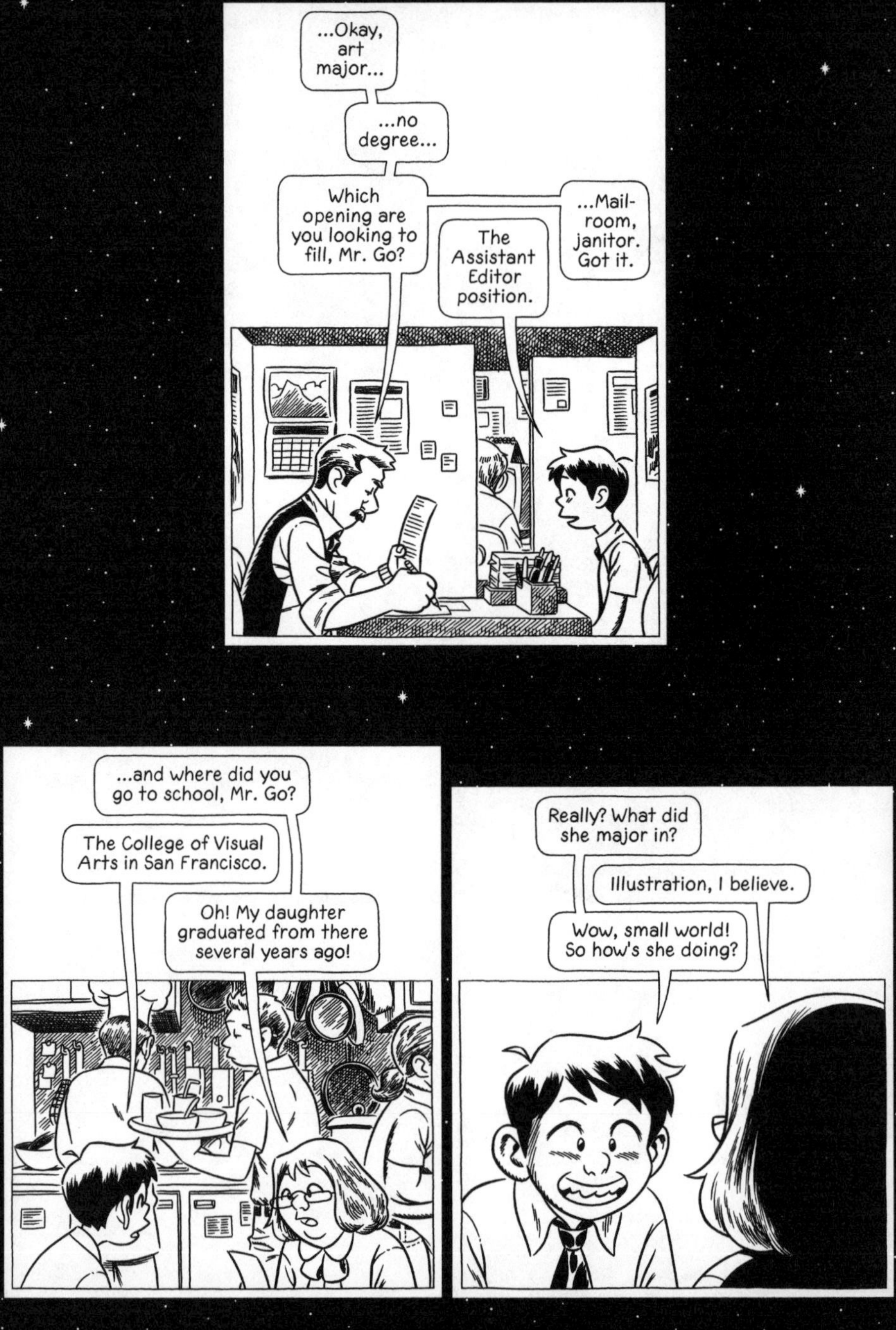
...Okay, art major...
...no degree...
Which opening are you looking to fill, Mr. Go?
The Assistant Editor position.
...Mail-room, janitor. Got it.
...and where did you go to school, Mr. Go?
The College of Visual Arts in San Francisco.
Oh! My daughter graduated from there several years ago!
Really? What did she major in?
Illustration, I believe.
Wow, small world! So how's she doing?

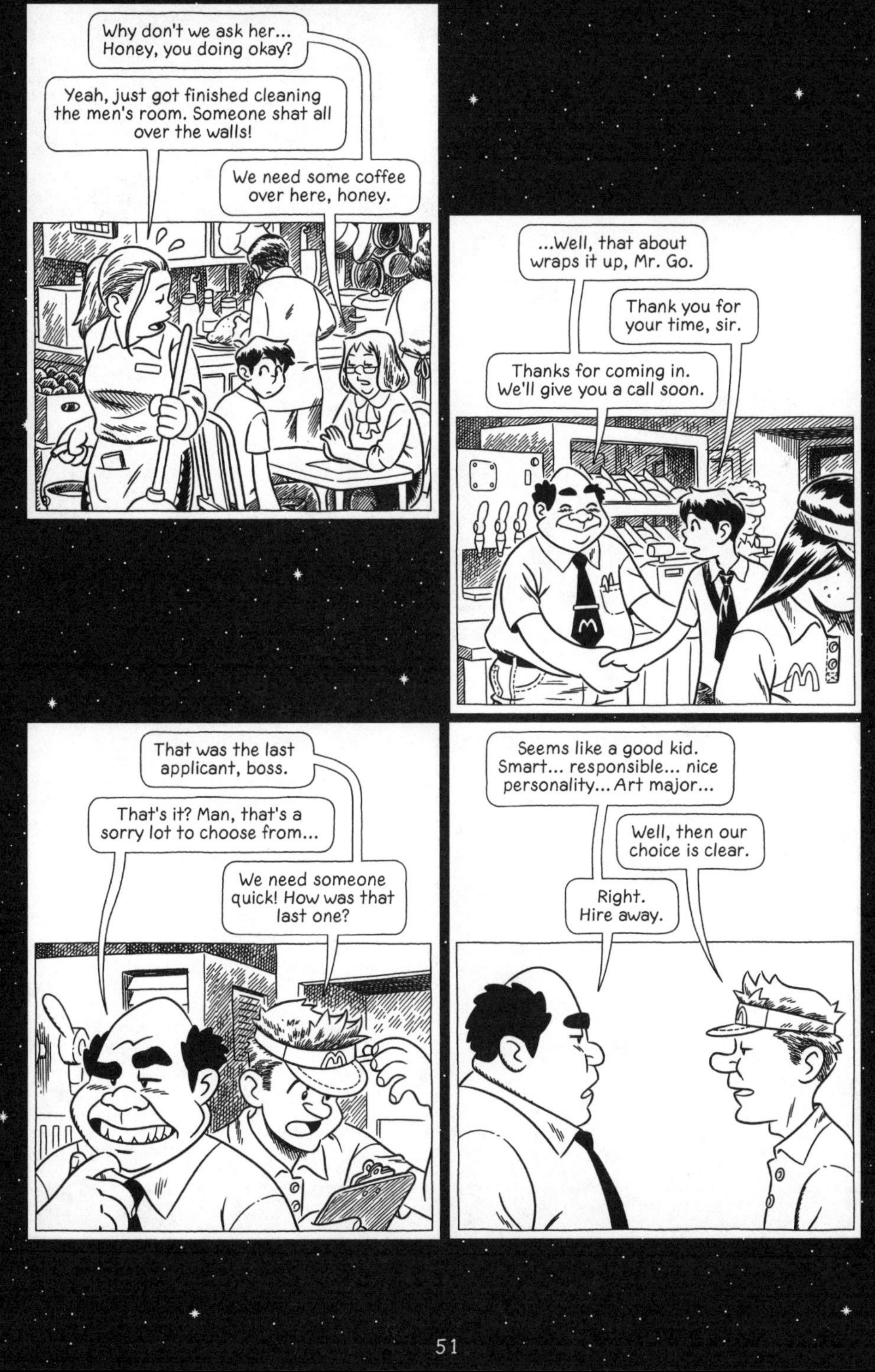
Why don't we ask her... Honey, you doing okay?
Yeah, just got finished cleaning the men's room. Someone shat all over the walls!
We need some coffee over here, honey.
...Well, that about wraps it up, Mr. Go.
Thank you for your time, sir.
Thanks for coming in. We'll give you a call soon.
That was the last applicant, boss.
That's it? Man, that's a sorry lot to choose from...
We need someone quick! How was that last one?
Seems like a good kid. Smart... responsible... nice personality... Art major...
Well, then our choice is clear.
Right. Hire away.

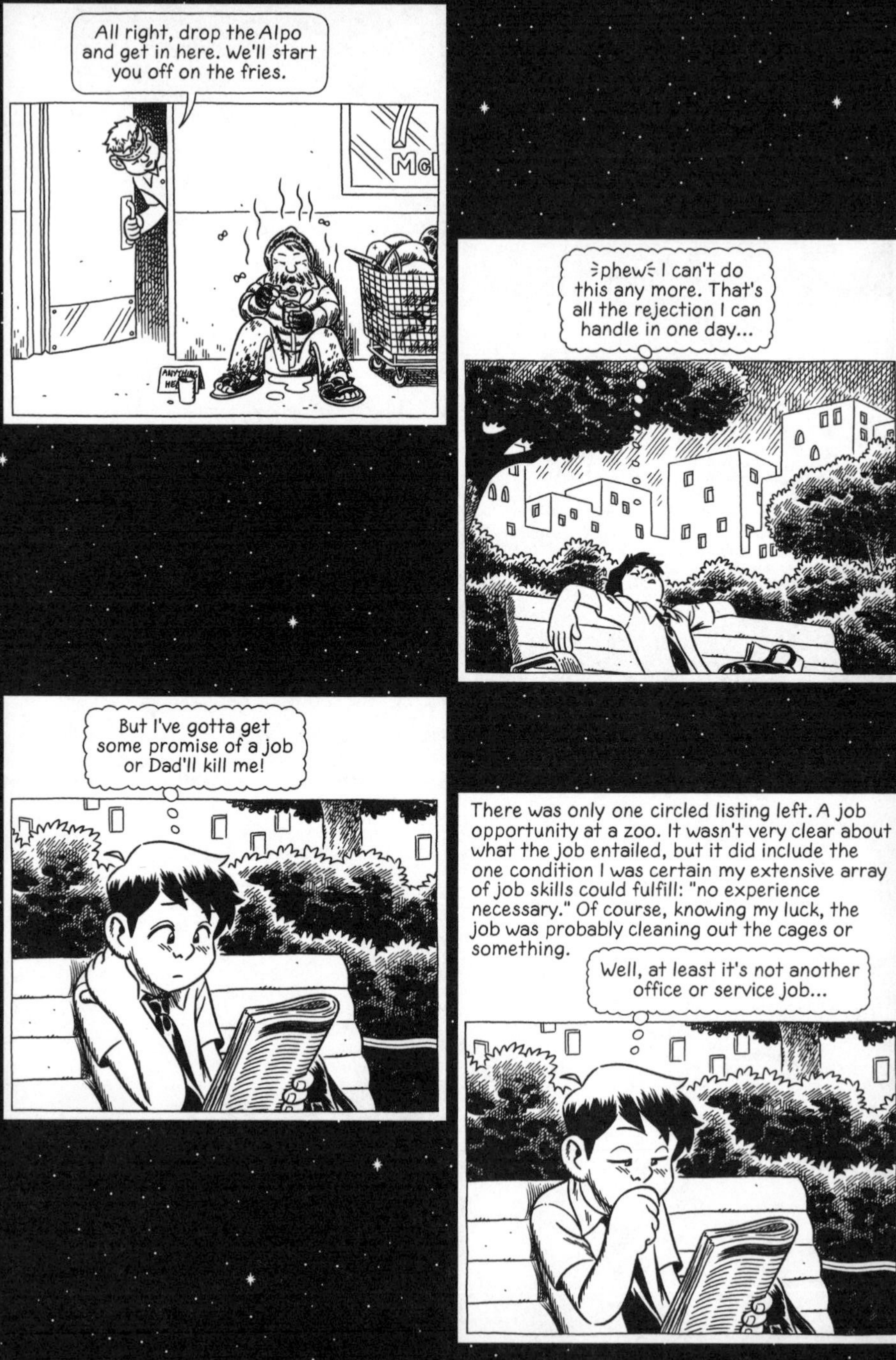
All right, drop the Alpo and get in here. We'll start you off on the fries.
phew I can't do this any more. That's all the rejection I can handle in one day...
But I've gotta get some promise of a job or Dad'll kill me!
There was only one circled listing left. A job opportunity at a zoo. It wasn't very clear about what the job entailed, but it did include the one condition I was certain my extensive array of job skills could fulfill: "no experience necessary." Of course, knowing my luck, the job was probably cleaning out the cages or something.
Well, at least it's not another office or service job...

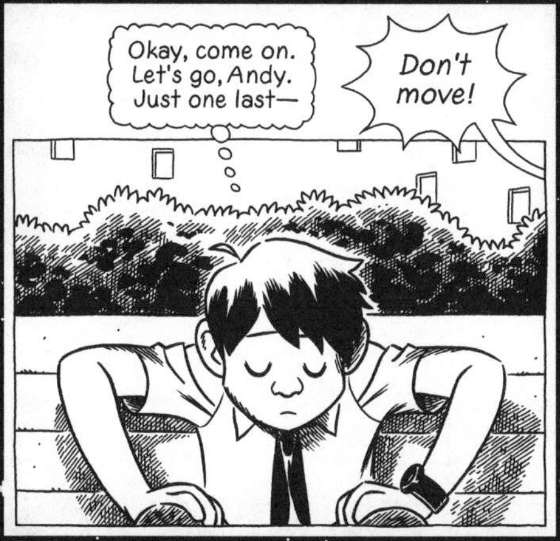
Okay, come on.
Let's go, Andy.
Just one last—
Don't move!

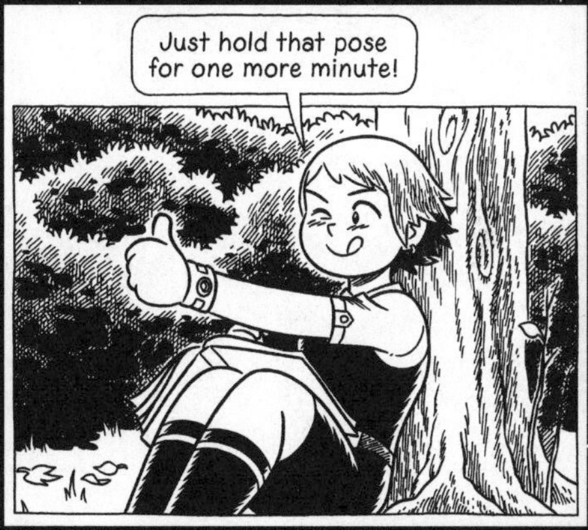
Just hold that pose for one more minute!

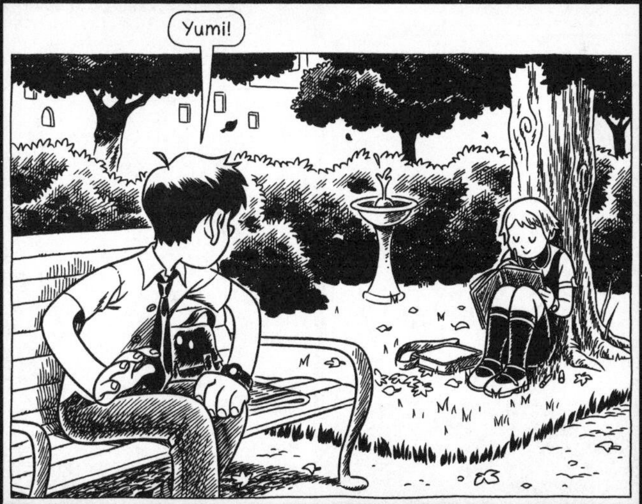
Yumi!

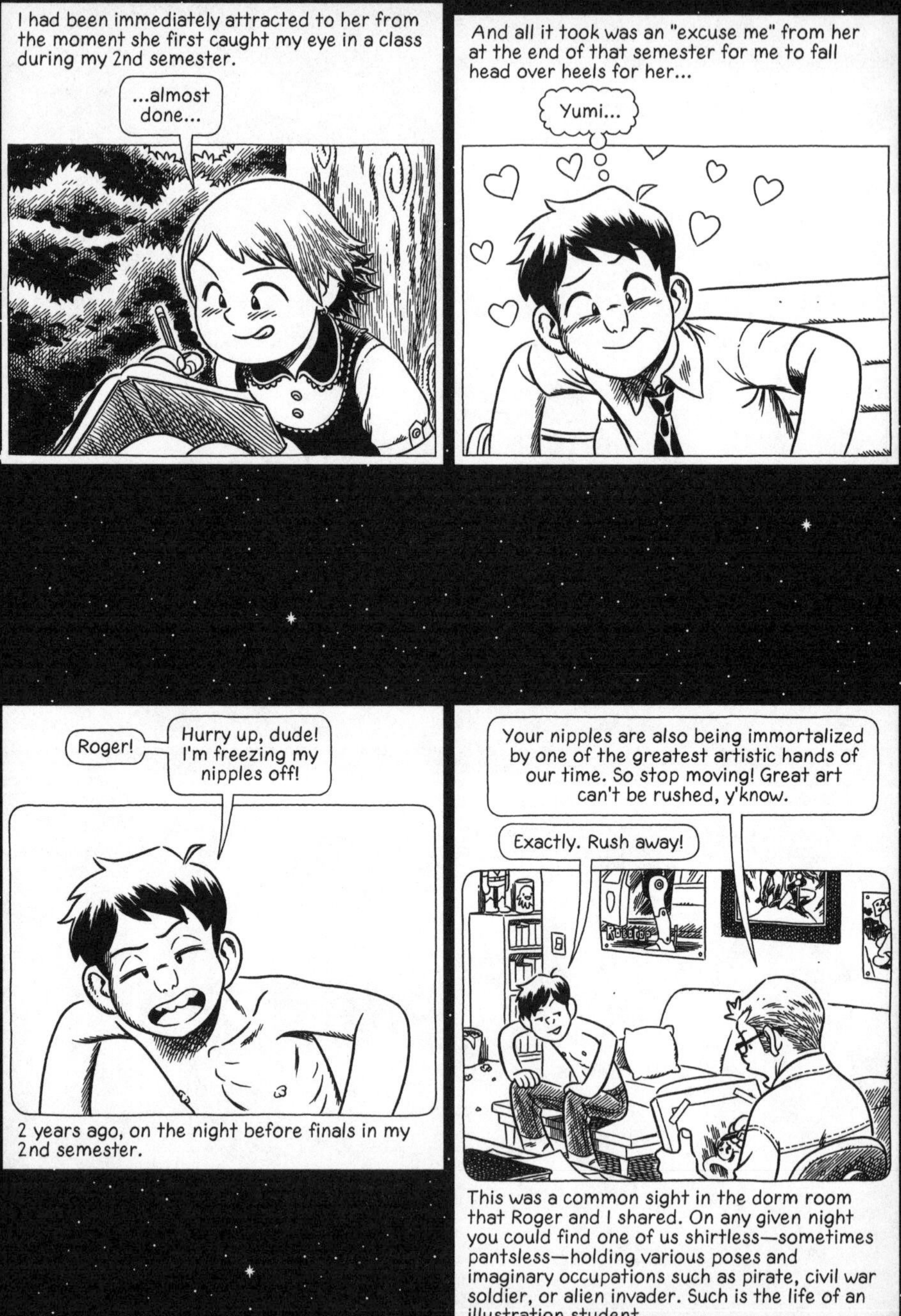

I had been immediately attracted to her from the moment she first caught my eye in a class during my 2nd semester.
...almost done...
And all it took was an "excuse me" from her at the end of that semester for me to fall head over heels for her...
Yumi...
Roger!
Hurry up, dude! I'm freezing my nipples off!
2 years ago, on the night before finals in my 2nd semester.
Your nipples are also being immortalized by one of the greatest artistic hands of our time. So stop moving! Great art can't be rushed, y'know.
Exactly. Rush away!
This was a common sight in the dorm room that Roger and I shared. On any given night you could find one of us shirtless—sometimes pantsless—holding various poses and imaginary occupations such as pirate, civil war soldier, or alien invader. Such is the life of an illustration student.

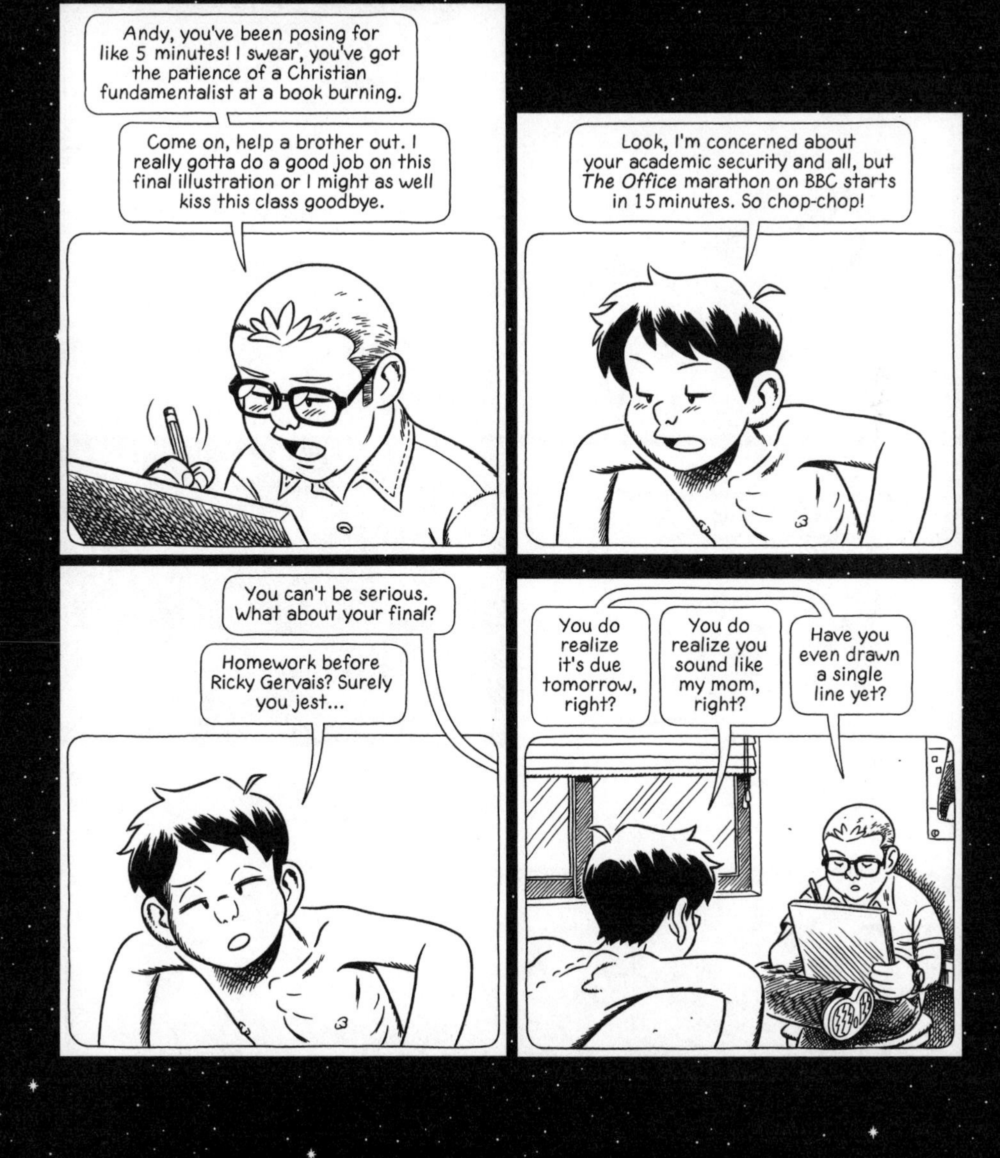
Andy, you've been posing for like 5 minutes! I swear, you've got the patience of a Christian fundamentalist at a book burning.
Come on, help a brother out. I really gotta do a good job on this final illustration or I might as well kiss this class goodbye.
Look, I'm concerned about your academic security and all, but *The Office* marathon on BBC starts in 15 minutes. So chop-chop!
You can't be serious. What about your final?
Homework before Ricky Gervais? Surely you jest...
You do realize it's due tomorrow, right?
You do realize you sound like my mom, right?
Have you even drawn a single line yet?

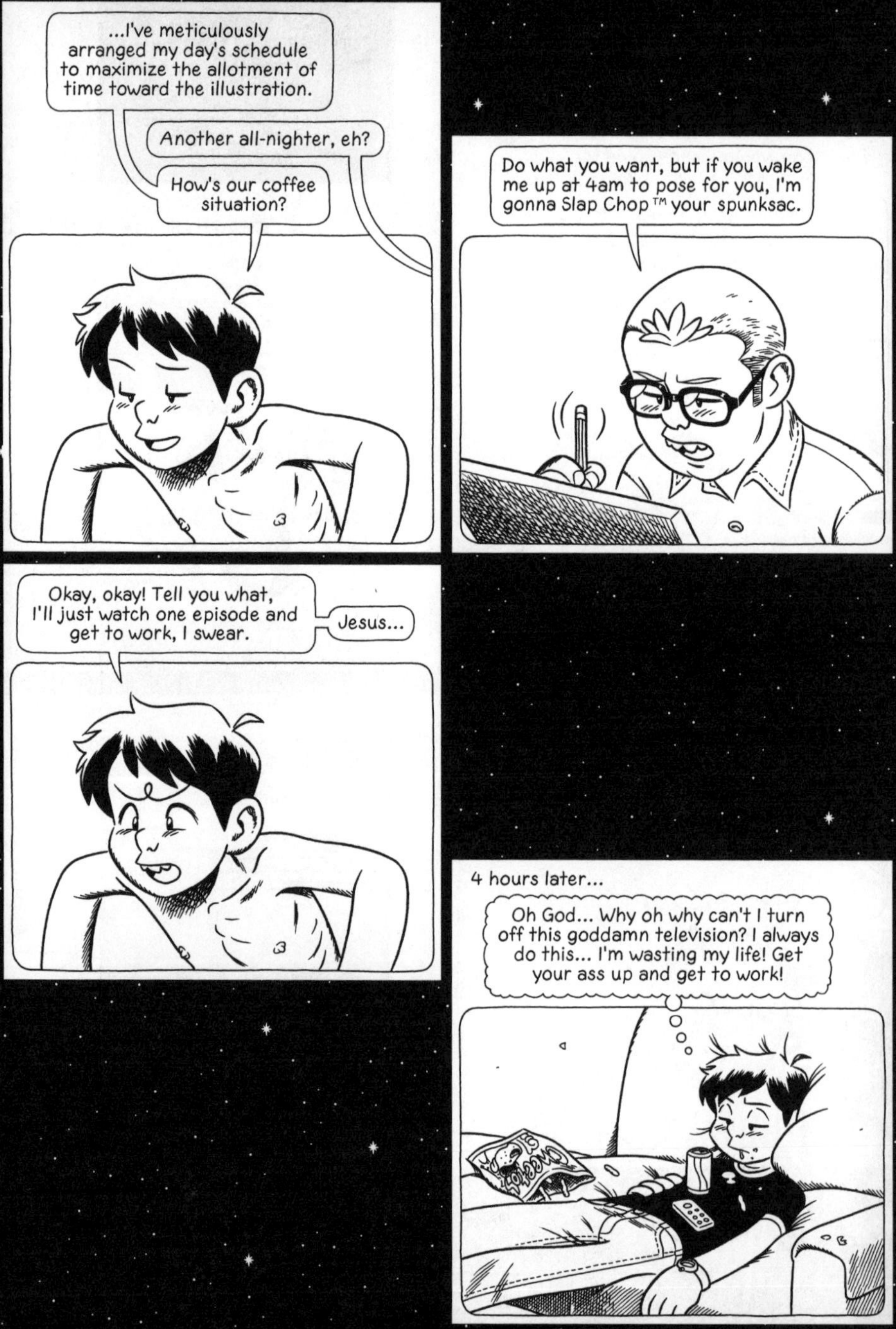
...I've meticulously arranged my day's schedule to maximize the allotment of time toward the illustration.
How's our coffee situation?
Another all-nighter, eh?
Do what you want, but if you wake me up at 4am to pose for you, I'm gonna Slap Chop ™ your spunksac.
Okay, okay! Tell you what, I'll just watch one episode and get to work, I swear.
Jesus...
4 hours later...
Oh God... Why oh why can't I turn off this goddamn television? I always do this... I'm wasting my life! Get your ass up and get to work!

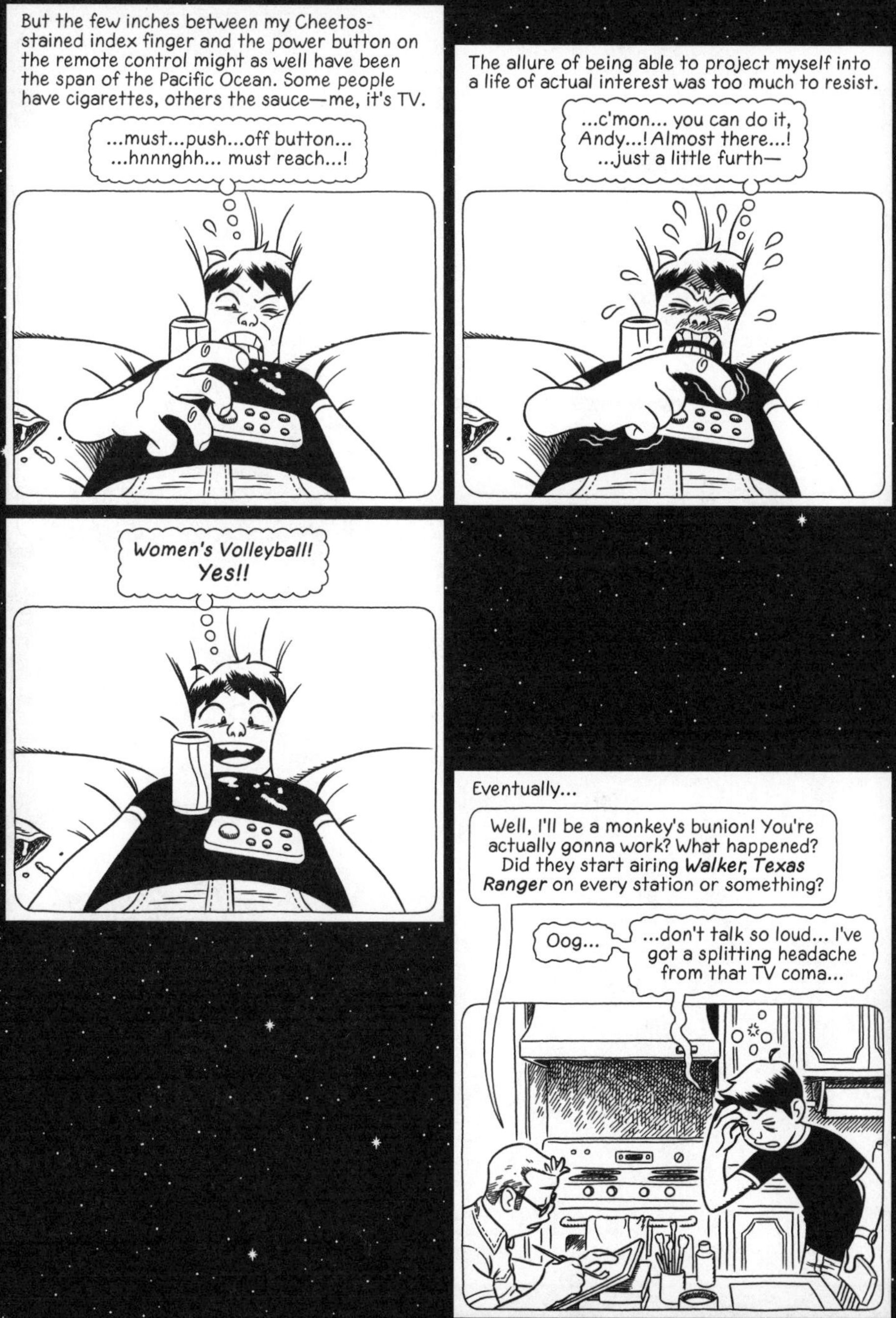
But the few inches between my Cheetos-stained index finger and the power button on the remote control might as well have been the span of the Pacific Ocean. Some people have cigarettes, others the sauce—me, it's TV.
...must...push...off button... ...hnnnghh... must reach...!
The allure of being able to project myself into a life of actual interest was too much to resist.
...c'mon... you can do it, Andy...! Almost there...! ...just a little furth—
Women's Volleyball! Yes!!
Eventually...
Well, I'll be a monkey's bunion! You're actually gonna work? What happened? Did they start airing Walker, Texas Ranger on every station or something?
Oog...
...don't talk so loud... I've got a splitting headache from that TV coma...

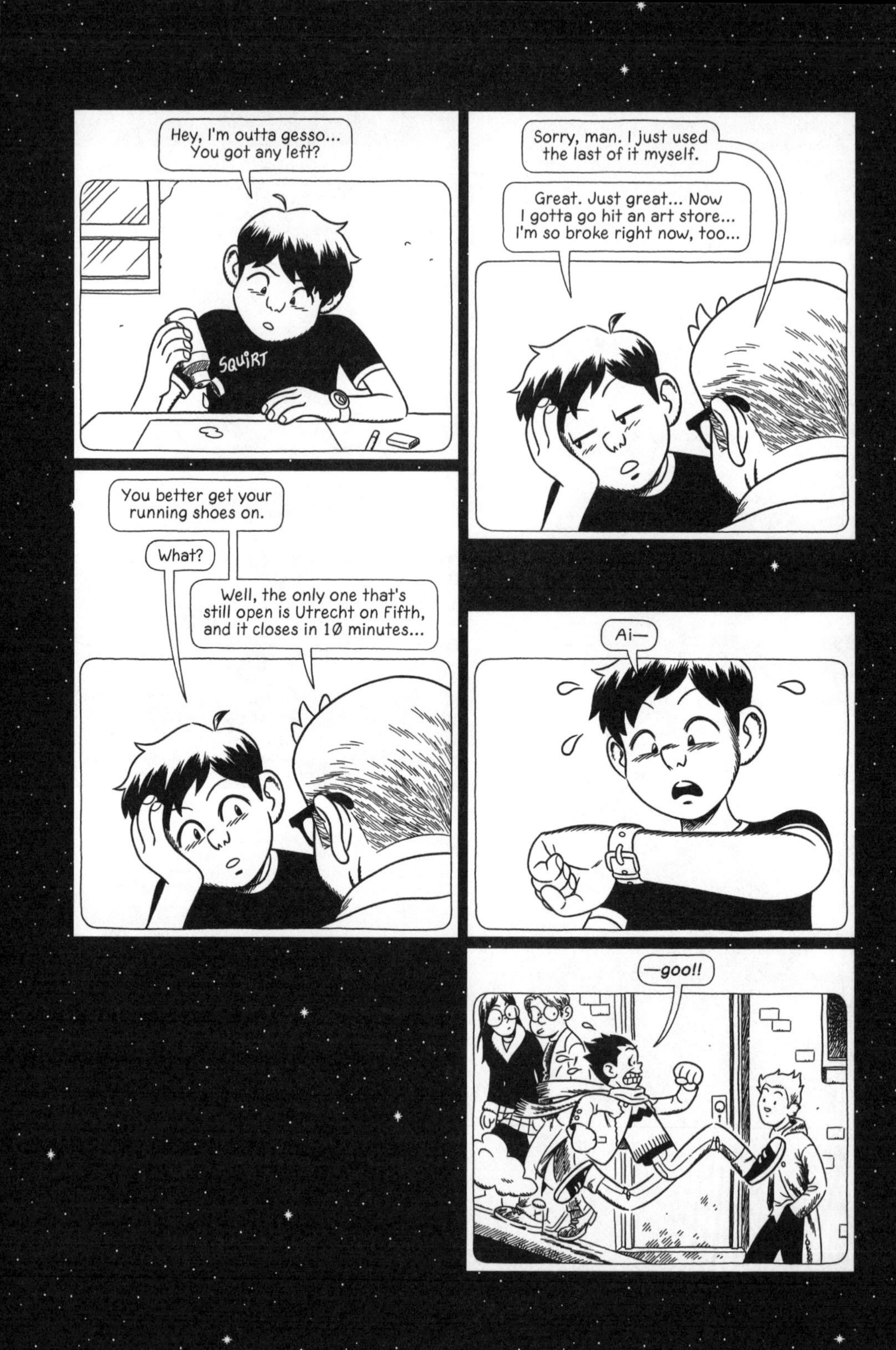
Hey, I'm outta gesso... You got any left?
SQUIRT
Sorry, man. I just used the last of it myself.
Great. Just great... Now I gotta go hit an art store... I'm so broke right now, too...
You better get your running shoes on.
What?
Well, the only one that's still open is Utrecht on Fifth, and it closes in 10 minutes...
Ai—
—goo!!

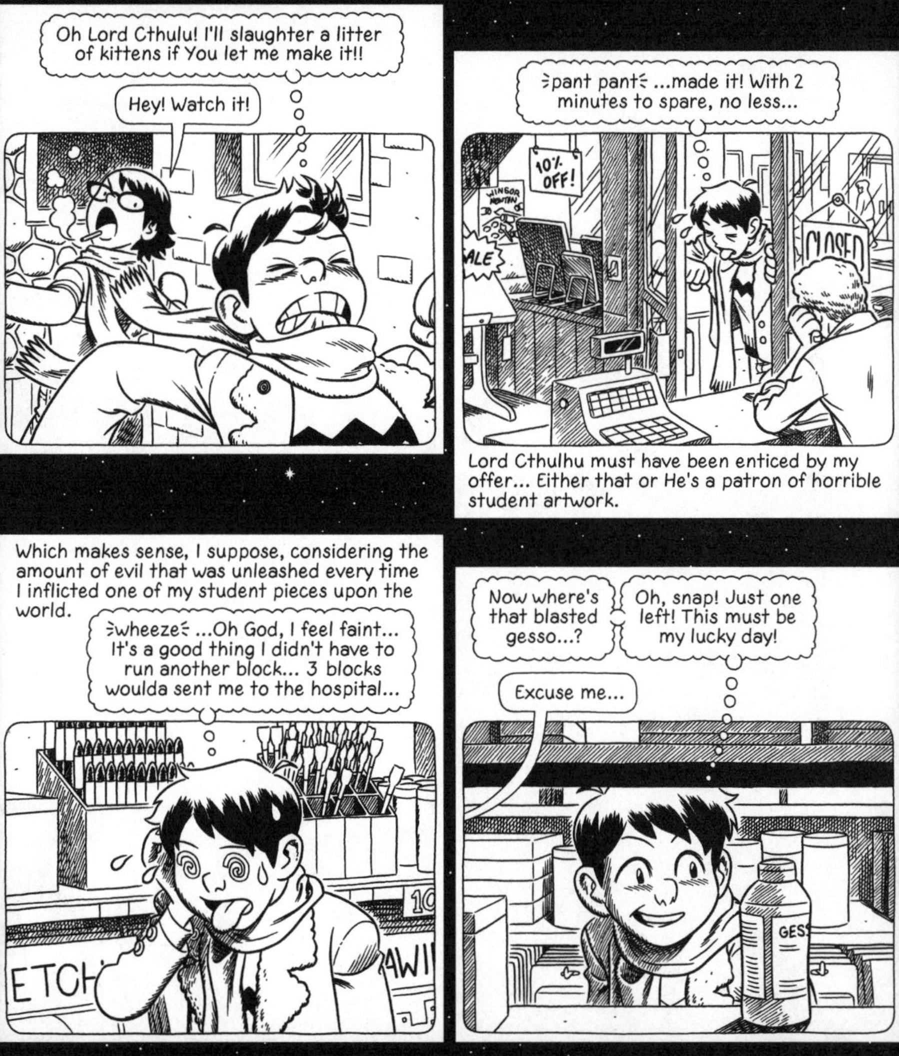

Oh Lord Cthulu! I'll slaughter a litter of kittens if You let me make it!!
Hey! Watch it!
⋛pant pant⋚ ...made it! With 2 minutes to spare, no less...
10% OFF!
CLOSED
Lord Cthulhu must have been enticed by my offer... Either that or He's a patron of horrible student artwork.
Which makes sense, I suppose, considering the amount of evil that was unleashed every time I inflicted one of my student pieces upon the world.
⋛wheeze⋚ ...Oh God, I feel faint... It's a good thing I didn't have to run another block... 3 blocks woulda sent me to the hospital...
Now where's that blasted gesso...?
Oh, snap! Just one left! This must be my lucky day!
Excuse me...

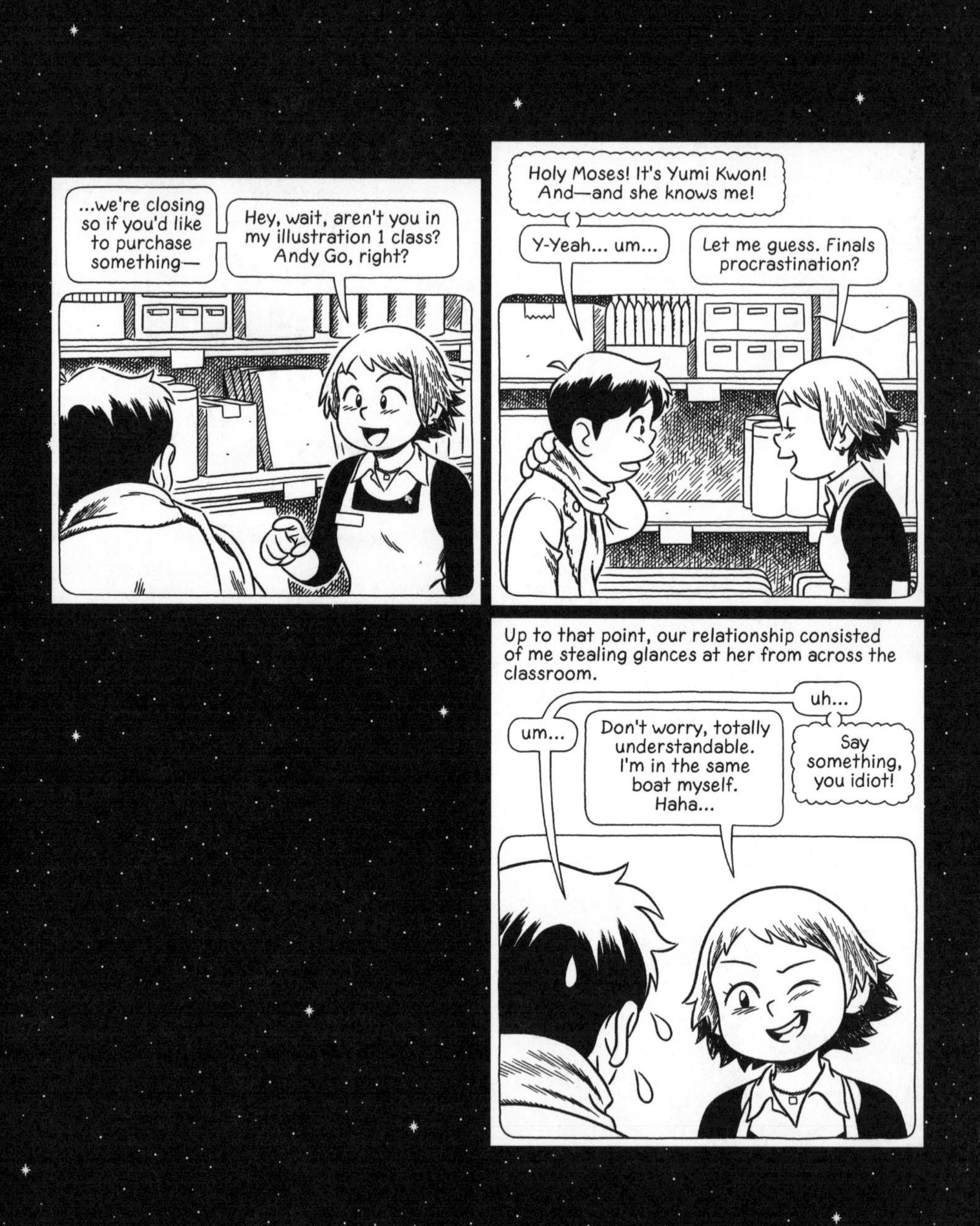
...we're closing so if you'd like to purchase something—
Hey, wait, aren't you in my illustration 1 class? Andy Go, right?
Holy Moses! It's Yumi Kwon! And—and she knows me!
Y-Yeah... um...
Let me guess. Finals procrastination?
Up to that point, our relationship consisted of me stealing glances at her from across the classroom.
um...
Don't worry, totally understandable. I'm in the same boat myself. Haha...
uh...
Say something, you idiot!

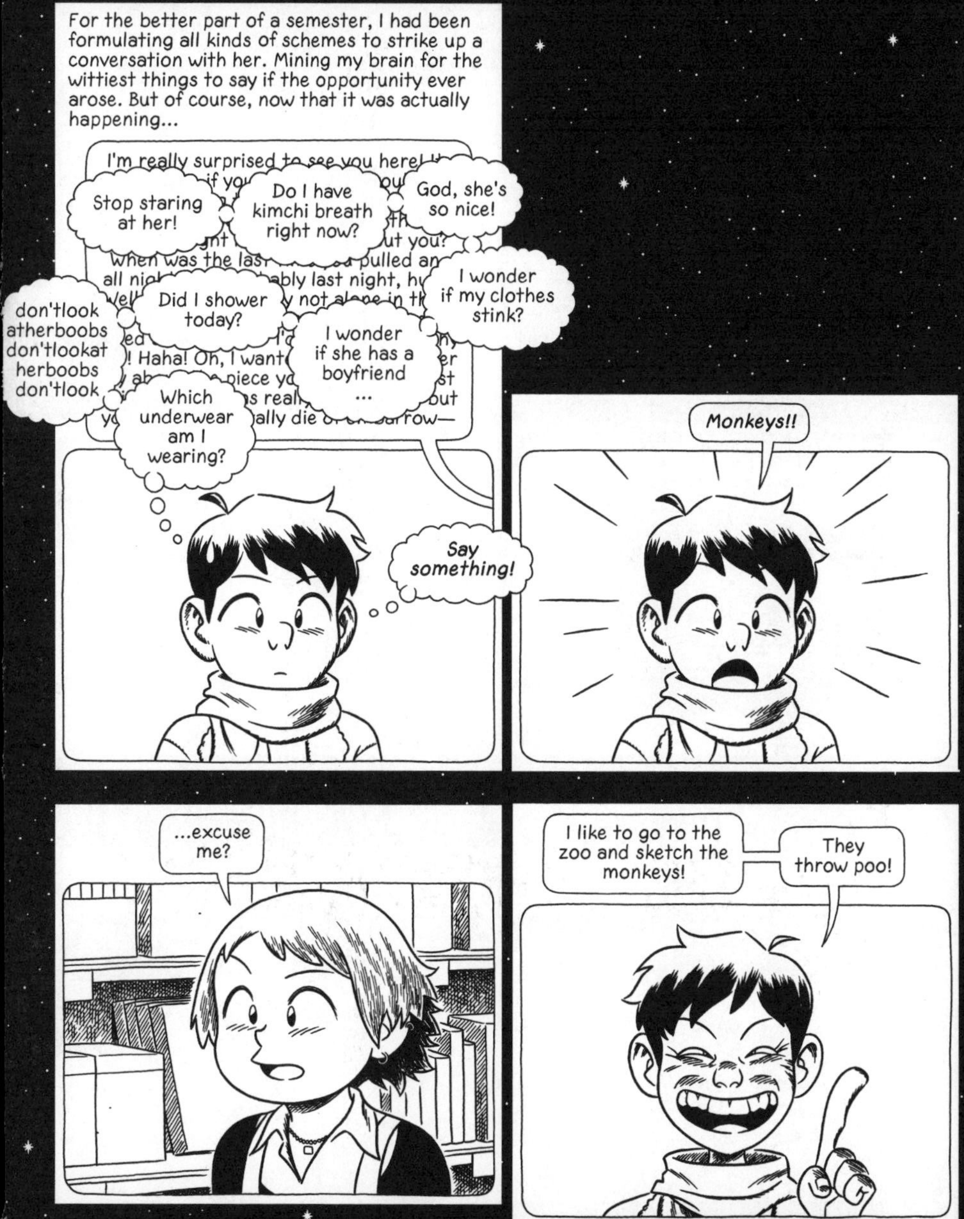
For the better part of a semester, I had been formulating all kinds of schemes to strike up a conversation with her. Mining my brain for the wittiest things to say if the opportunity ever arose. But of course, now that it was actually happening...
I'm really surprised to see you here!
Stop staring at her!
Do I have kimchi breath right now?
God, she's so nice!
I wonder if my clothes stink?
don'tlook atherboobs don'tlookat herboobs don'tlook
Did I shower today?
I wonder if she has a boyfriend ...
Which underwear am I wearing?
Say something!
Monkeys!!
...excuse me?
I like to go to the zoo and sketch the monkeys!
They throw poo!

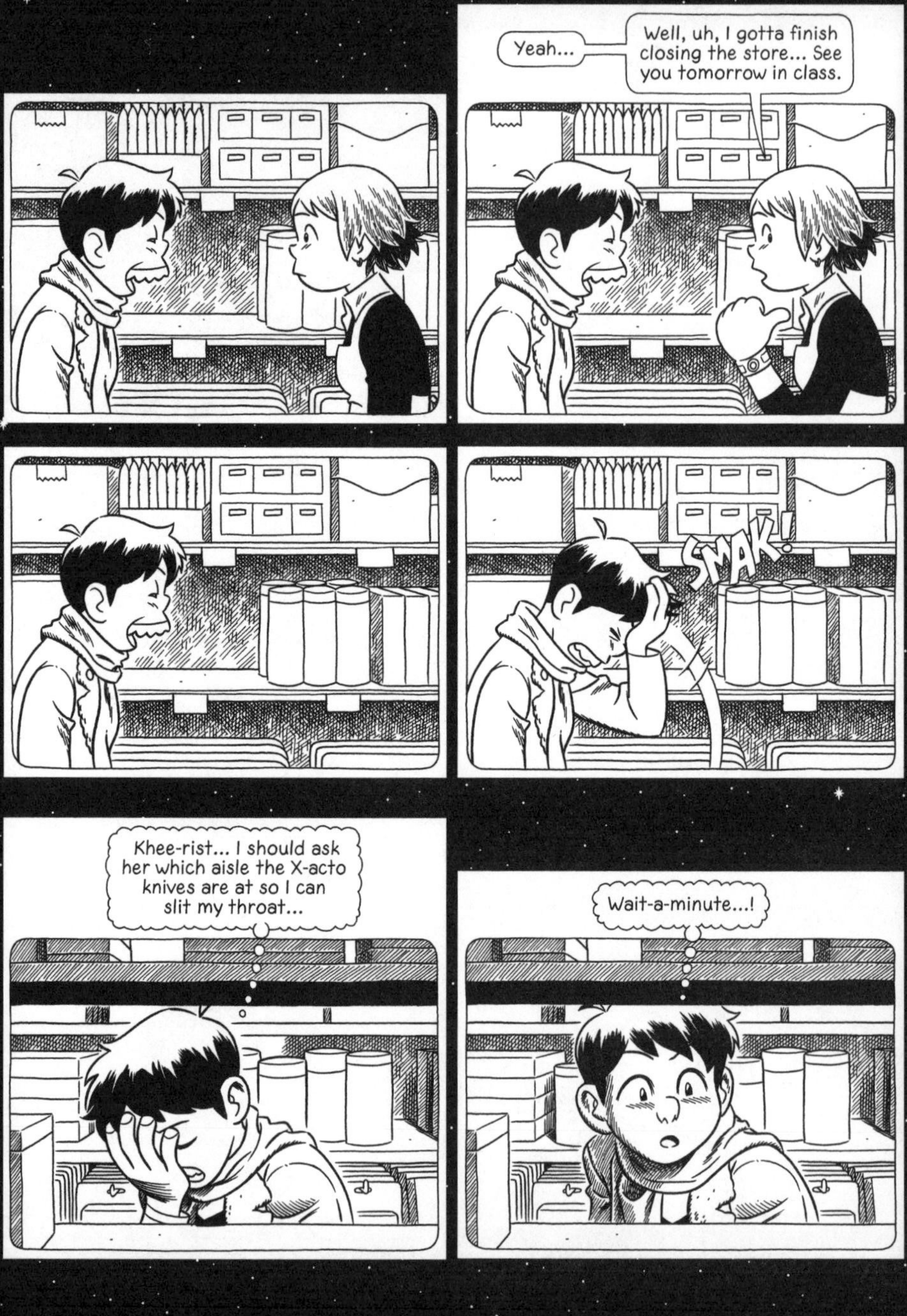
Yeah...
Well, uh, I gotta finish closing the store... See you tomorrow in class.
SMAK!
Khee-rist... I should ask her which aisle the X-acto knives are at so I can slit my throat...
Wait-a-minute...!

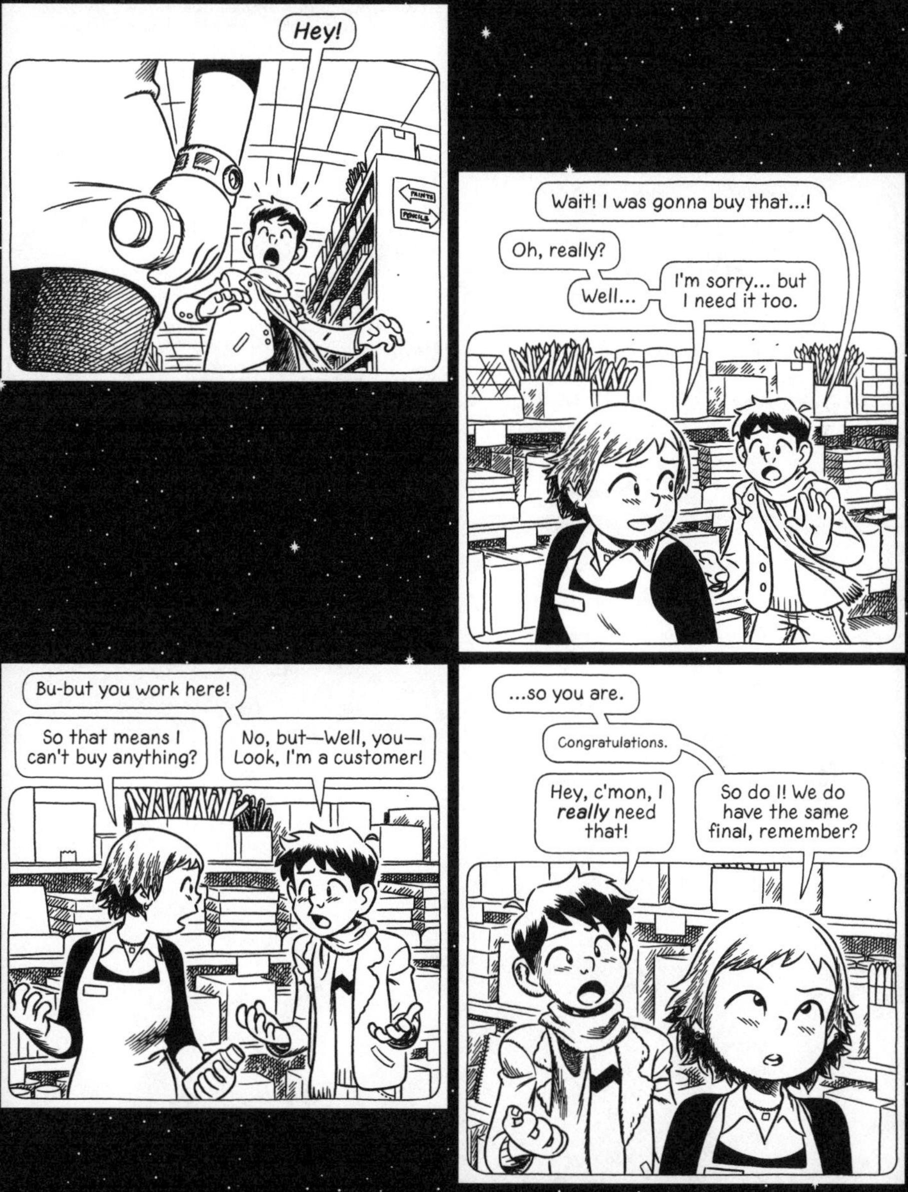
Hey!
PAINTS
PENCILS
Wait! I was gonna buy that...!
Oh, really?
Well...
I'm sorry... but I need it too.
Bu-but you work here!
So that means I can't buy anything?
No, but—Well, you— Look, I'm a customer!
...so you are.
Congratulations.
Hey, c'mon, I *really* need that!
So do I! We do have the same final, remember?

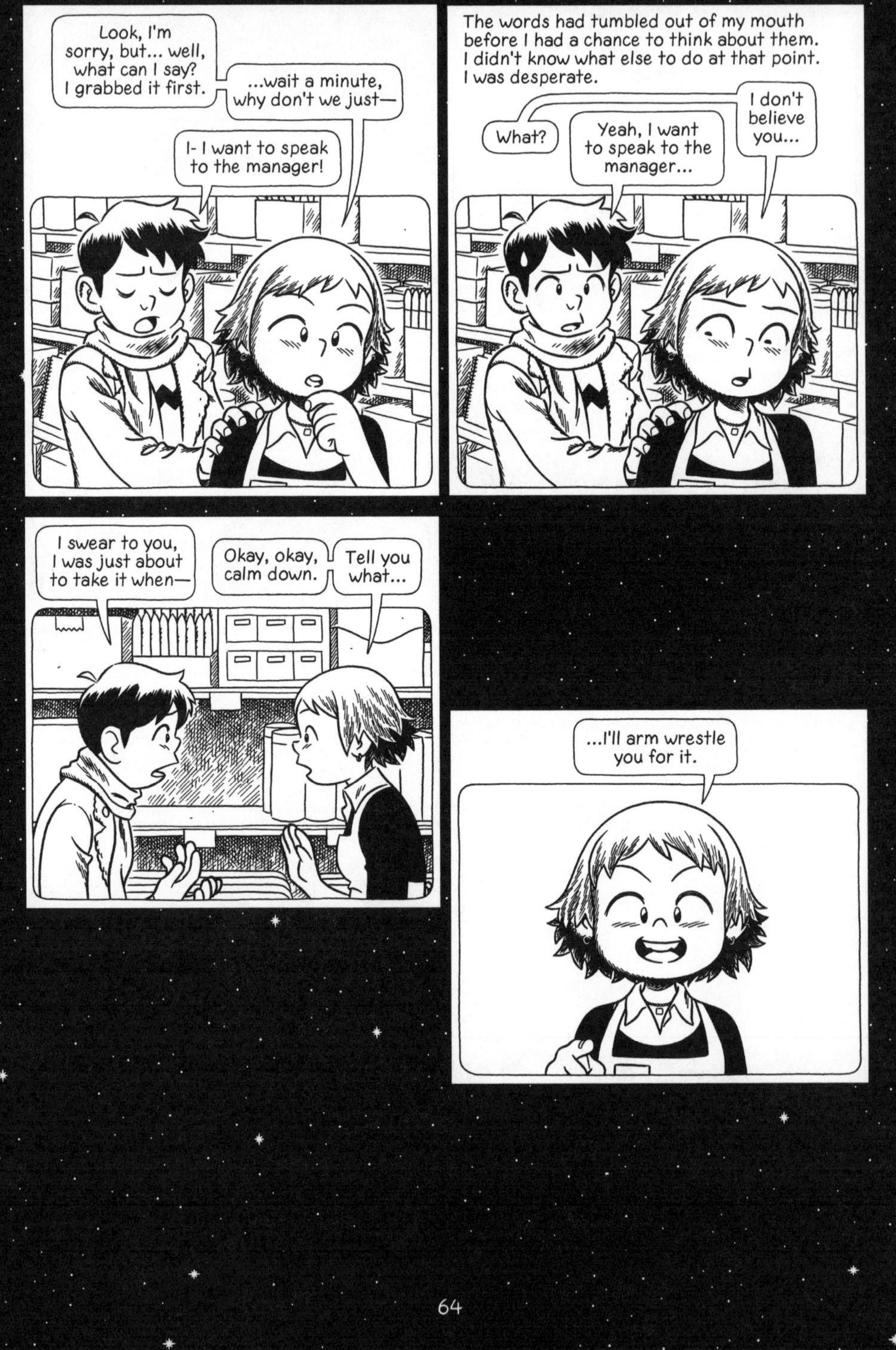
Look, I'm sorry, but... well, what can I say? I grabbed it first.
...wait a minute, why don't we just—
I- I want to speak to the manager!
The words had tumbled out of my mouth before I had a chance to think about them. I didn't know what else to do at that point. I was desperate.
What?
I don't believe you...
Yeah, I want to speak to the manager...
I swear to you, I was just about to take it when—
Okay, okay, calm down.
Tell you what...
...I'll arm wrestle you for it.

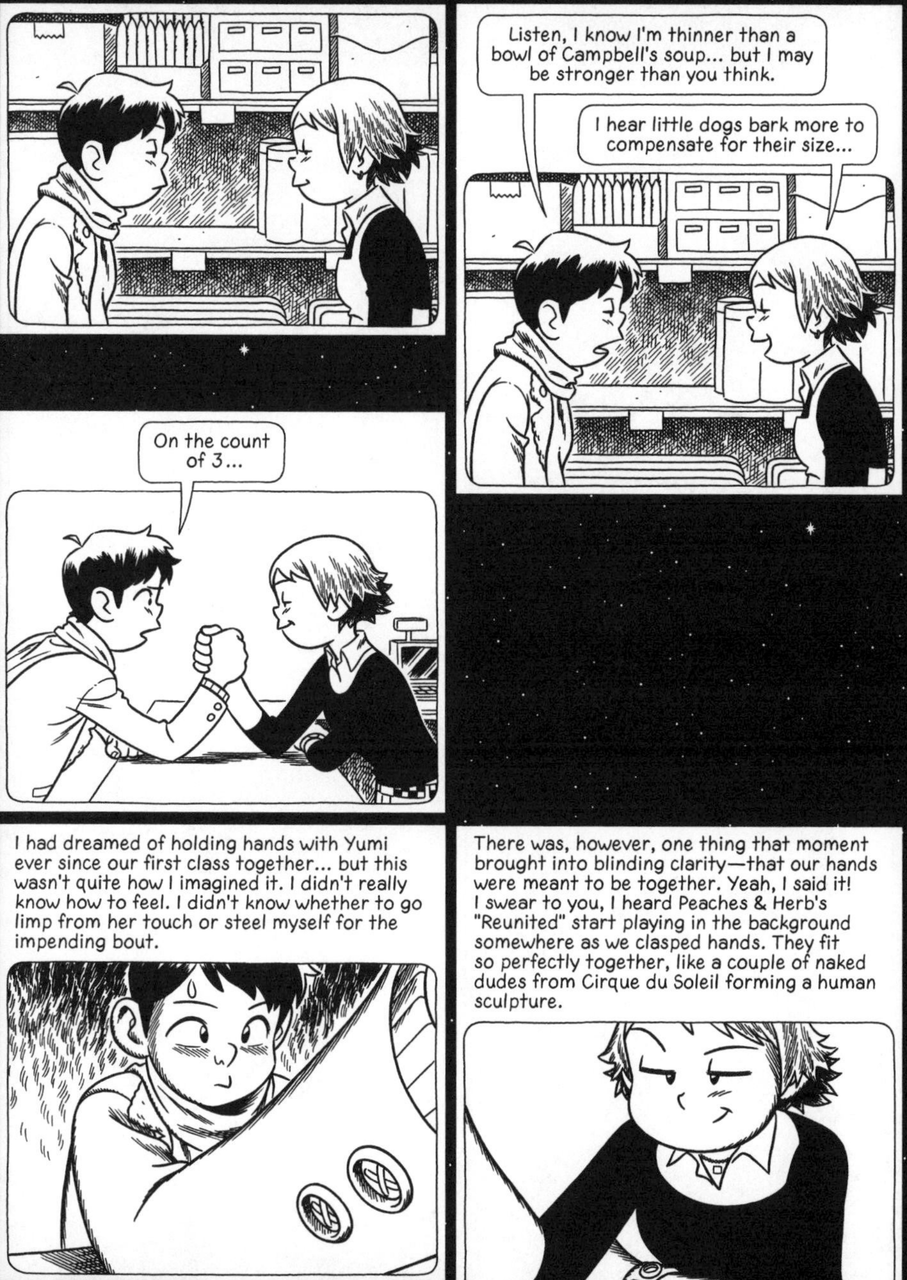
Listen, I know I'm thinner than a bowl of Campbell's soup... but I may be stronger than you think.
I hear little dogs bark more to compensate for their size...
On the count of 3...
I had dreamed of holding hands with Yumi ever since our first class together... but this wasn't quite how I imagined it. I didn't really know how to feel. I didn't know whether to go limp from her touch or steel myself for the impending bout.
There was, however, one thing that moment brought into blinding clarity—that our hands were meant to be together. Yeah, I said it! I swear to you, I heard Peaches & Herb's "Reunited" start playing in the background somewhere as we clasped hands. They fit so perfectly together, like a couple of naked dudes from Cirque du Soleil forming a human sculpture.

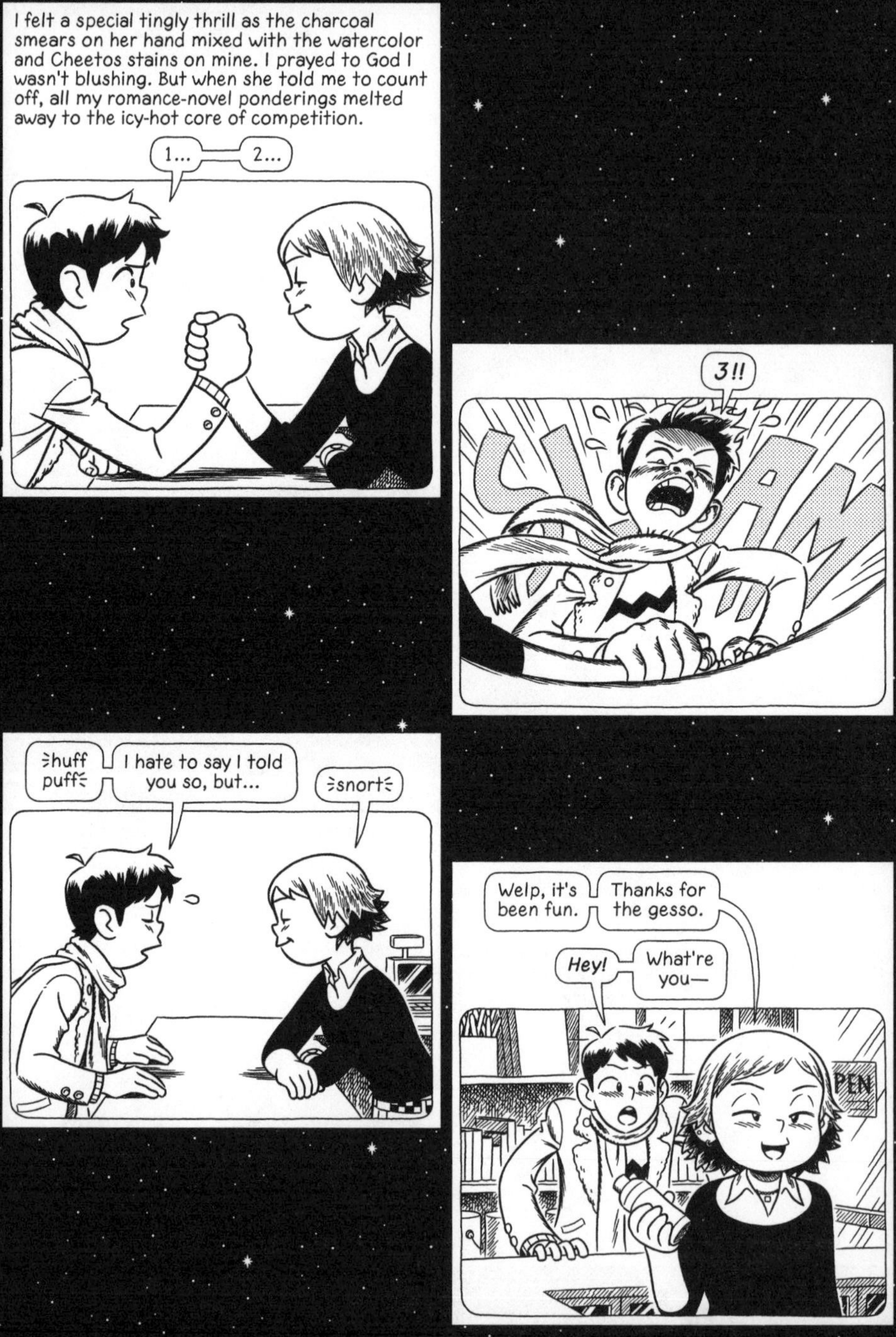
I felt a special tingly thrill as the charcoal smears on her hand mixed with the watercolor and Cheetos stains on mine. I prayed to God I wasn't blushing. But when she told me to count off, all my romance-novel ponderings melted away to the icy-hot core of competition.
1...
2...
3!!
SLAM
≑huff puff≑
I hate to say I told you so, but...
≑snort≑
Welp, it's been fun.
Thanks for the gesso.
Hey!
What're you—

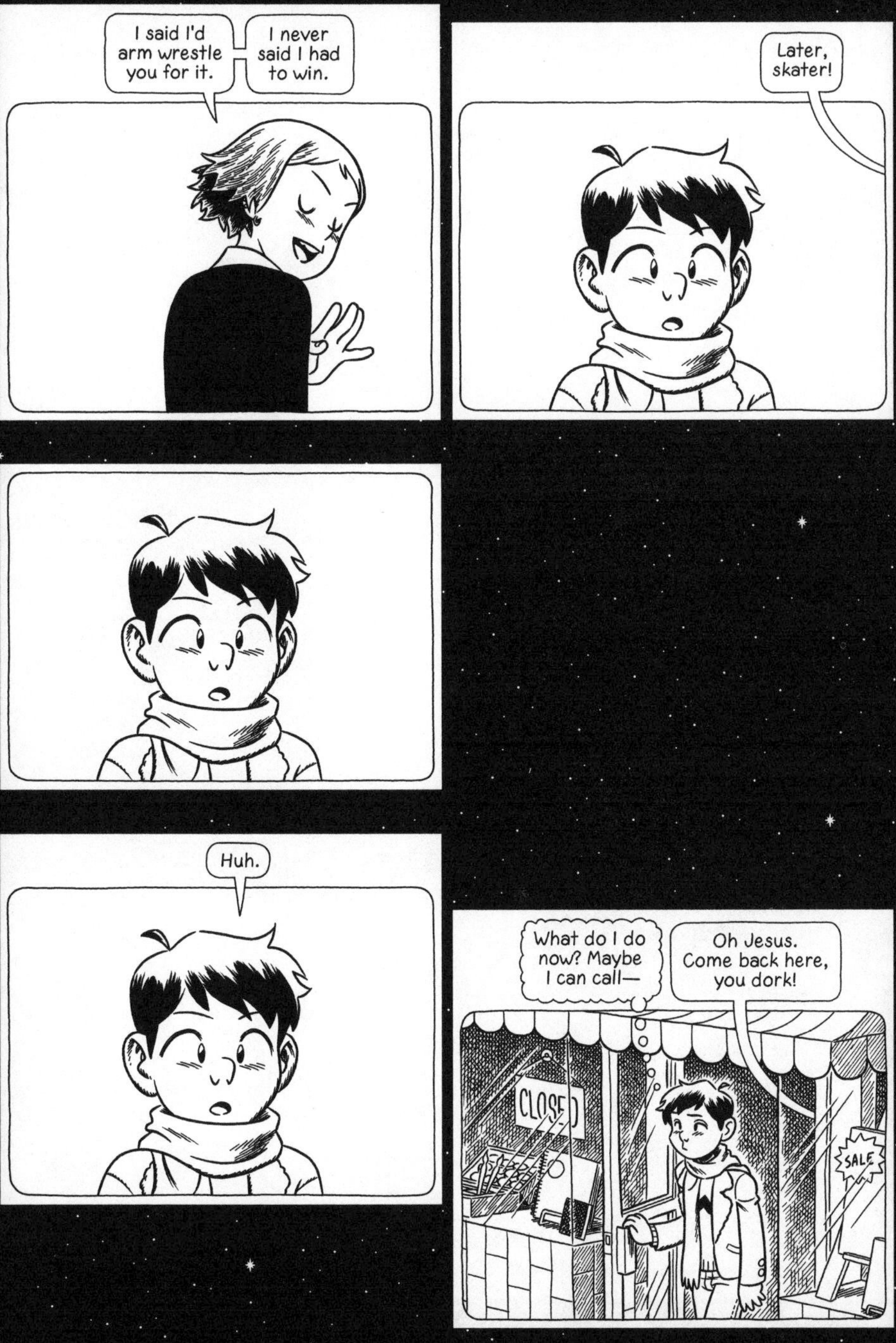
I said I'd arm wrestle you for it.
I never said I had to win.
Later, skater!
Huh.
What do I do now? Maybe I can call—
Oh Jesus. Come back here, you dork!
CLOSED
SALE

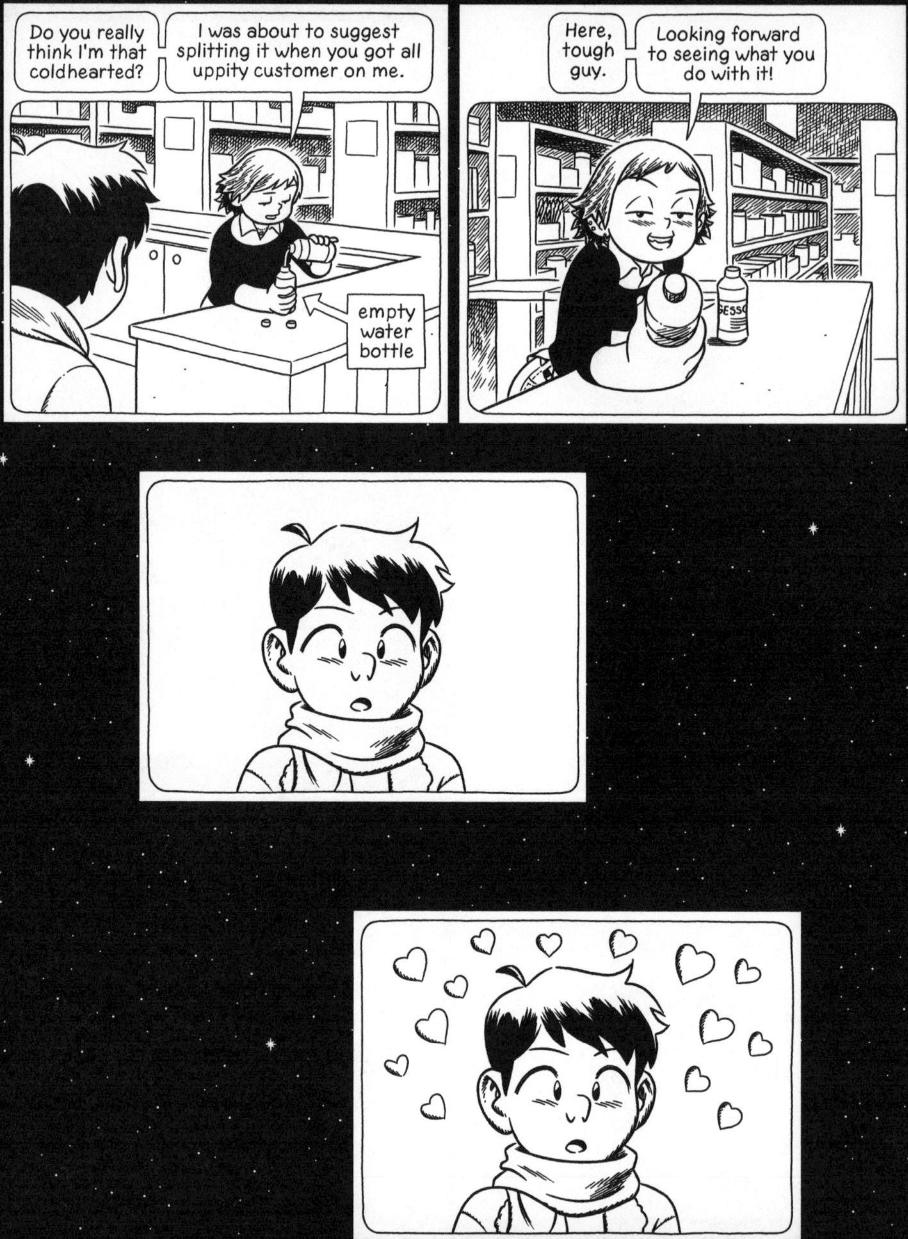
Do you really think I'm that coldhearted?
I was about to suggest splitting it when you got all uppity customer on me.
empty water bottle
Here, tough guy.
Looking forward to seeing what you do with it!
GESSO

CHAPTER
06

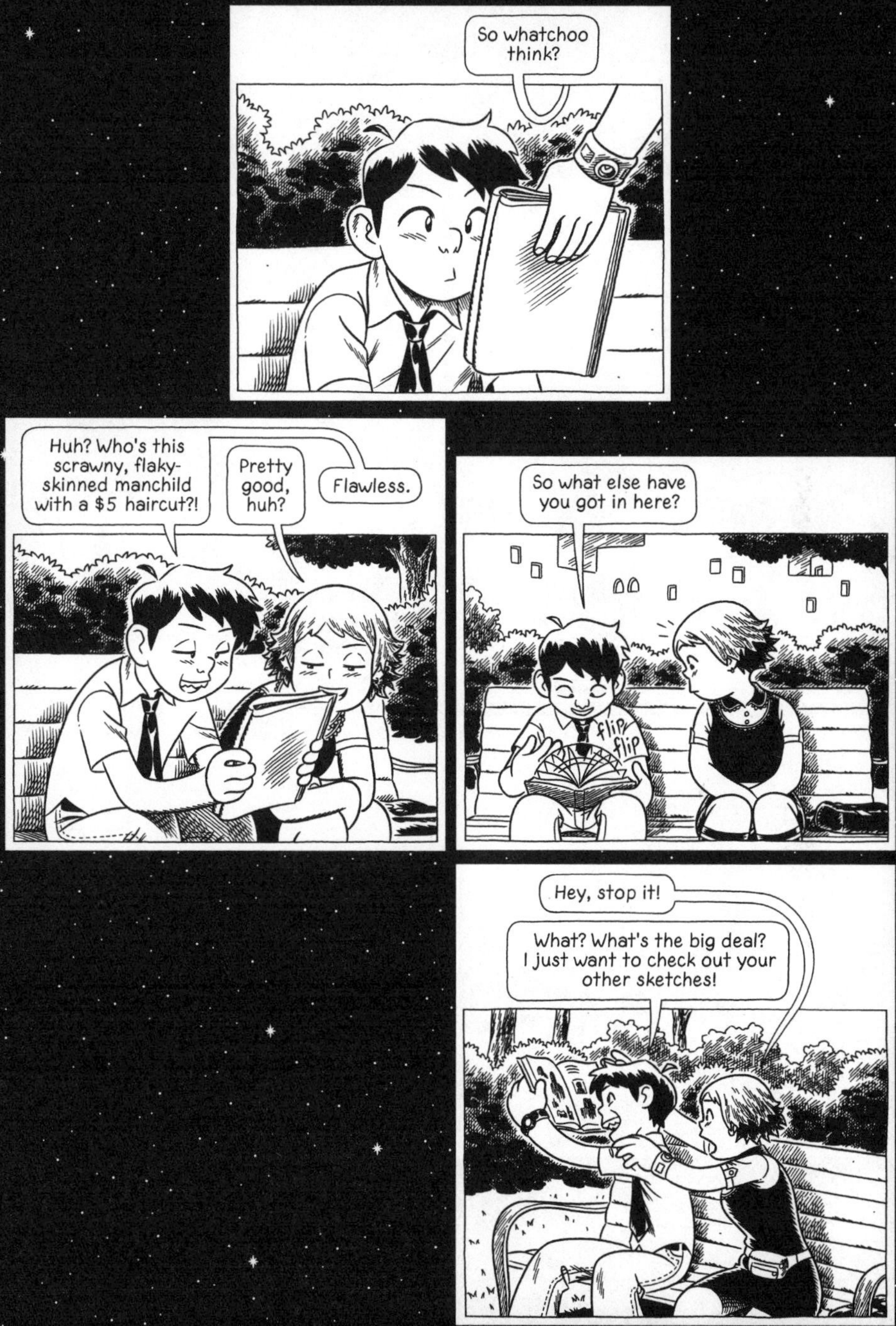

So whatchoo think?
Huh? Who's this scrawny, flaky-skinned manchild with a $5 haircut?!
Pretty good, huh?
Flawless.
So what else have you got in here?
flip flip
Hey, stop it!
What? What's the big deal? I just want to check out your other sketches!

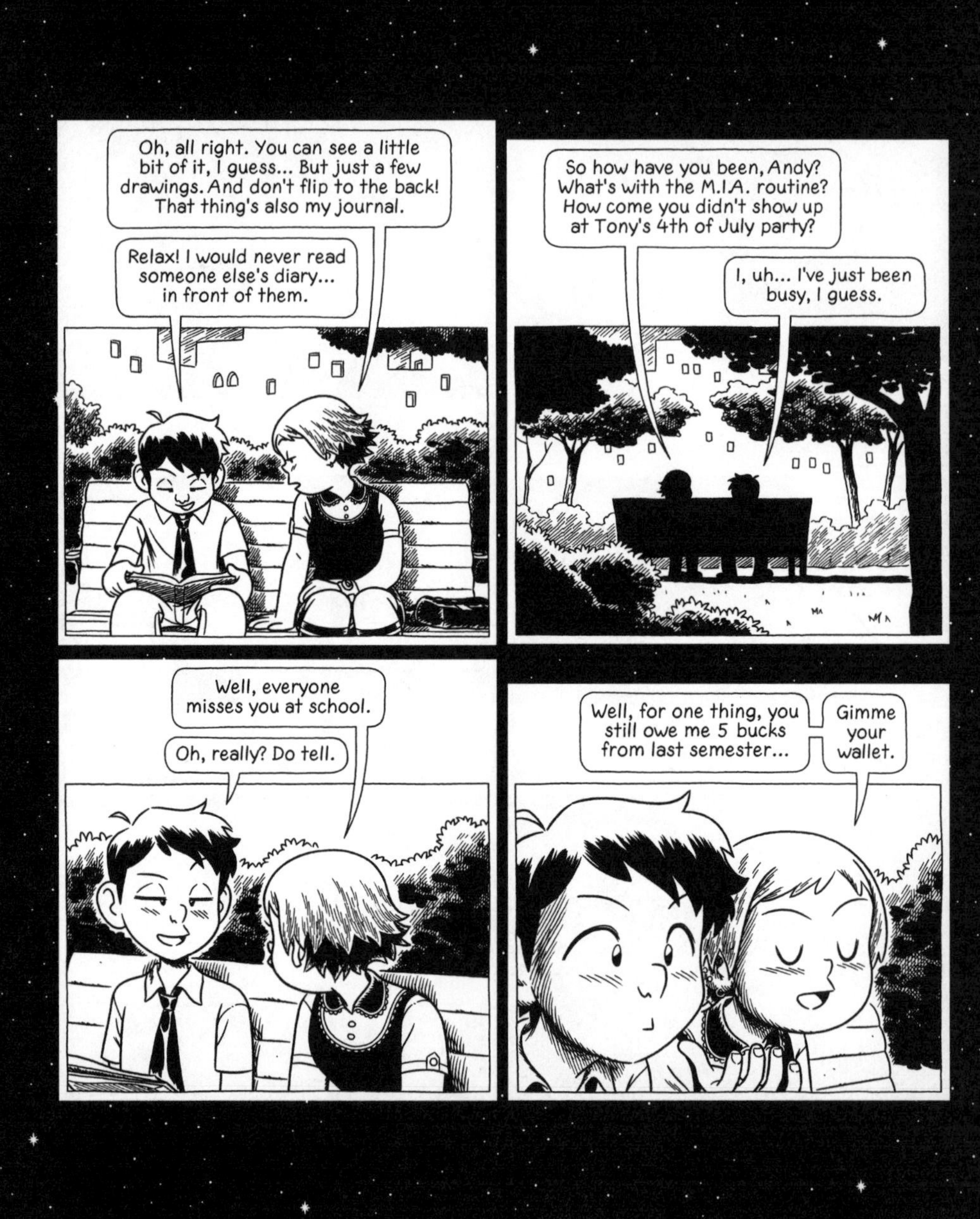
Oh, all right. You can see a little bit of it, I guess... But just a few drawings. And don't flip to the back! That thing's also my journal.
Relax! I would never read someone else's diary... in front of them.
So how have you been, Andy? What's with the M.I.A. routine? How come you didn't show up at Tony's 4th of July party?
I, uh... I've just been busy, I guess.
Well, everyone misses you at school.
Oh, really? Do tell.
Well, for one thing, you still owe me 5 bucks from last semester...
Gimme your wallet.

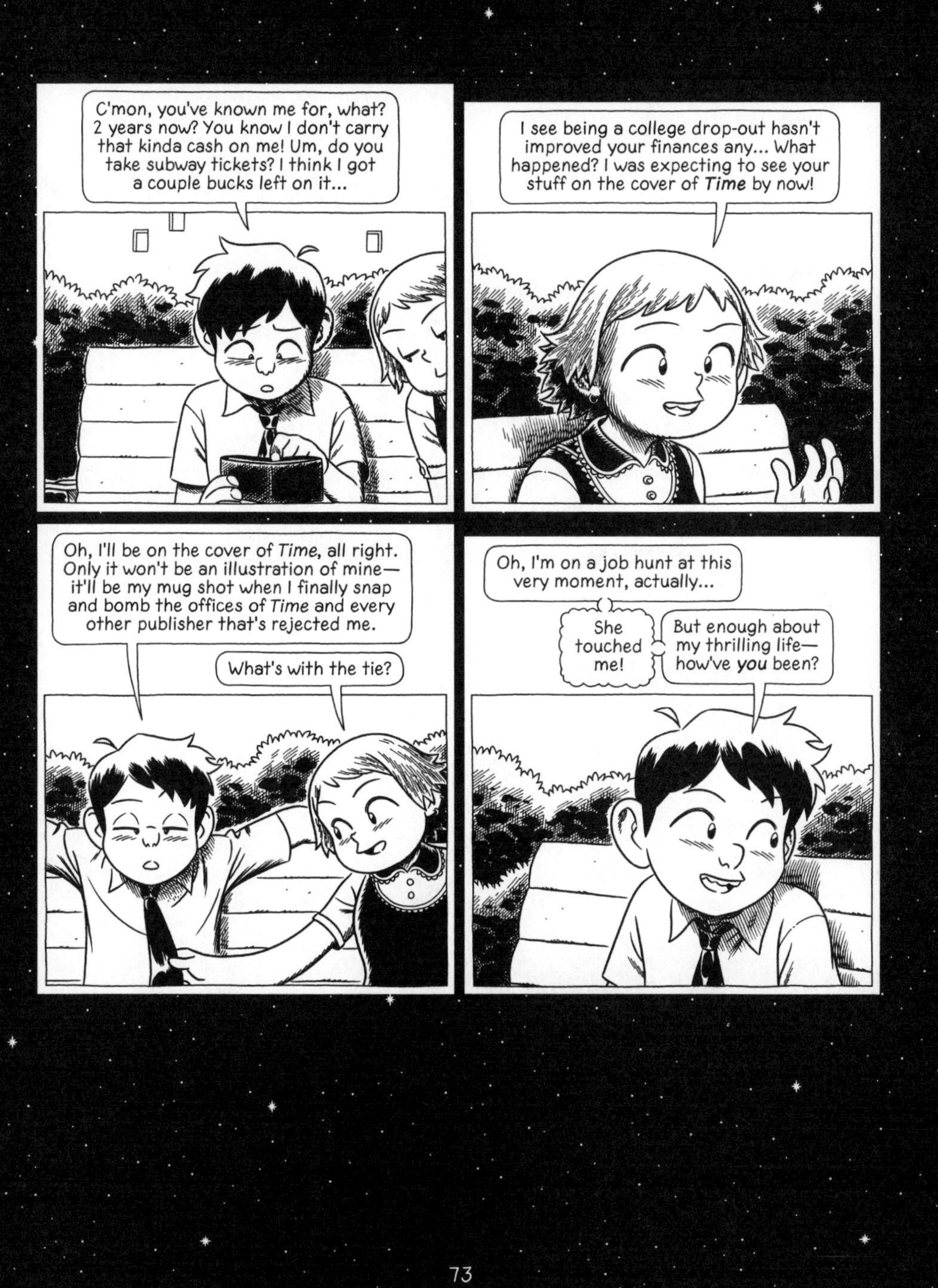
C'mon, you've known me for, what? 2 years now? You know I don't carry that kinda cash on me! Um, do you take subway tickets? I think I got a couple bucks left on it...
I see being a college drop-out hasn't improved your finances any... What happened? I was expecting to see your stuff on the cover of Time by now!
Oh, I'll be on the cover of Time, all right. Only it won't be an illustration of mine—it'll be my mug shot when I finally snap and bomb the offices of Time and every other publisher that's rejected me.
What's with the tie?
Oh, I'm on a job hunt at this very moment, actually...
She touched me!
But enough about my thrilling life—how've you been?

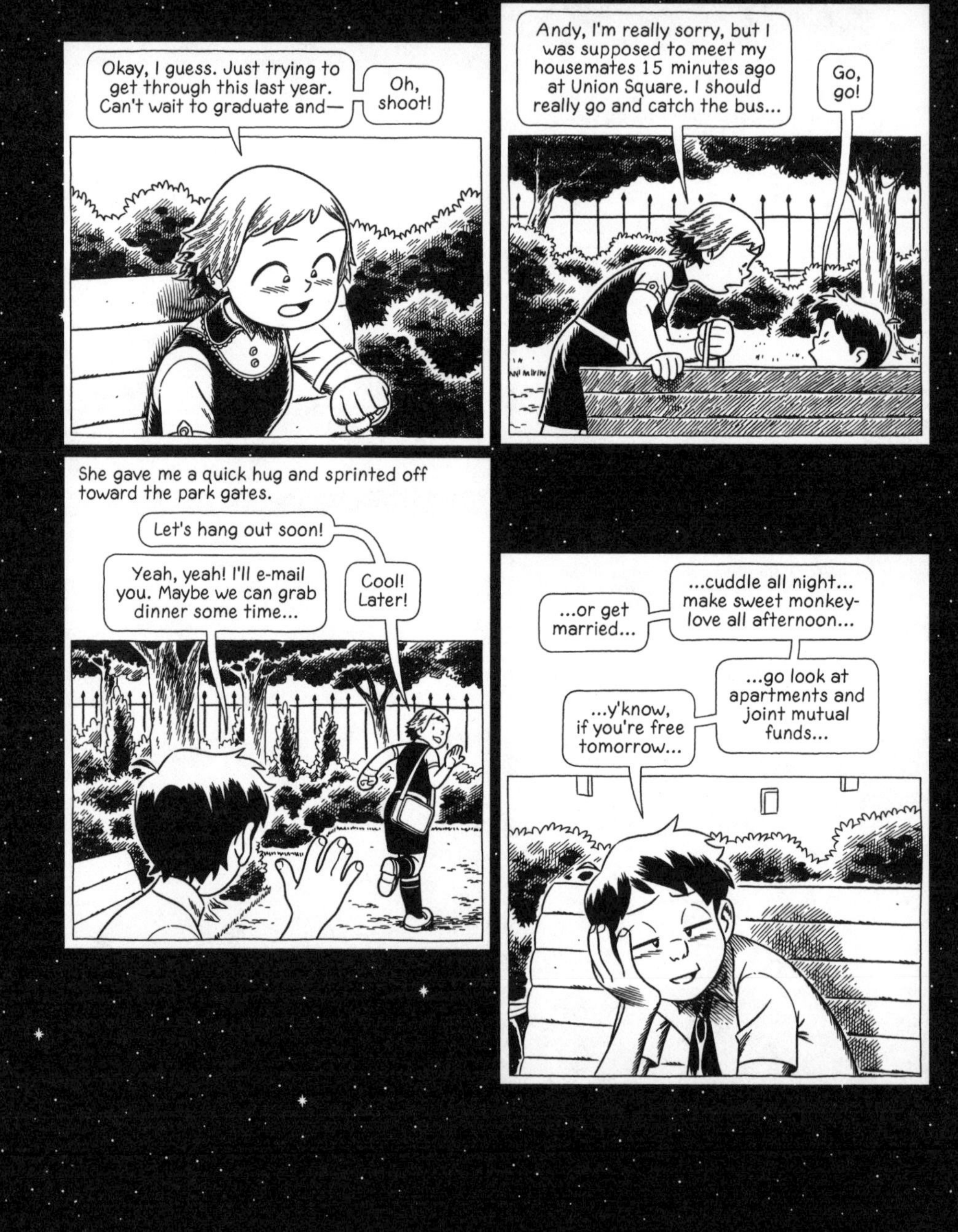
Okay, I guess. Just trying to get through this last year. Can't wait to graduate and—
Oh, shoot!
Andy, I'm really sorry, but I was supposed to meet my housemates 15 minutes ago at Union Square. I should really go and catch the bus...
Go, go!
She gave me a quick hug and sprinted off toward the park gates.
Let's hang out soon!
Yeah, yeah! I'll e-mail you. Maybe we can grab dinner some time...
Cool! Later!
...y'know, if you're free tomorrow...
...go look at apartments and joint mutual funds...
...cuddle all night... make sweet monkey-love all afternoon...
...or get married...

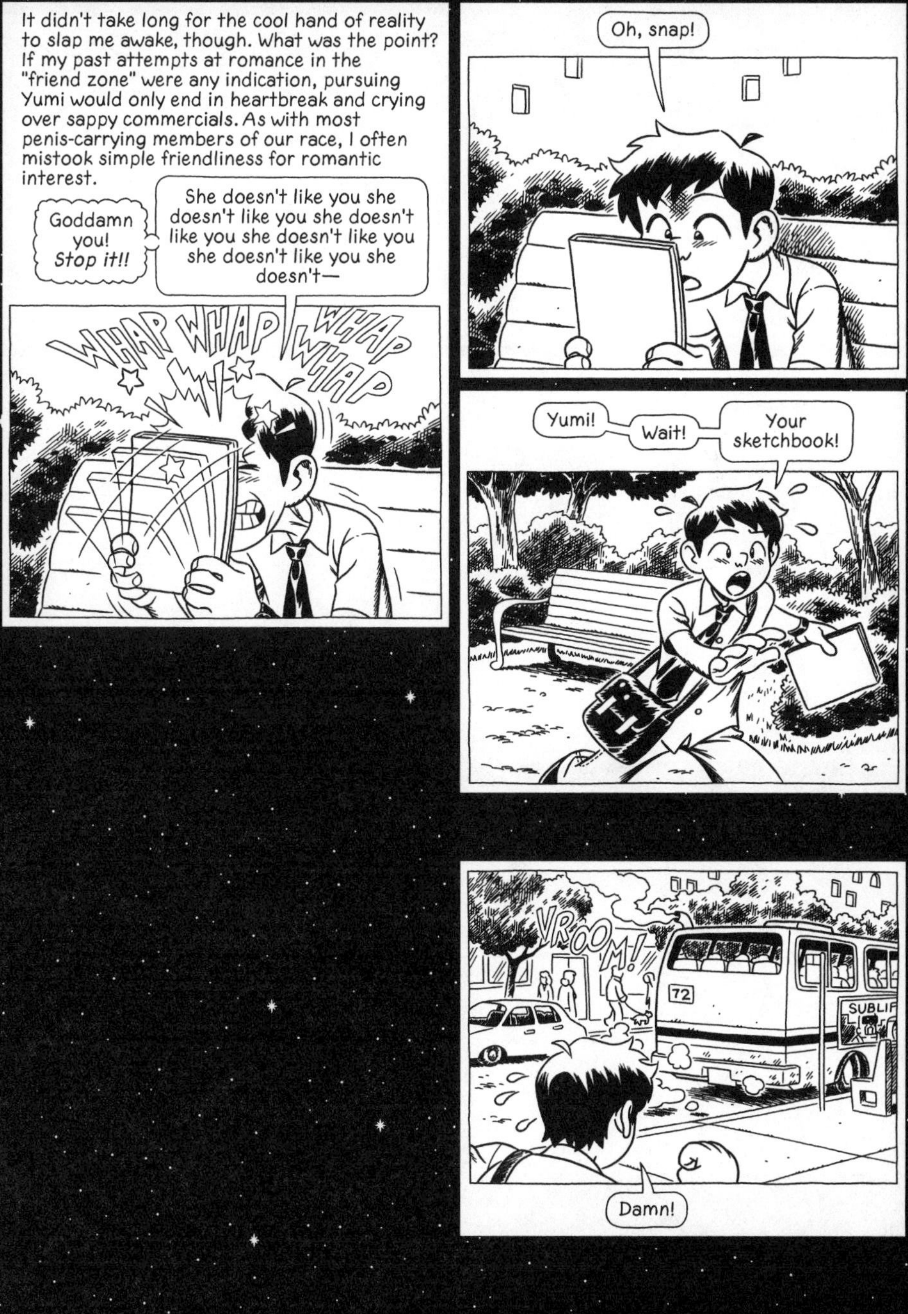
It didn't take long for the cool hand of reality to slap me awake, though. What was the point? If my past attempts at romance in the "friend zone" were any indication, pursuing Yumi would only end in heartbreak and crying over sappy commercials. As with most penis-carrying members of our race, I often mistook simple friendliness for romantic interest.
Goddamn you! *Stop it!!*
She doesn't like you she doesn't like you she doesn't like you she doesn't like you she doesn't like you she doesn't—
WHAP WHAP WHAP WHAP WHAP
Oh, snap!
Yumi!
Wait!
Your sketchbook!
VROOM!
72
Damn!

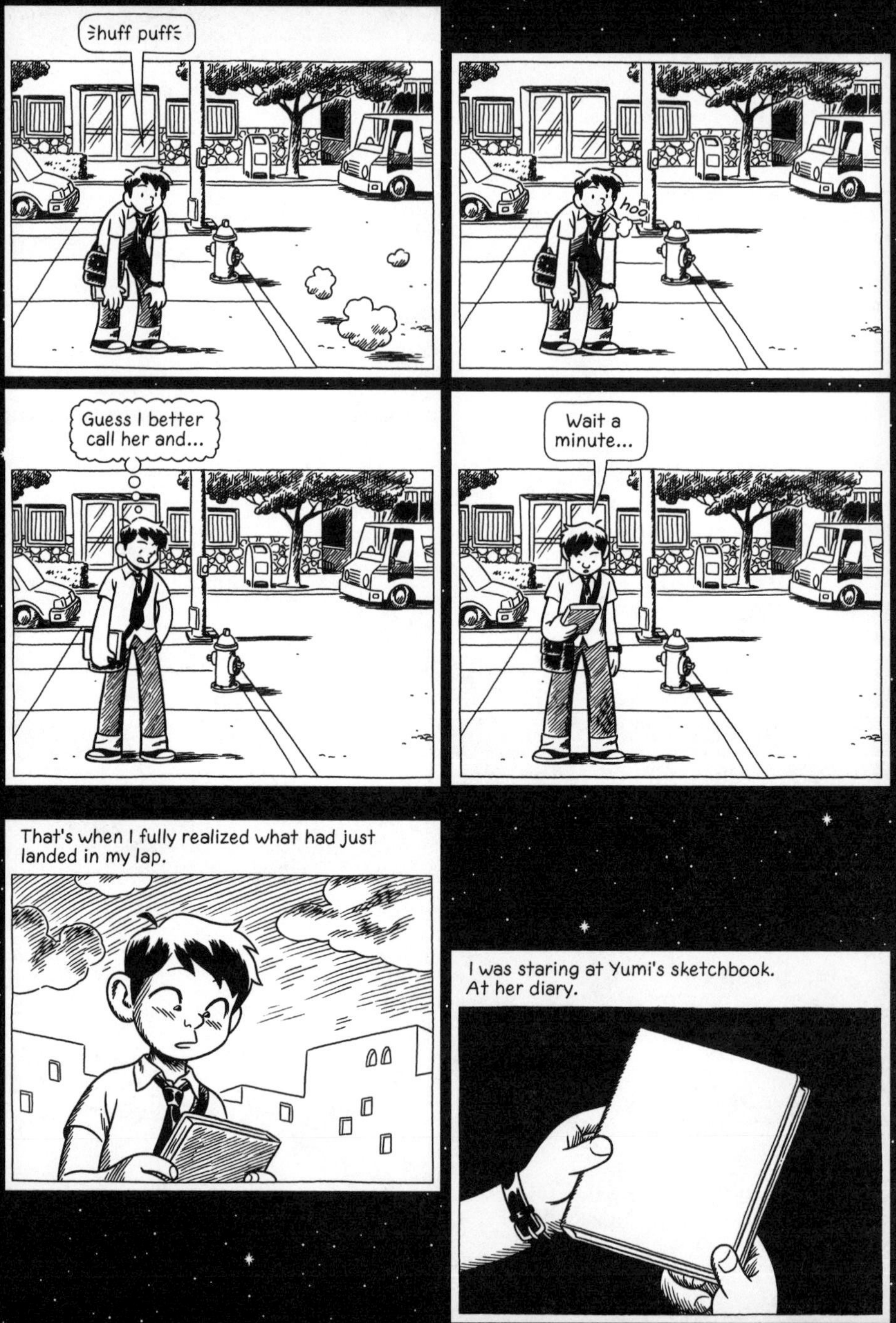
huff puff
hoo
Guess I better call her and...
Wait a minute...
That's when I fully realized what had just landed in my lap.
I was staring at Yumi's sketchbook. At her diary.

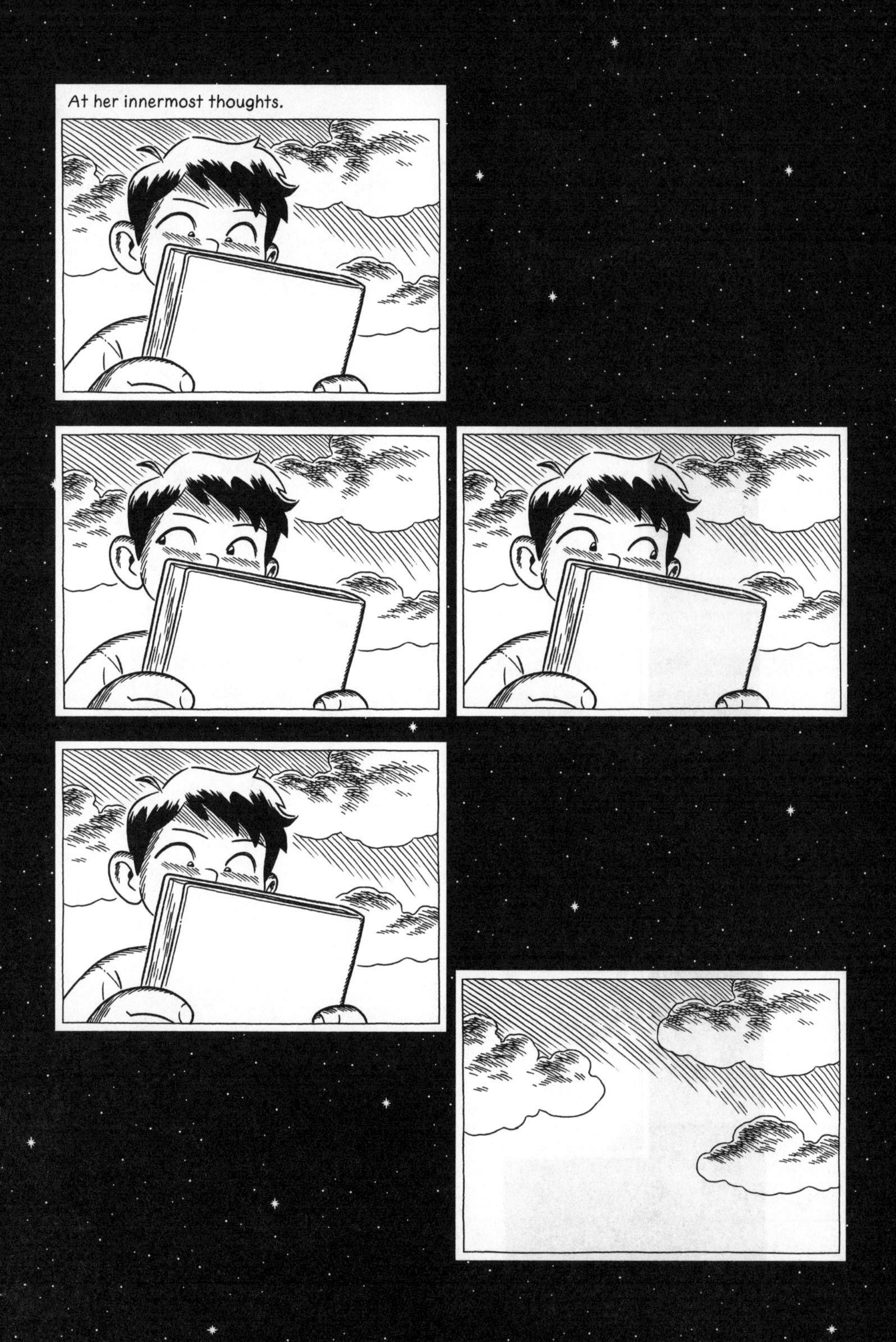
At her innermost thoughts.

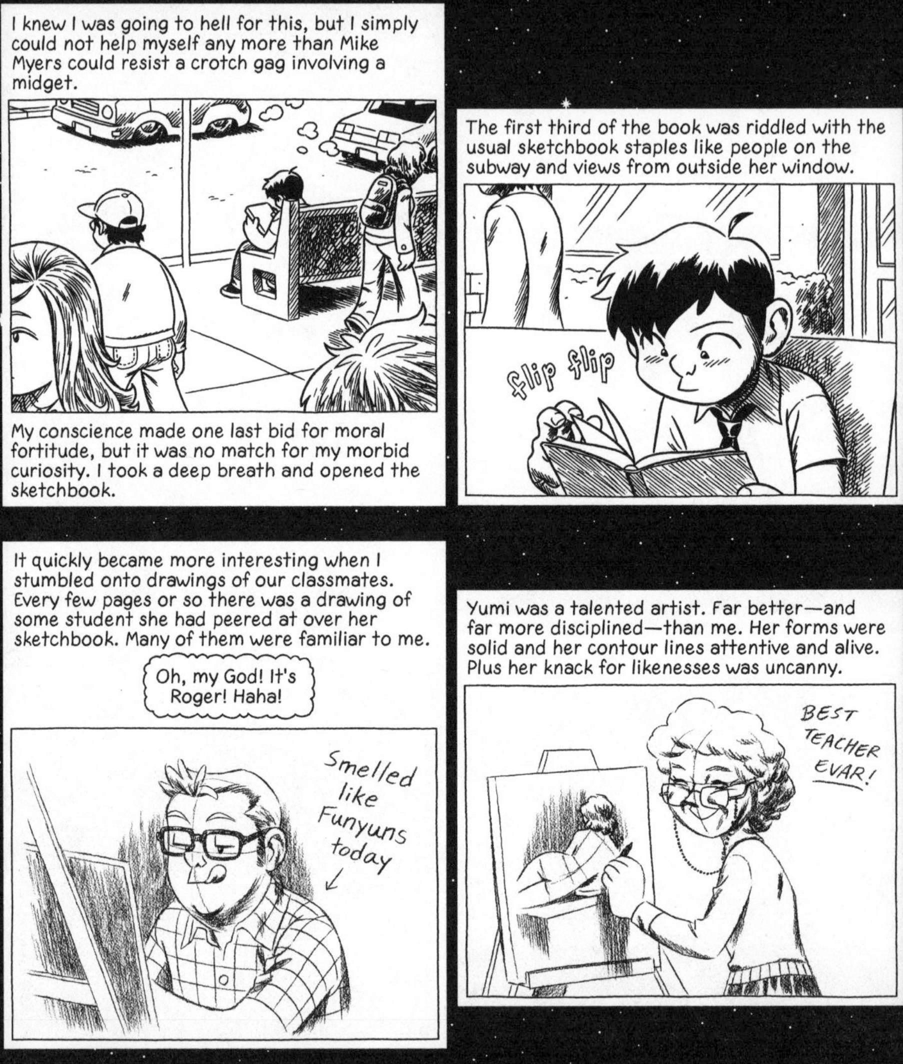
I knew I was going to hell for this, but I simply could not help myself any more than Mike Myers could resist a crotch gag involving a midget.
My conscience made one last bid for moral fortitude, but it was no match for my morbid curiosity. I took a deep breath and opened the sketchbook.
The first third of the book was riddled with the usual sketchbook staples like people on the subway and views from outside her window.
flip flip
It quickly became more interesting when I stumbled onto drawings of our classmates. Every few pages or so there was a drawing of some student she had peered at over her sketchbook. Many of them were familiar to me.
Oh, my God! It's Roger! Haha!
Smelled like Funyuns today
Yumi was a talented artist. Far better—and far more disciplined—than me. Her forms were solid and her contour lines attentive and alive. Plus her knack for likenesses was uncanny.
BEST TEACHER EVAR!

As I studied a particularly dead-on sketch of our Figure Drawing 1 teacher, I almost missed a drawing on the facing page. I flipped back and the drawing stopped me in my tracks.

Holy shit! It's me!

It was dated a couple years back so I assumed she must have drawn it close to when we first met. I felt strangely excited that she had been looking at me long enough to draw it. I also felt a little uncomfortable as I was completely oblivious to it at the time. Then again, I had done the same thing to hundreds of subjects myself, so I was in no position to complain.

I flipped past a couple more pages and found a drawing of Tony too.

Bwa ha ha! This is great!

Had a boner the whole class

He was also in his ever-present Batman shirt, of course. (I wasn't sure whether he simply had a closet full of the same shirt—much like Batman himself—or if it was just the same one worn over and over again.)

Next came a loose drawing of a kitchen, then of a cat napping on a window. My imagination whirled... Was this her kitchen and her cat that I was seeing? Although we were pretty good friends, most of our interactions had been limited to school. Many details of her private life—like the inside of her apartment—were still agonizing mysteries to me.

These smudged, 2-dimensional glimpses into her life had me curling my toes in nervous excitement. I was starting to feel really guilty for invading her privacy like this.

But not enough to stop me from poring over every scrap of it like it was the Dead Sea Scrolls.

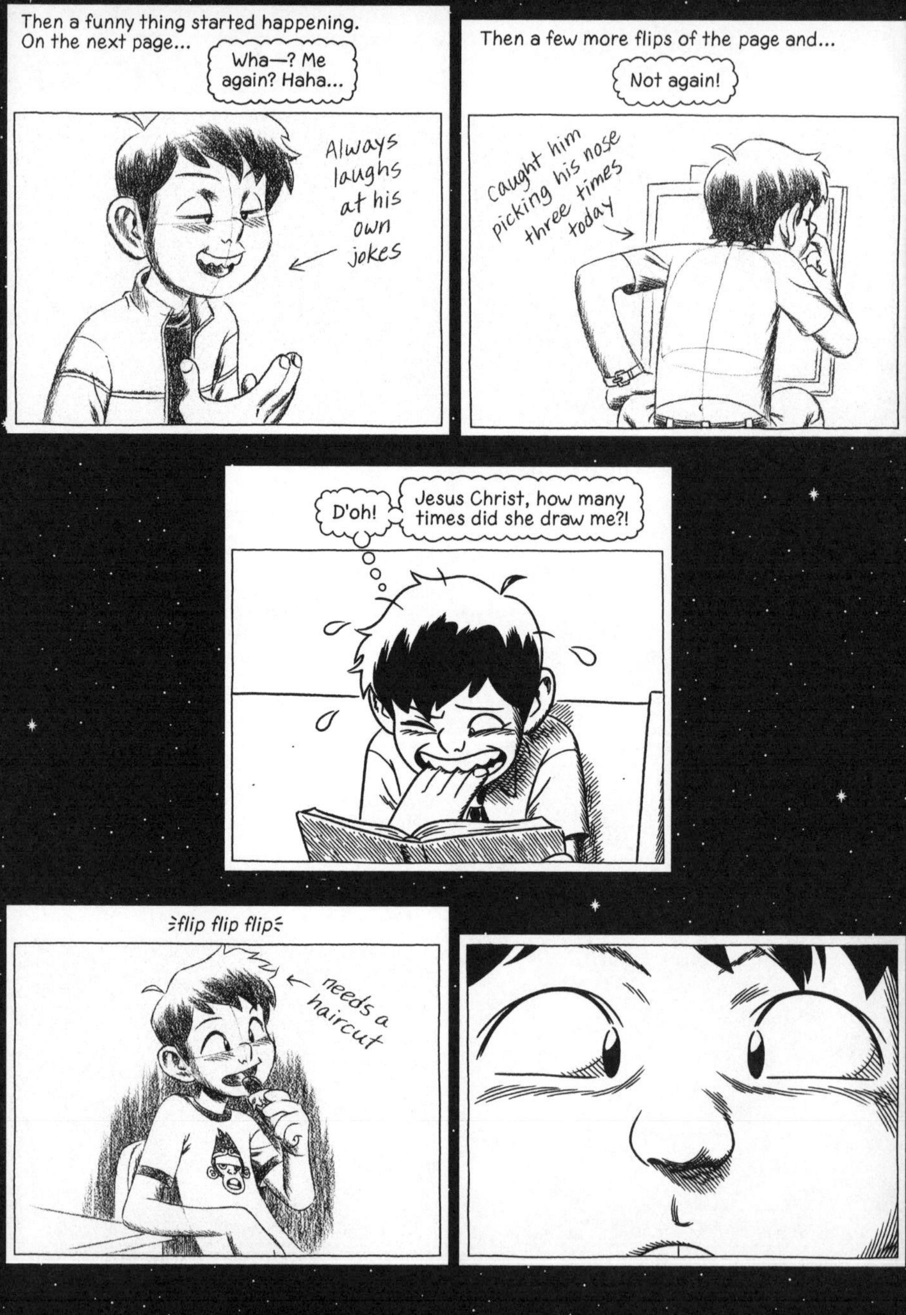
Then a funny thing started happening.
On the next page...
Wha—? Me again? Haha...
Always laughs at his own jokes
Then a few more flips of the page and...
Not again!
Caught him picking his nose three times today
D'oh!
Jesus Christ, how many times did she draw me?!
flip flip flip
needs a haircut

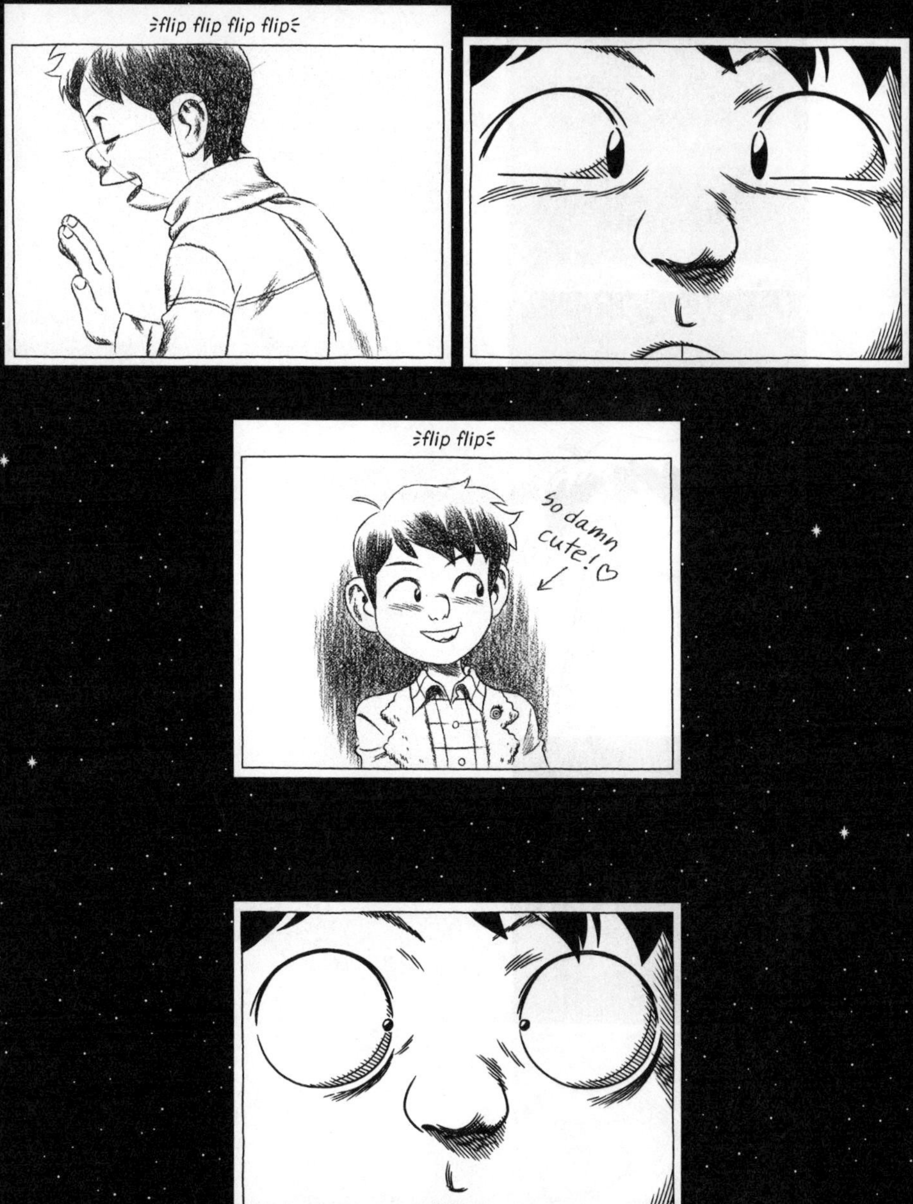
flip flip flip flip
flip flip
So damn cute! ♡

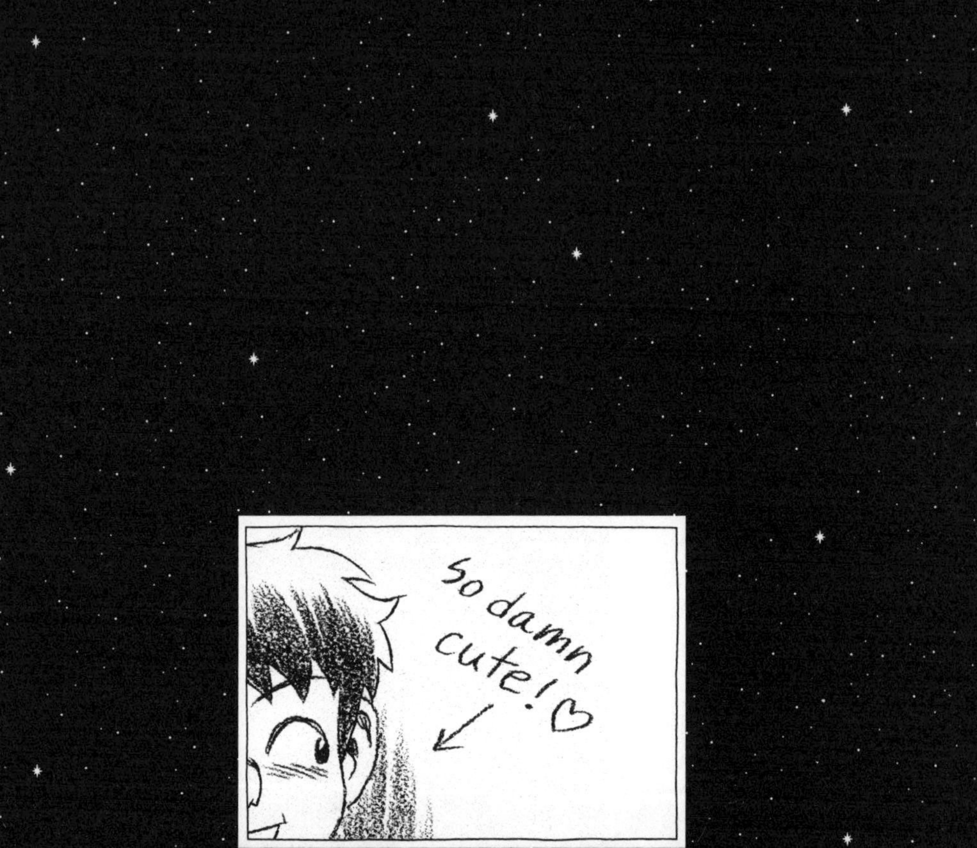
So damn cute! ♡

CHAPTER 07

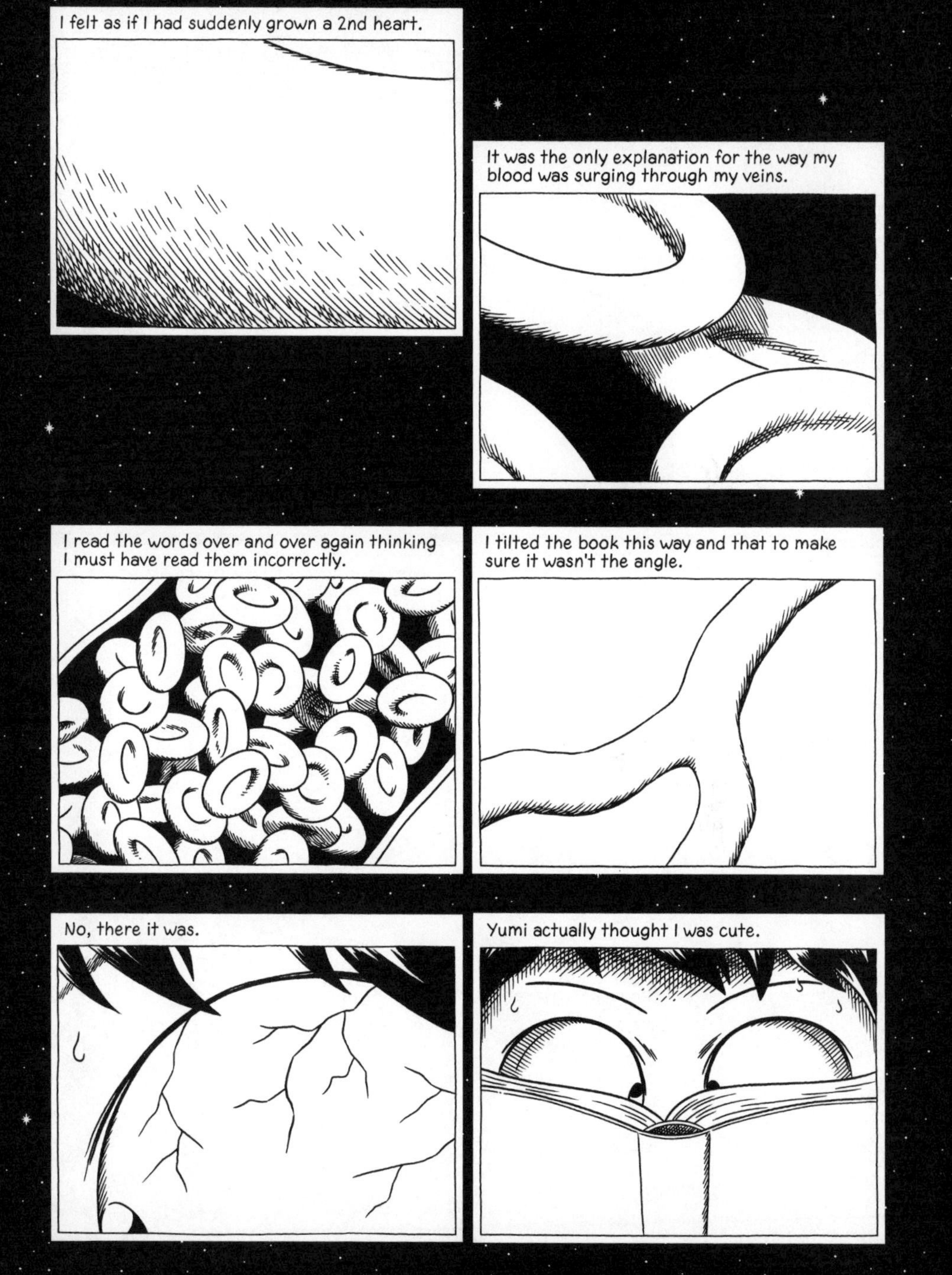
I felt as if I had suddenly grown a 2nd heart.
It was the only explanation for the way my blood was surging through my veins.
I read the words over and over again thinking I must have read them incorrectly.
I tilted the book this way and that to make sure it wasn't the angle.
No, there it was.
Yumi actually thought I was cute.

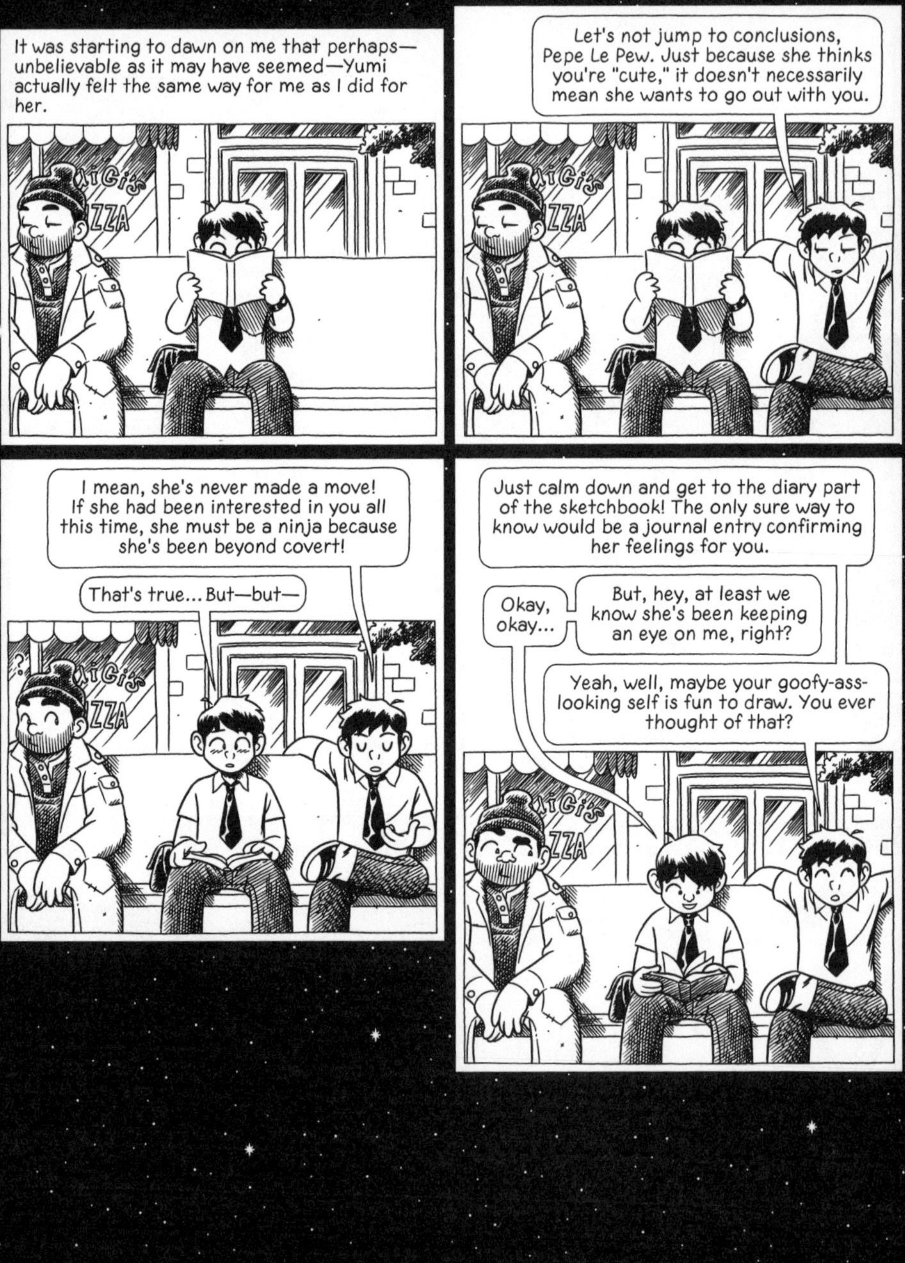
It was starting to dawn on me that perhaps—unbelievable as it may have seemed—Yumi actually felt the same way for me as I did for her.
Let's not jump to conclusions, Pepe Le Pew. Just because she thinks you're "cute," it doesn't necessarily mean she wants to go out with you.
I mean, she's never made a move! If she had been interested in you all this time, she must be a ninja because she's been beyond covert!
That's true... But—but—
Just calm down and get to the diary part of the sketchbook! The only sure way to know would be a journal entry confirming her feelings for you.
Okay, okay...
But, hey, at least we know she's been keeping an eye on me, right?
Yeah, well, maybe your goofy-ass-looking self is fun to draw. You ever thought of that?

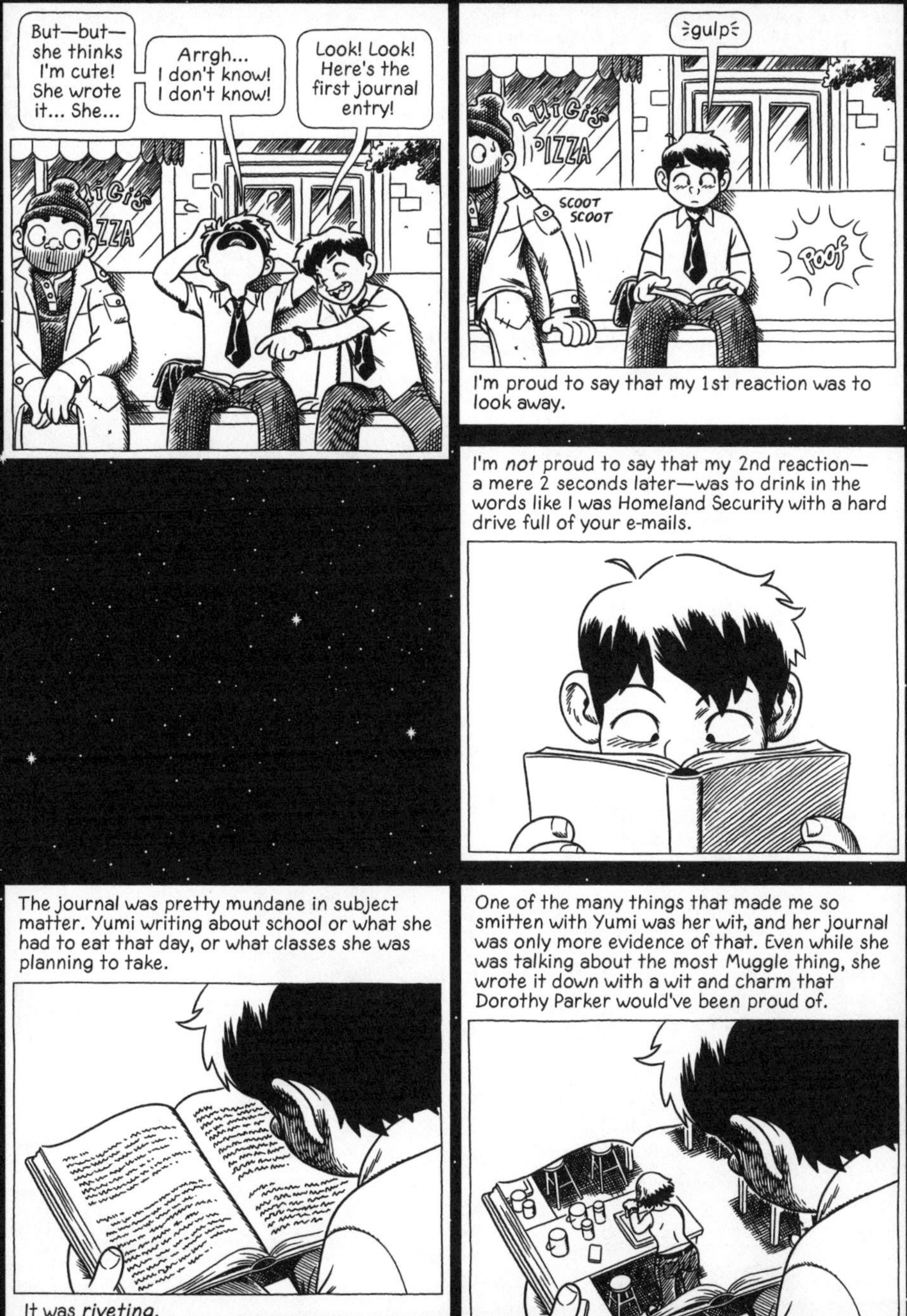

But—but—she thinks I'm cute! She wrote it... She...
Arrgh... I don't know! I don't know!
Look! Look! Here's the first journal entry!
ǂgulpǂ
Luigi's
PIZZA
SCOOT SCOOT
Poof
I'm proud to say that my 1st reaction was to look away.
I'm *not* proud to say that my 2nd reaction—a mere 2 seconds later—was to drink in the words like I was Homeland Security with a hard drive full of your e-mails.
The journal was pretty mundane in subject matter. Yumi writing about school or what she had to eat that day, or what classes she was planning to take.
It was *riveting*.
One of the many things that made me so smitten with Yumi was her wit, and her journal was only more evidence of that. Even while she was talking about the most Muggle thing, she wrote it down with a wit and charm that Dorothy Parker would've been proud of.

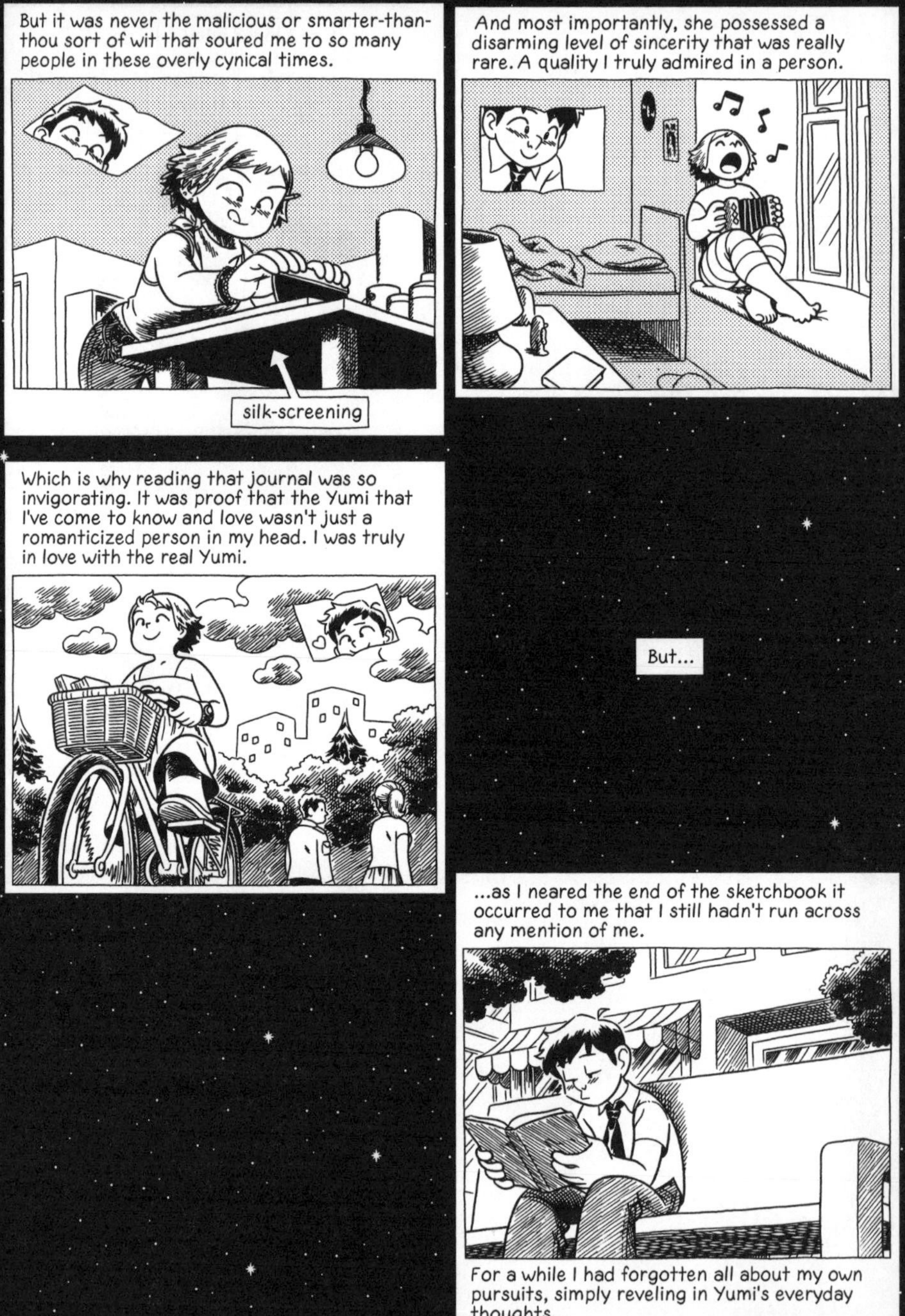
But it was never the malicious or smarter-than-thou sort of wit that soured me to so many people in these overly cynical times.
silk-screening
And most importantly, she possessed a disarming level of sincerity that was really rare. A quality I truly admired in a person.
Which is why reading that journal was so invigorating. It was proof that the Yumi that I've come to know and love wasn't just a romanticized person in my head. I was truly in love with the real Yumi.
But...
...as I neared the end of the sketchbook it occurred to me that I still hadn't run across any mention of me.
For a while I had forgotten all about my own pursuits, simply reveling in Yumi's everyday thoughts.

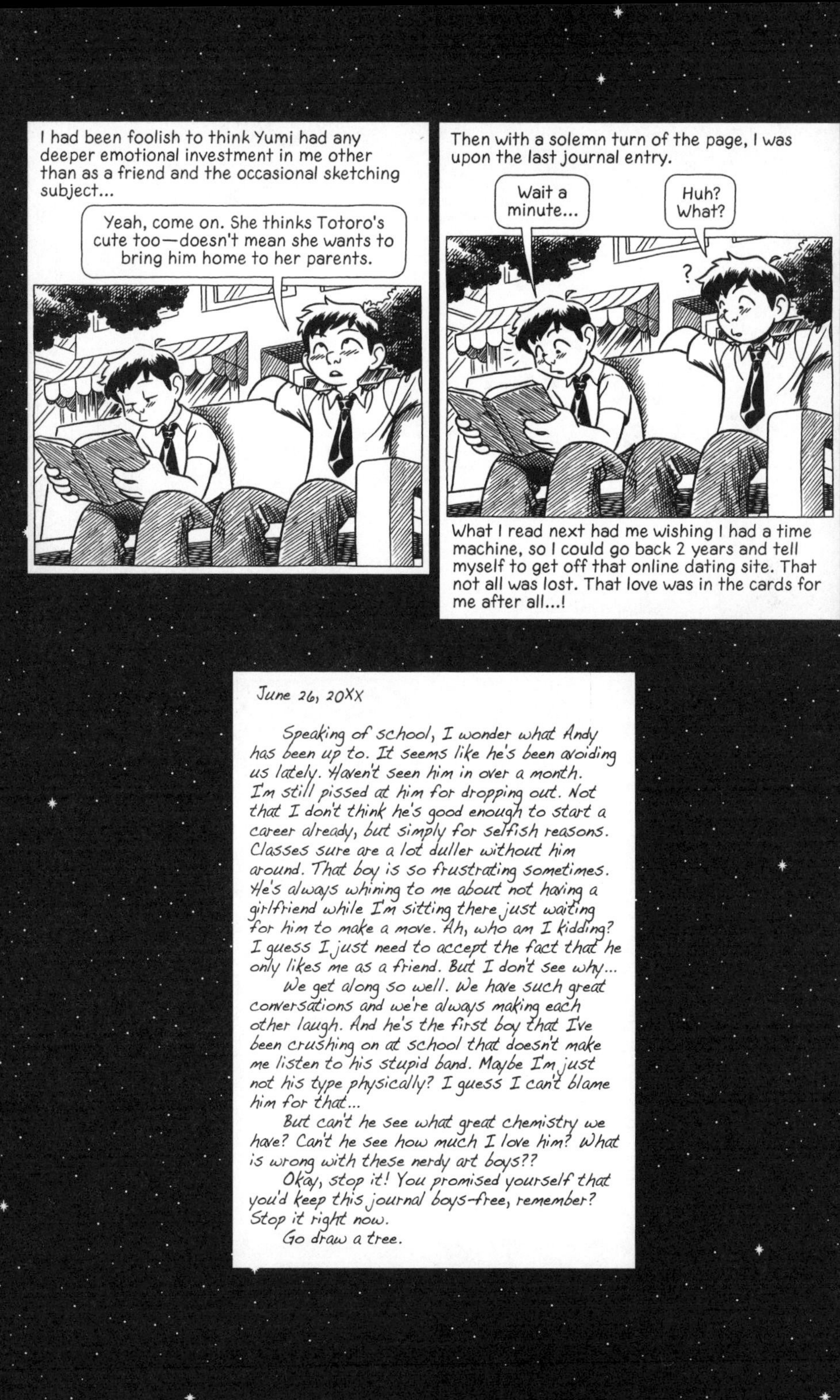
I had been foolish to think Yumi had any deeper emotional investment in me other than as a friend and the occasional sketching subject...
Yeah, come on. She thinks Totoro's cute too—doesn't mean she wants to bring him home to her parents.
Then with a solemn turn of the page, I was upon the last journal entry.
Wait a minute...
Huh? What?
?
What I read next had me wishing I had a time machine, so I could go back 2 years and tell myself to get off that online dating site. That not all was lost. That love was in the cards for me after all...!
June 26, 20XX
Speaking of school, I wonder what Andy has been up to. It seems like he's been avoiding us lately. Haven't seen him in over a month. I'm still pissed at him for dropping out. Not that I don't think he's good enough to start a career already, but simply for selfish reasons. Classes sure are a lot duller without him around. That boy is so frustrating sometimes. He's always whining to me about not having a girlfriend while I'm sitting there just waiting for him to make a move. Ah, who am I kidding? I guess I just need to accept the fact that he only likes me as a friend. But I don't see why...
We get along so well. We have such great conversations and we're always making each other laugh. And he's the first boy that I've been crushing on at school that doesn't make me listen to his stupid band. Maybe I'm just not his type physically? I guess I can't blame him for that...
But can't he see what great chemistry we have? Can't he see how much I love him? What is wrong with these nerdy art boys??
Okay, stop it! You promised yourself that you'd keep this journal boys-free, remember? Stop it right now.
Go draw a tree.

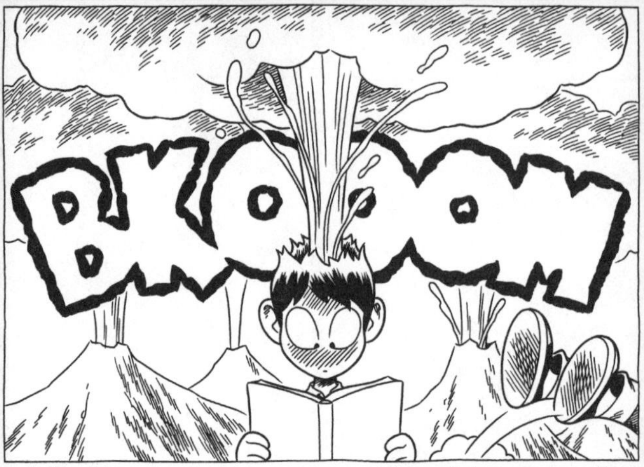
BKOOOM

I don't quite remember the next moment immediately upon reading those words because my spirit left my body for a second. I read the entry over and over, I don't know how many times.

You know how you're not supposed to feed a starving person a steak? Well, this was just like that. But when I finally digested the words, I felt as if my entire body was about to explode into a thousand little heart-shaped candies that had "Yumi loves you" printed on them.

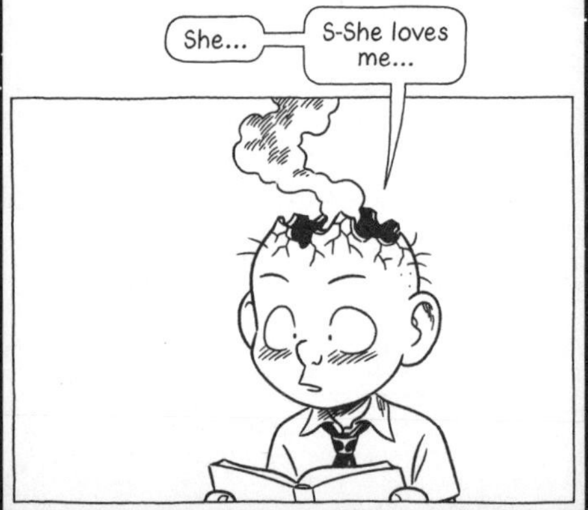
She...
S-She loves me...

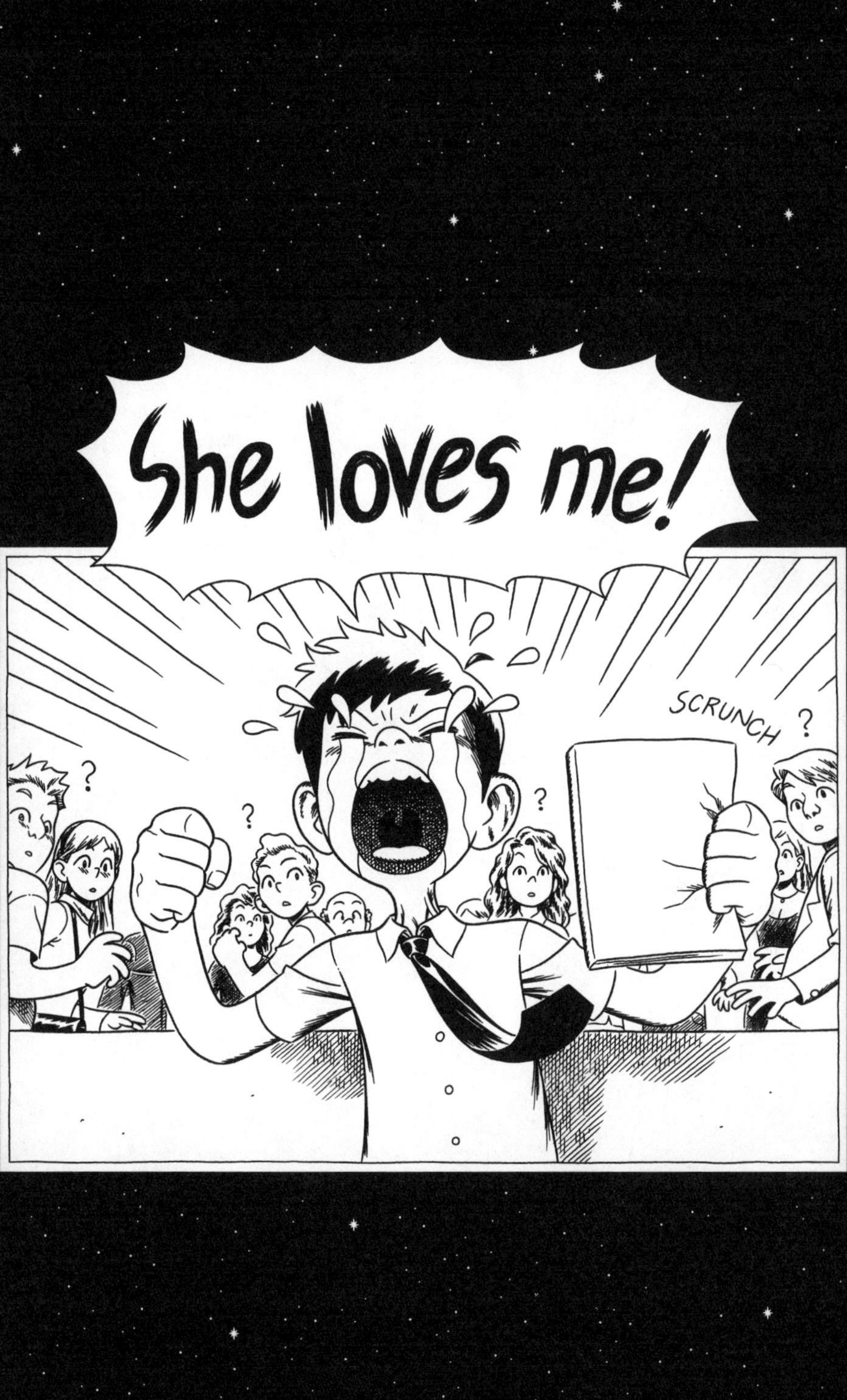
She loves me!
SCRUNCH
?
?
?
?

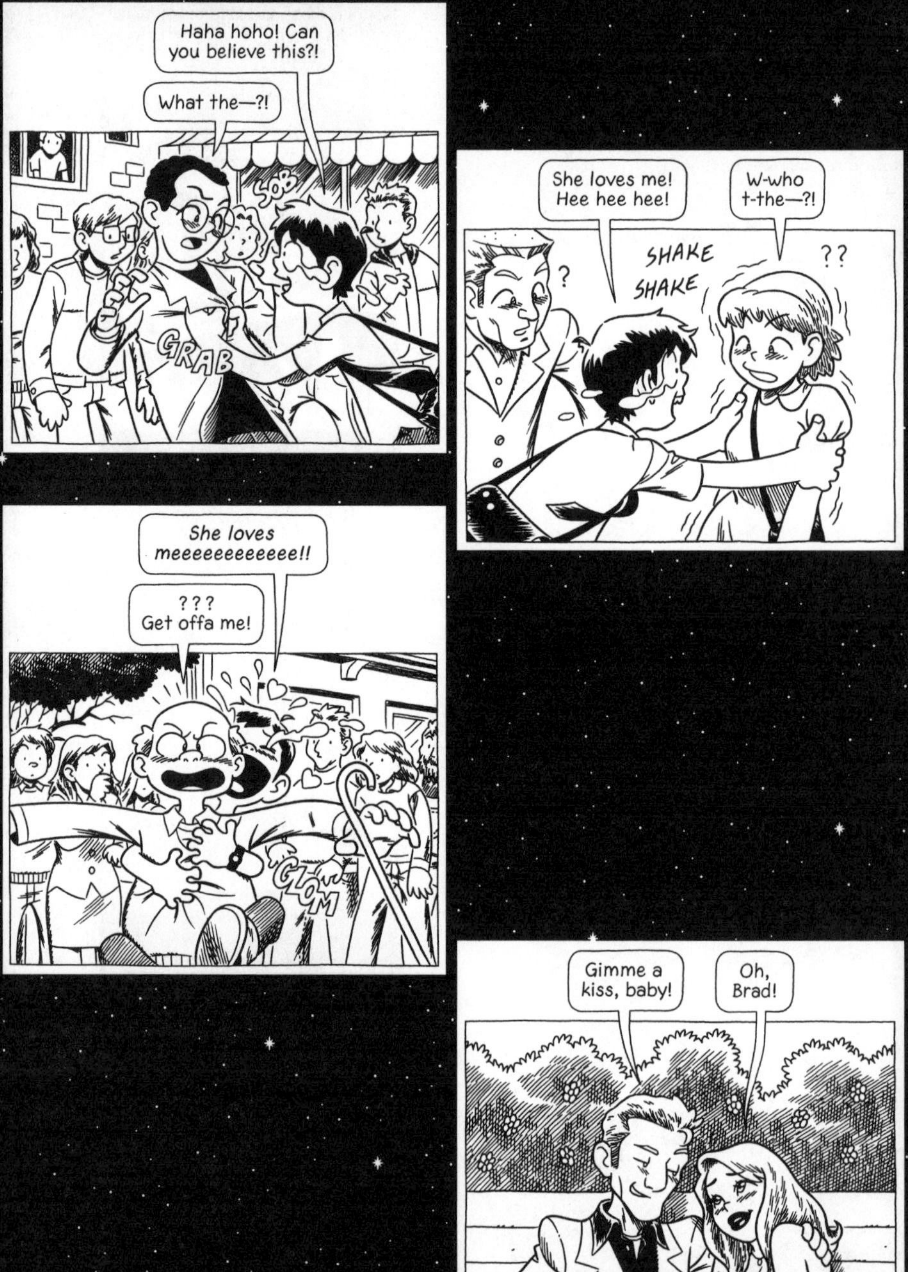
Haha hoho! Can you believe this?!
What the—?!
SOB
GRAB
She loves me! Hee hee hee!
W-who t-the—?!
SHAKE
SHAKE
?
??
She loves meeeeeeeeeeee!!
??? Get offa me!
GLOM
Gimme a kiss, baby!
Oh, Brad!

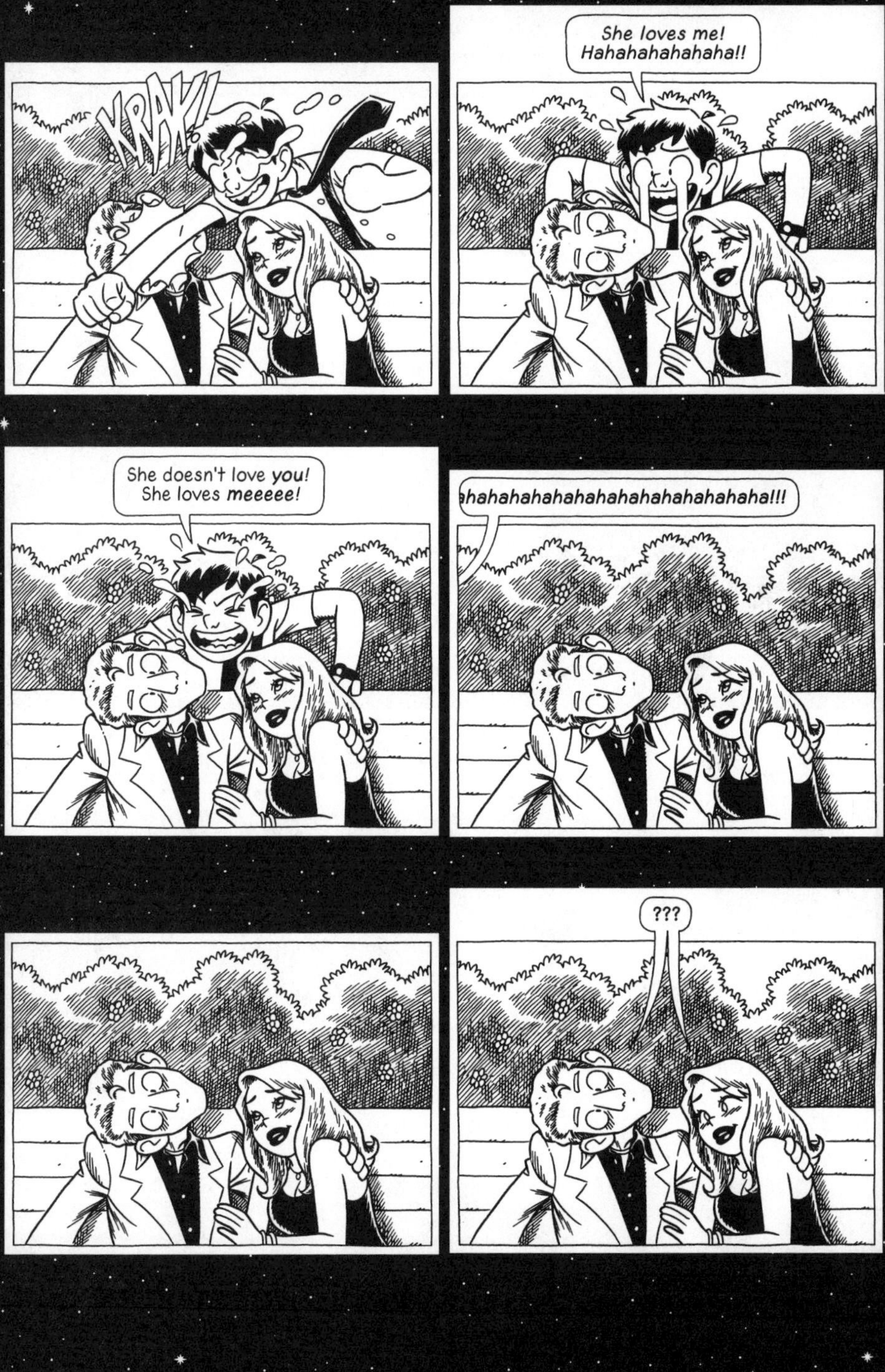
KRAK!!
She loves me! Hahahahahahaha!!
She doesn't love you! She loves meeeee!
ahahahahahahahahahahahahahaha!!!
???

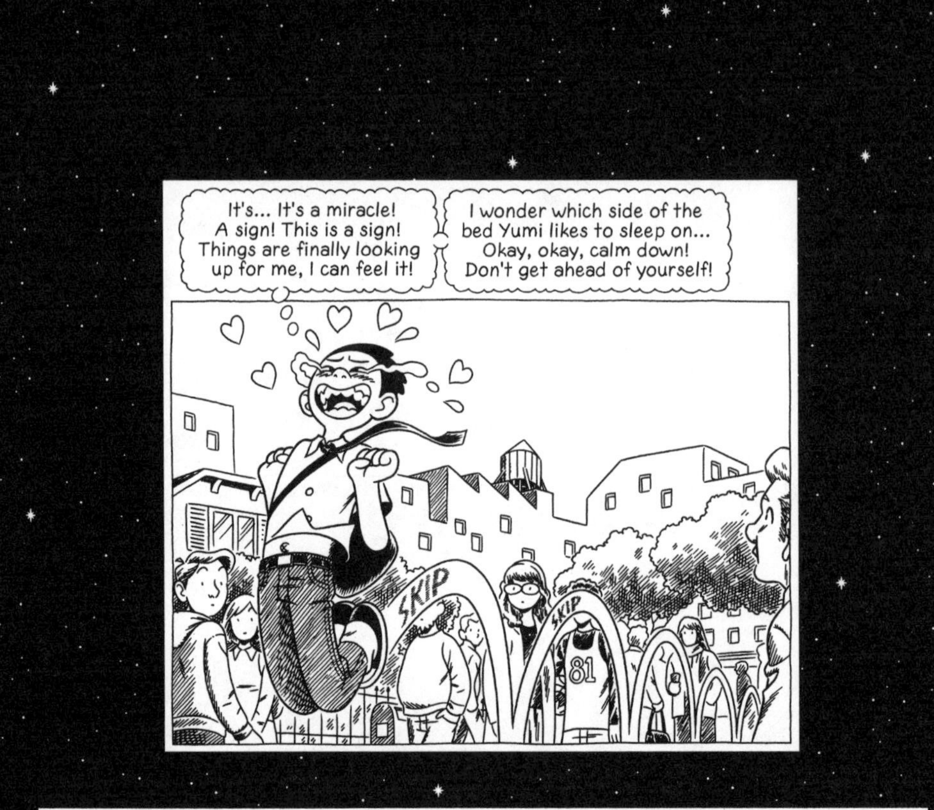
It's... It's a miracle! A sign! This is a sign! Things are finally looking up for me, I can feel it!
I wonder which side of the bed Yumi likes to sleep on... Okay, okay, calm down! Don't get ahead of yourself!
SKIP
SKIP
81

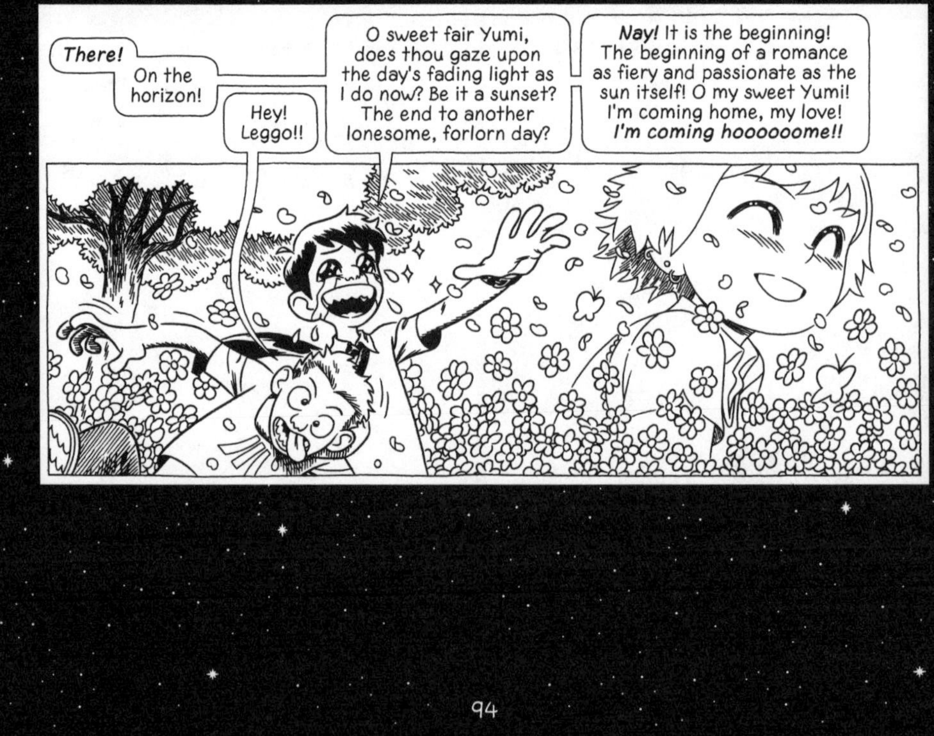
There!
On the horizon!
Hey! Leggo!!
O sweet fair Yumi, does thou gaze upon the day's fading light as I do now? Be it a sunset? The end to another lonesome, forlorn day?
Nay! It is the beginning! The beginning of a romance as fiery and passionate as the sun itself! O my sweet Yumi! I'm coming home, my love! ***I'm coming hoooooome!!***

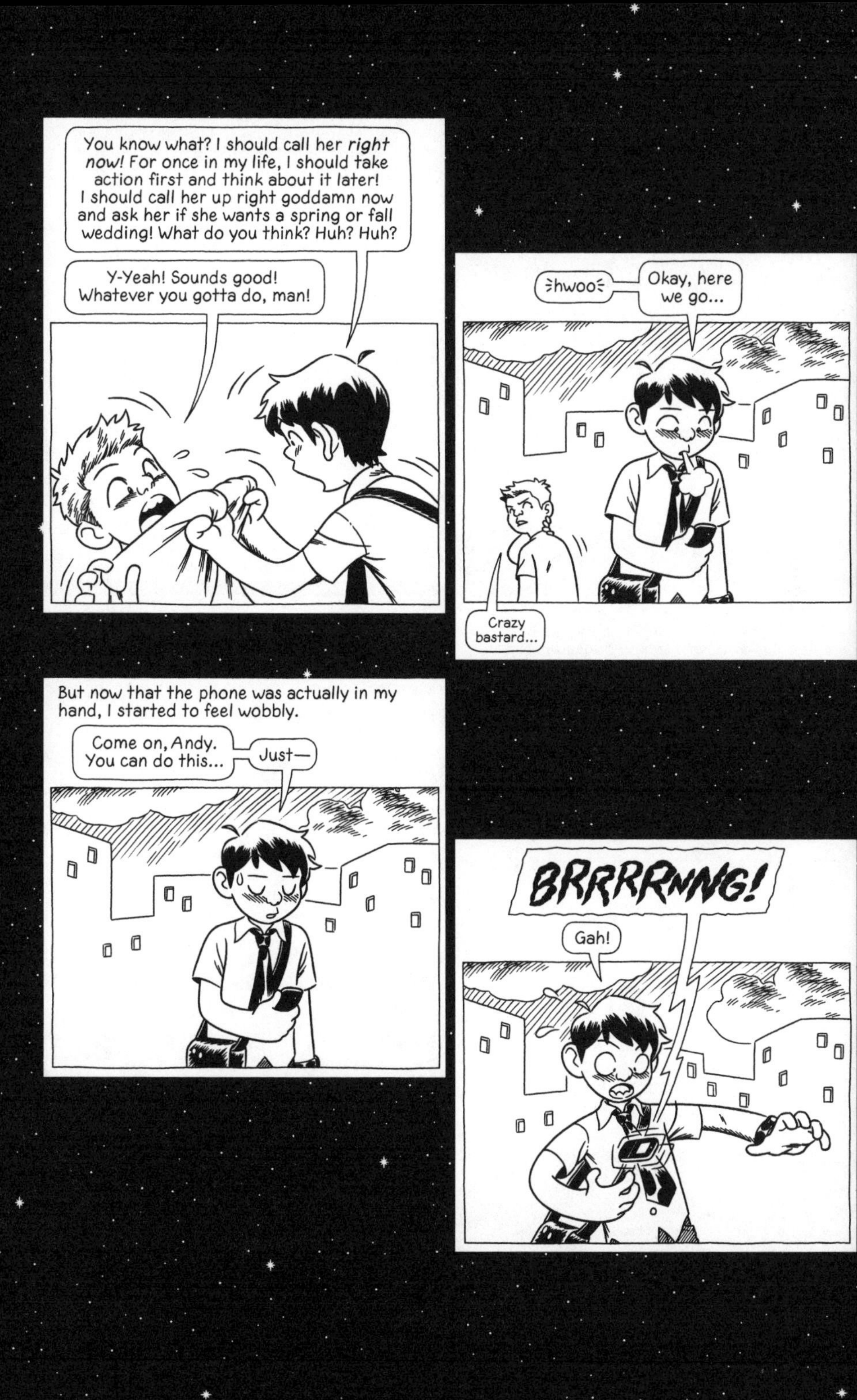

You know what? I should call her *right now!* For once in my life, I should take action first and think about it later! I should call her up right goddamn now and ask her if she wants a spring or fall wedding! What do you think? Huh? Huh?
Y-Yeah! Sounds good! Whatever you gotta do, man!
hwoo
Okay, here we go...
Crazy bastard...
But now that the phone was actually in my hand, I started to feel wobbly.
Come on, Andy. You can do this...
Just—
BRRRRNNG!
Gah!

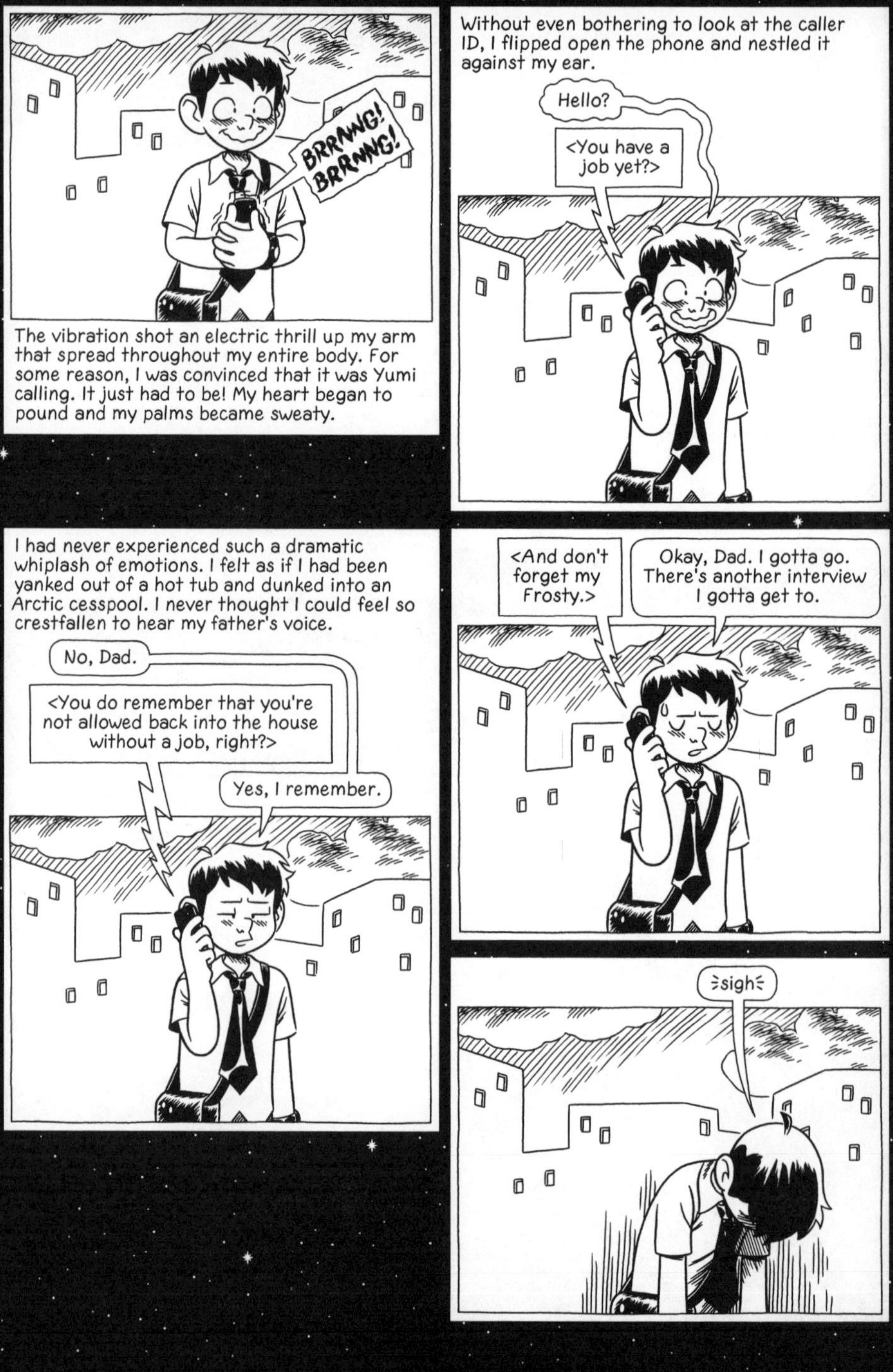
BRRNNG! BRRNNG!
The vibration shot an electric thrill up my arm that spread throughout my entire body. For some reason, I was convinced that it was Yumi calling. It just had to be! My heart began to pound and my palms became sweaty.
Without even bothering to look at the caller ID, I flipped open the phone and nestled it against my ear.
Hello?
<You have a job yet?>
I had never experienced such a dramatic whiplash of emotions. I felt as if I had been yanked out of a hot tub and dunked into an Arctic cesspool. I never thought I could feel so crestfallen to hear my father's voice.
No, Dad.
<You do remember that you're not allowed back into the house without a job, right?>
Yes, I remember.
<And don't forget my Frosty.>
Okay, Dad. I gotta go. There's another interview I gotta get to.
sigh

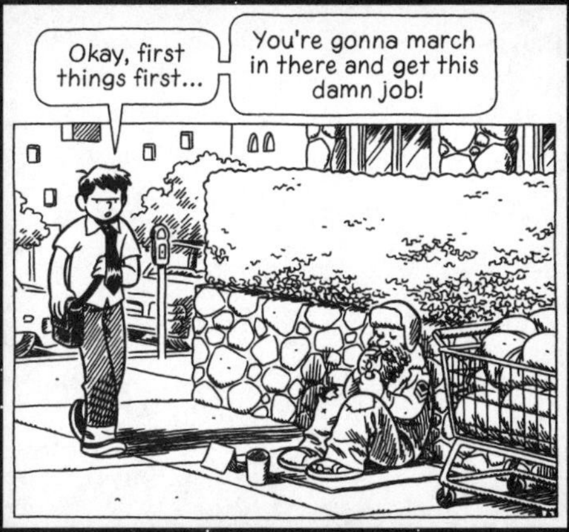
Okay, first things first...
You're gonna march in there and get this damn job!

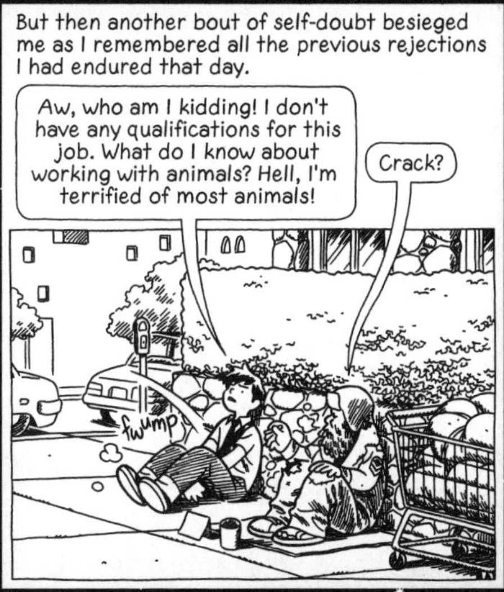
But then another bout of self-doubt besieged me as I remembered all the previous rejections I had endured that day.
Aw, who am I kidding! I don't have any qualifications for this job. What do I know about working with animals? Hell, I'm terrified of most animals!
Crack?
fwump

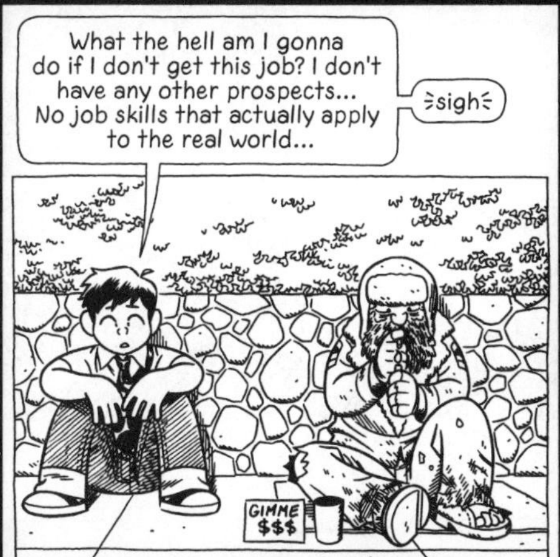
What the hell am I gonna do if I don't get this job? I don't have any other prospects... No job skills that actually apply to the real world...
sigh
GIMME $$$

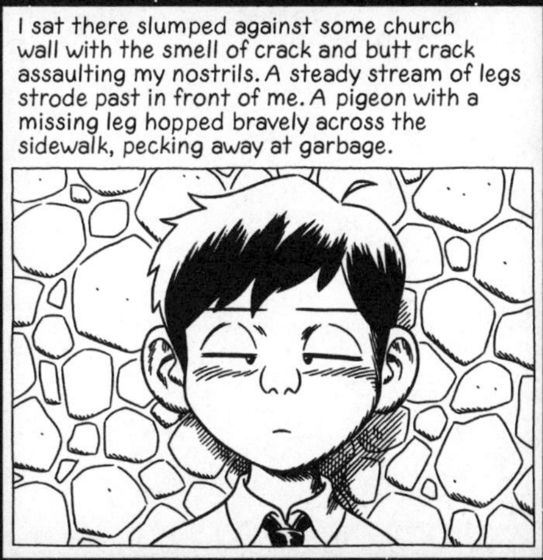
I sat there slumped against some church wall with the smell of crack and butt crack assaulting my nostrils. A steady stream of legs strode past in front of me. A pigeon with a missing leg hopped bravely across the sidewalk, pecking away at garbage.

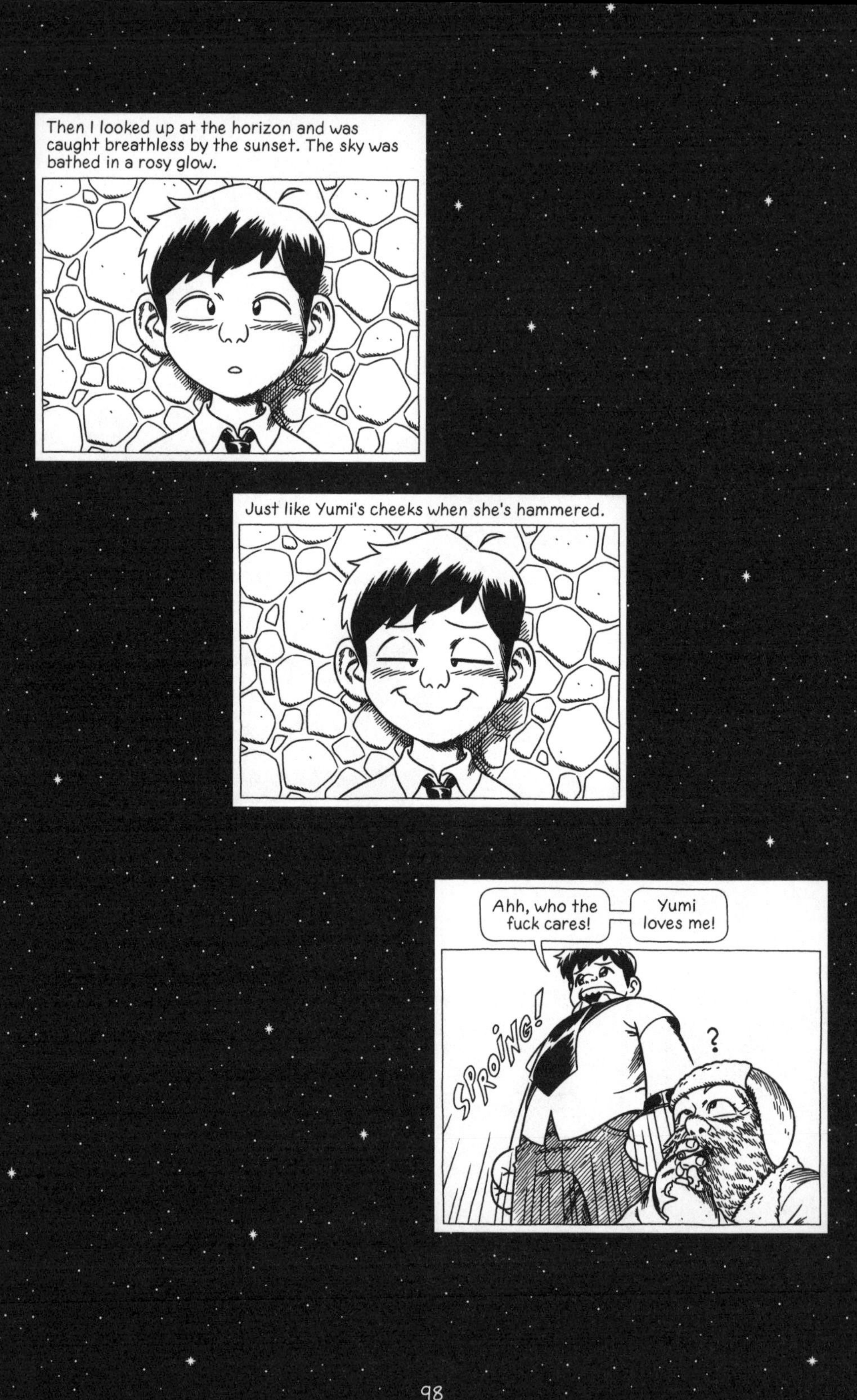
Then I looked up at the horizon and was caught breathless by the sunset. The sky was bathed in a rosy glow.
Just like Yumi's cheeks when she's hammered.
Ahh, who the fuck cares!
Yumi loves me!
SPROING!
?

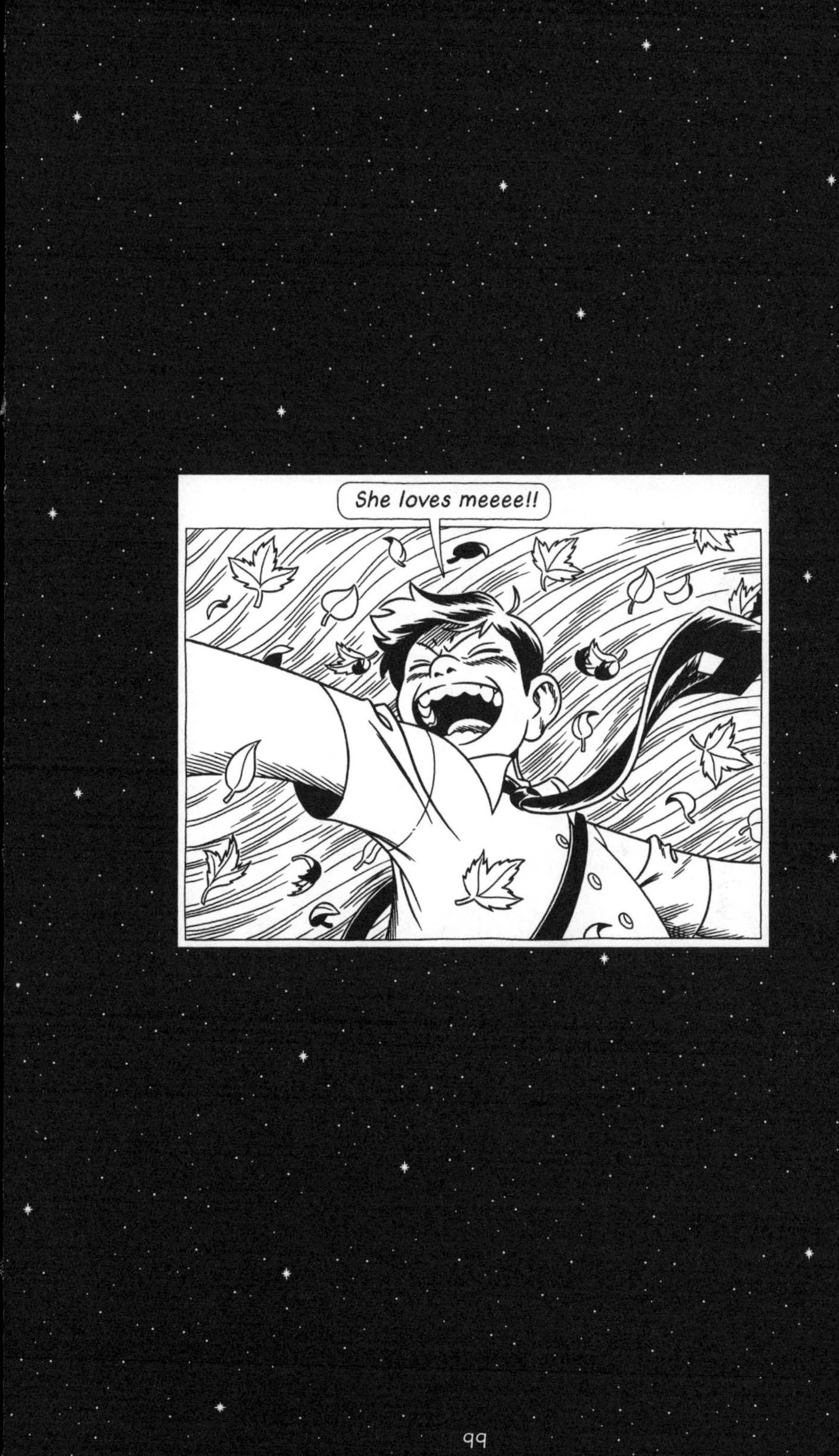
She loves meeeee!!

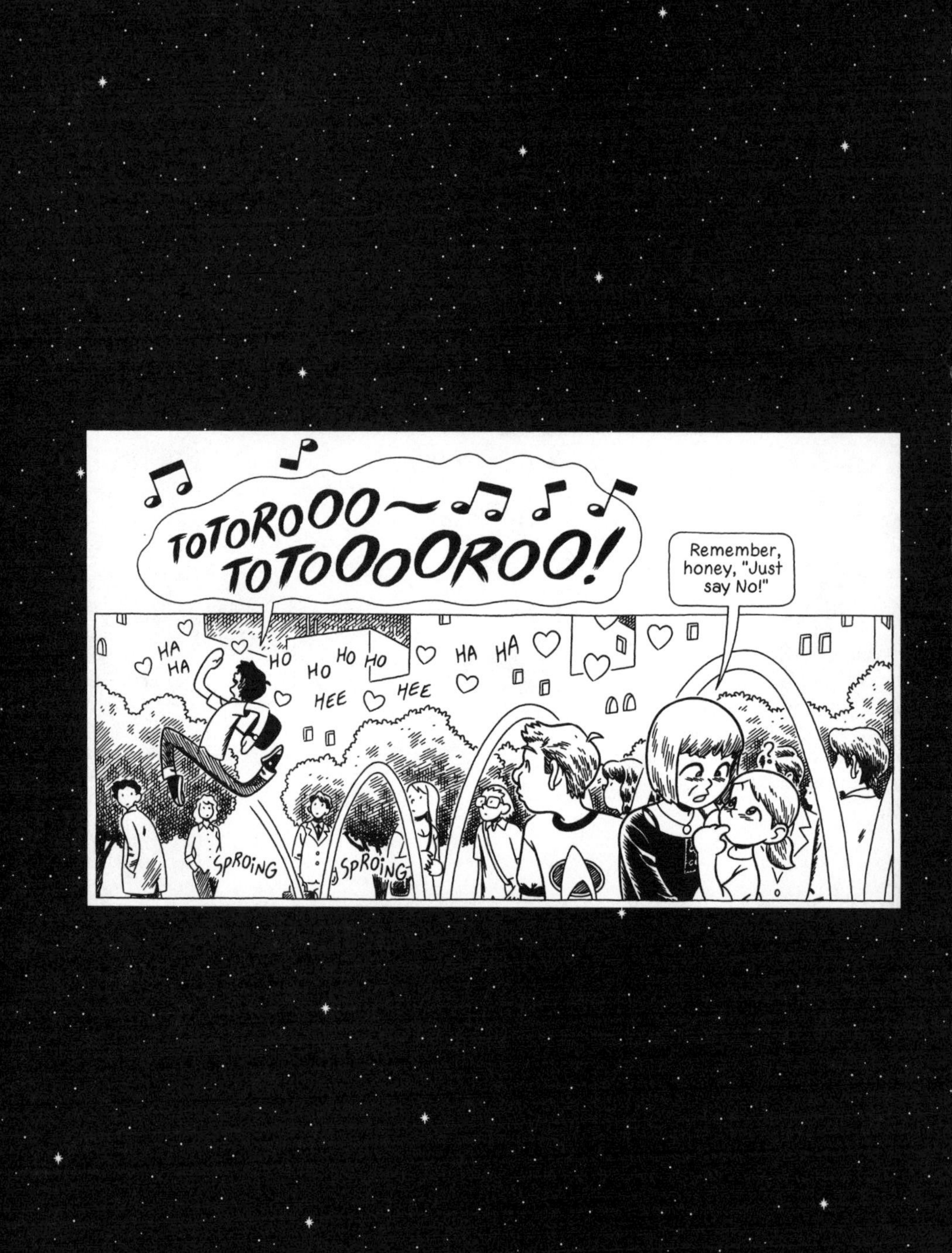
TOTOROOO~ TOTOOOOROO!
HA HA
HO HO HO HO
HEE HEE
HA HA
Remember, honey, "Just say No!"
SPROING
SPROING

CHAPTER
08

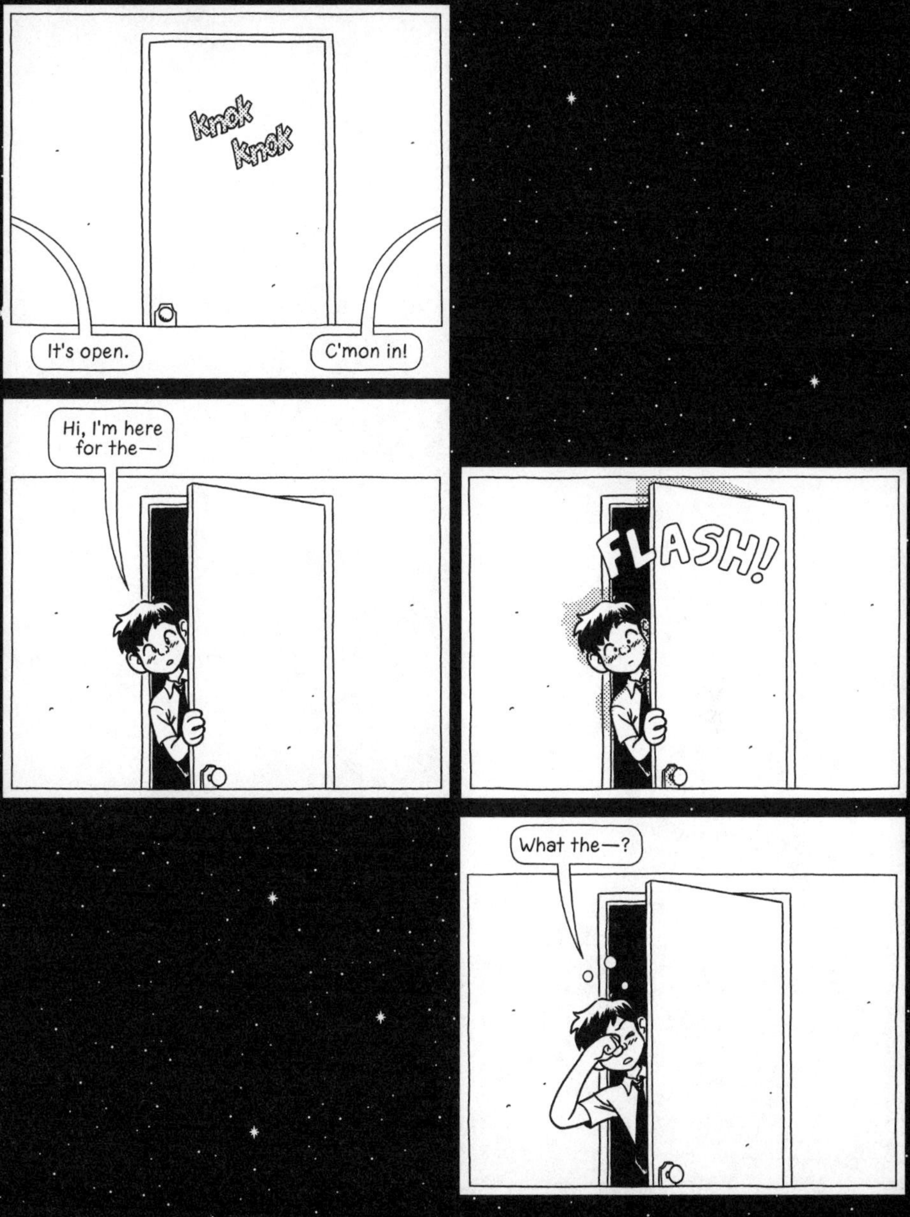
Knok
Knok
It's open.
C'mon in!
Hi, I'm here for the—
FLASH!
What the—?

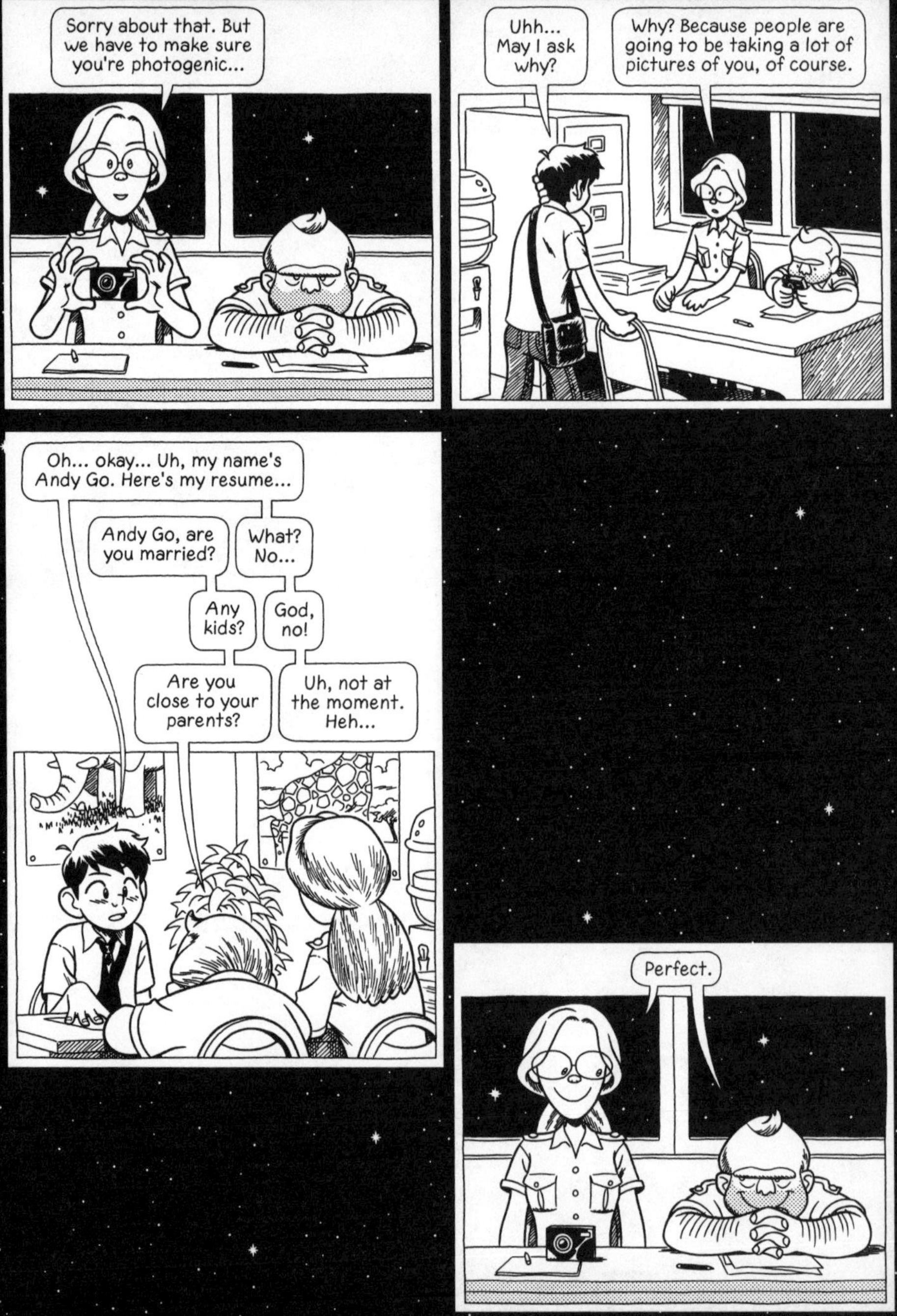

Sorry about that. But we have to make sure you're photogenic...
Uhh... May I ask why?
Why? Because people are going to be taking a lot of pictures of you, of course.
Oh... okay... Uh, my name's Andy Go. Here's my resume...
Andy Go, are you married?
What? No...
Any kids?
God, no!
Are you close to your parents?
Uh, not at the moment. Heh...
Perfect.

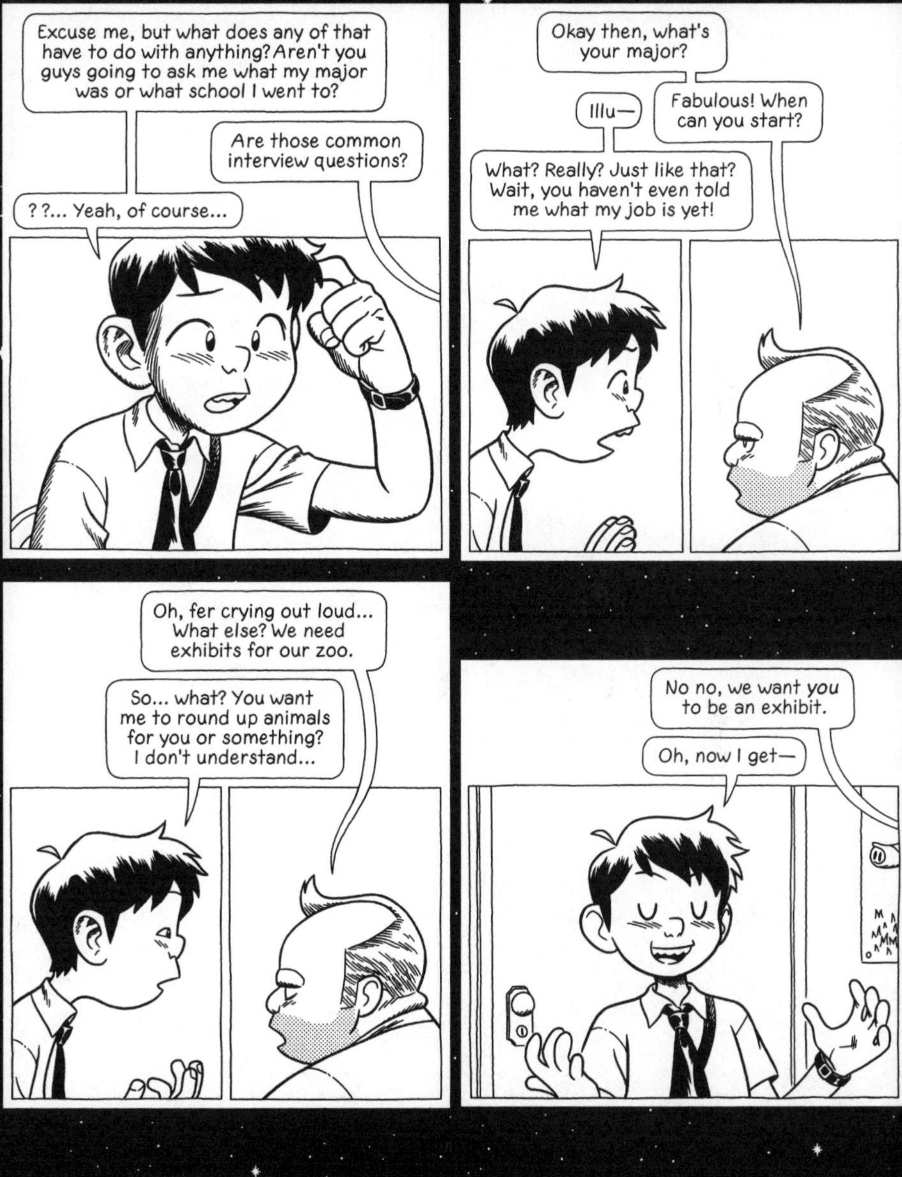
Excuse me, but what does any of that have to do with anything? Aren't you guys going to ask me what my major was or what school I went to?
Are those common interview questions?
??... Yeah, of course...
Okay then, what's your major?
Illu—
Fabulous! When can you start?
What? Really? Just like that? Wait, you haven't even told me what my job is yet!
Oh, fer crying out loud... What else? We need exhibits for our zoo.
So... what? You want me to round up animals for you or something? I don't understand...
No no, we want *you* to be an exhibit.
Oh, now I get—

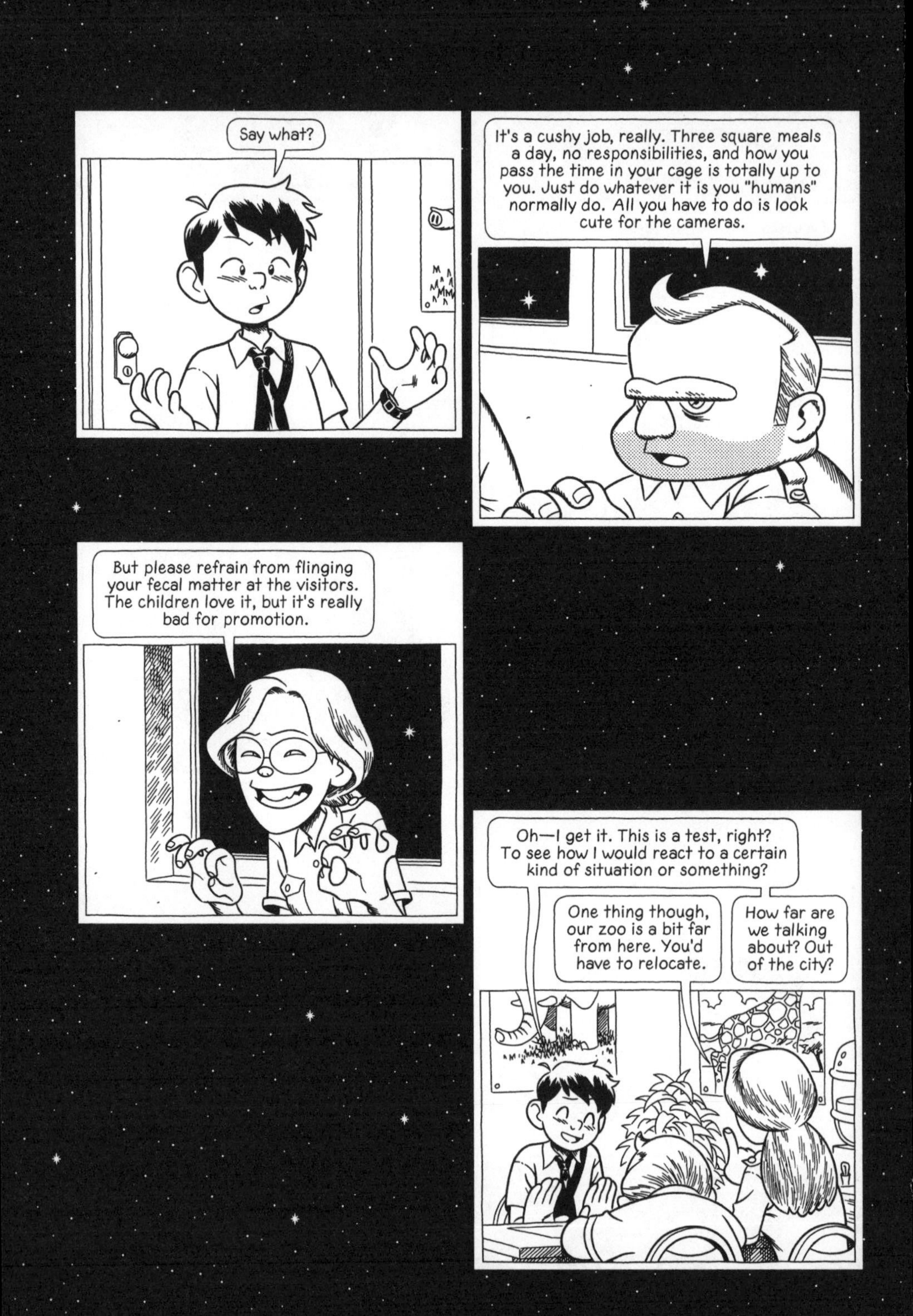
Say what?
It's a cushy job, really. Three square meals a day, no responsibilities, and how you pass the time in your cage is totally up to you. Just do whatever it is you "humans" normally do. All you have to do is look cute for the cameras.
But please refrain from flinging your fecal matter at the visitors. The children love it, but it's really bad for promotion.
Oh—I get it. This is a test, right? To see how I would react to a certain kind of situation or something?
One thing though, our zoo is a bit far from here. You'd have to relocate.
How far are we talking about? Out of the city?

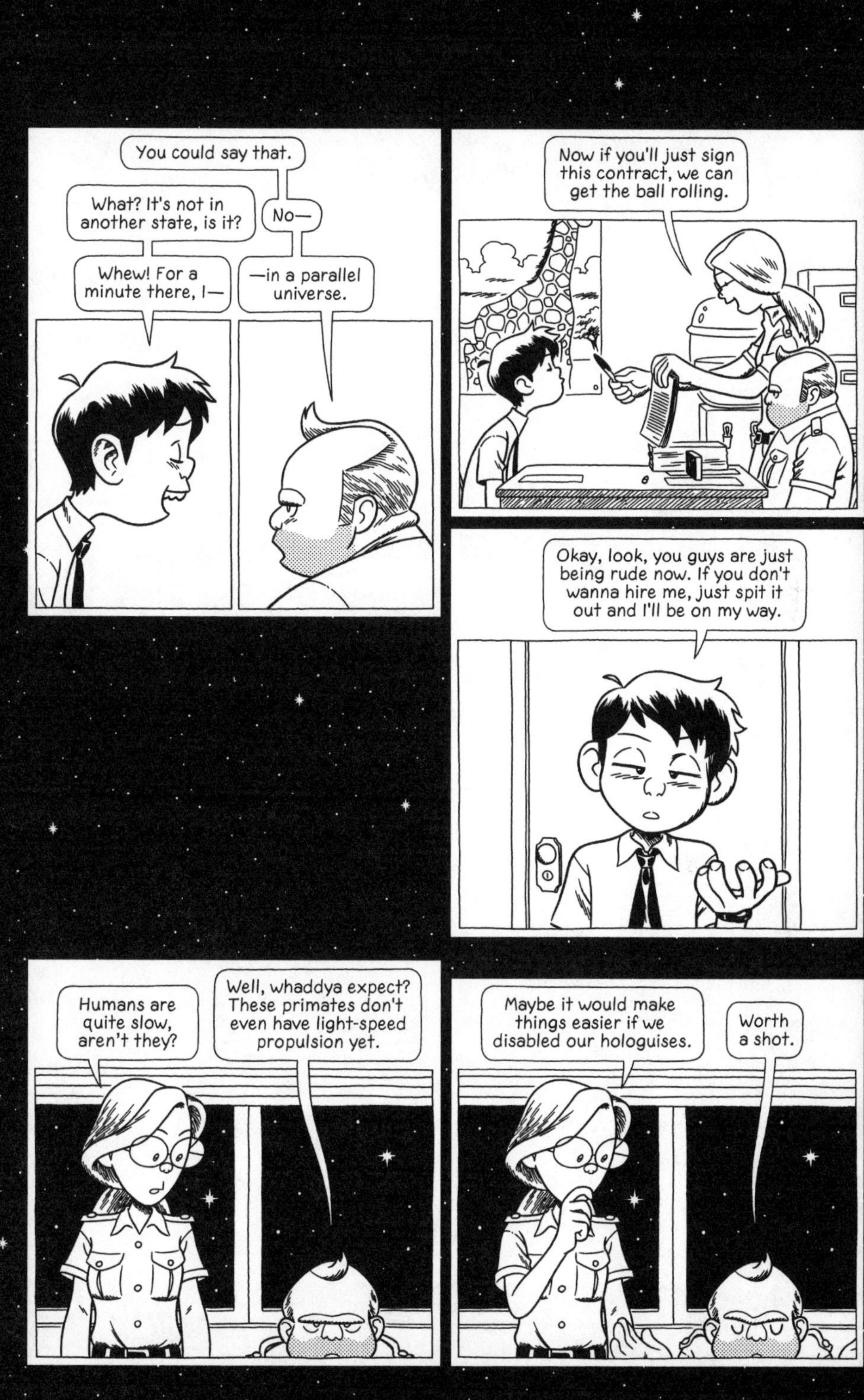
You could say that.
What? It's not in another state, is it?
No—
Whew! For a minute there, I—
—in a parallel universe.
Now if you'll just sign this contract, we can get the ball rolling.
Okay, look, you guys are just being rude now. If you don't wanna hire me, just spit it out and I'll be on my way.
Humans are quite slow, aren't they?
Well, whaddya expect? These primates don't even have light-speed propulsion yet.
Maybe it would make things easier if we disabled our hologuises.
Worth a shot.

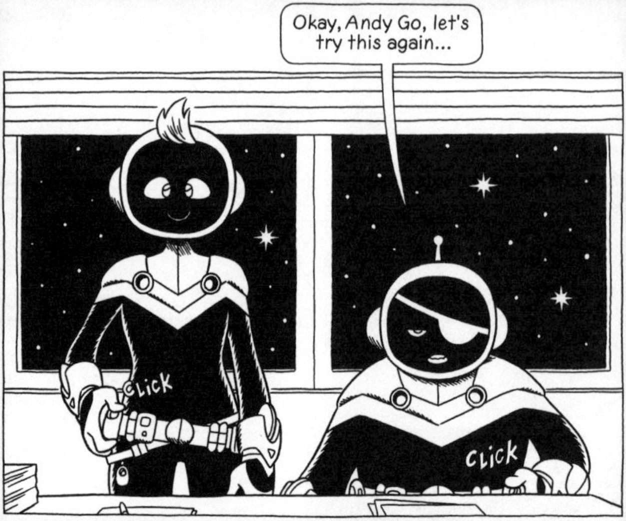
Okay, Andy Go, let's try this again...
CLICK
CLICK

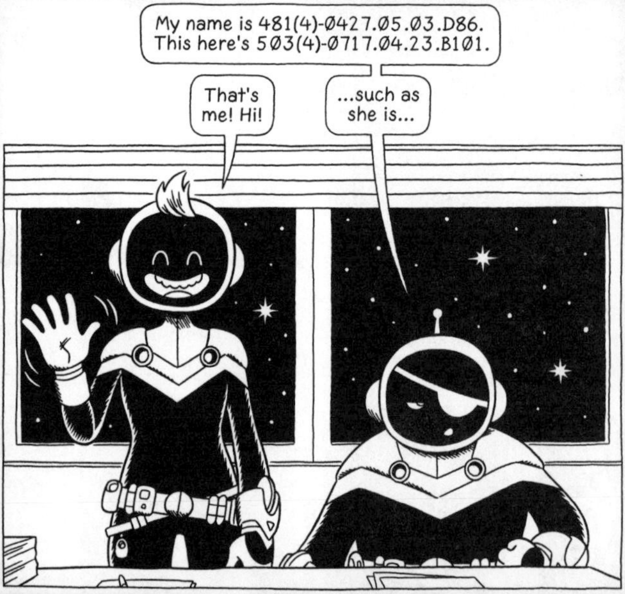
My name is 481(4)-Ø427.Ø5.Ø3.D86. This here's 5Ø3(4)-Ø717.Ø4.23.B1Ø1.
That's me! Hi!
...such as she is...

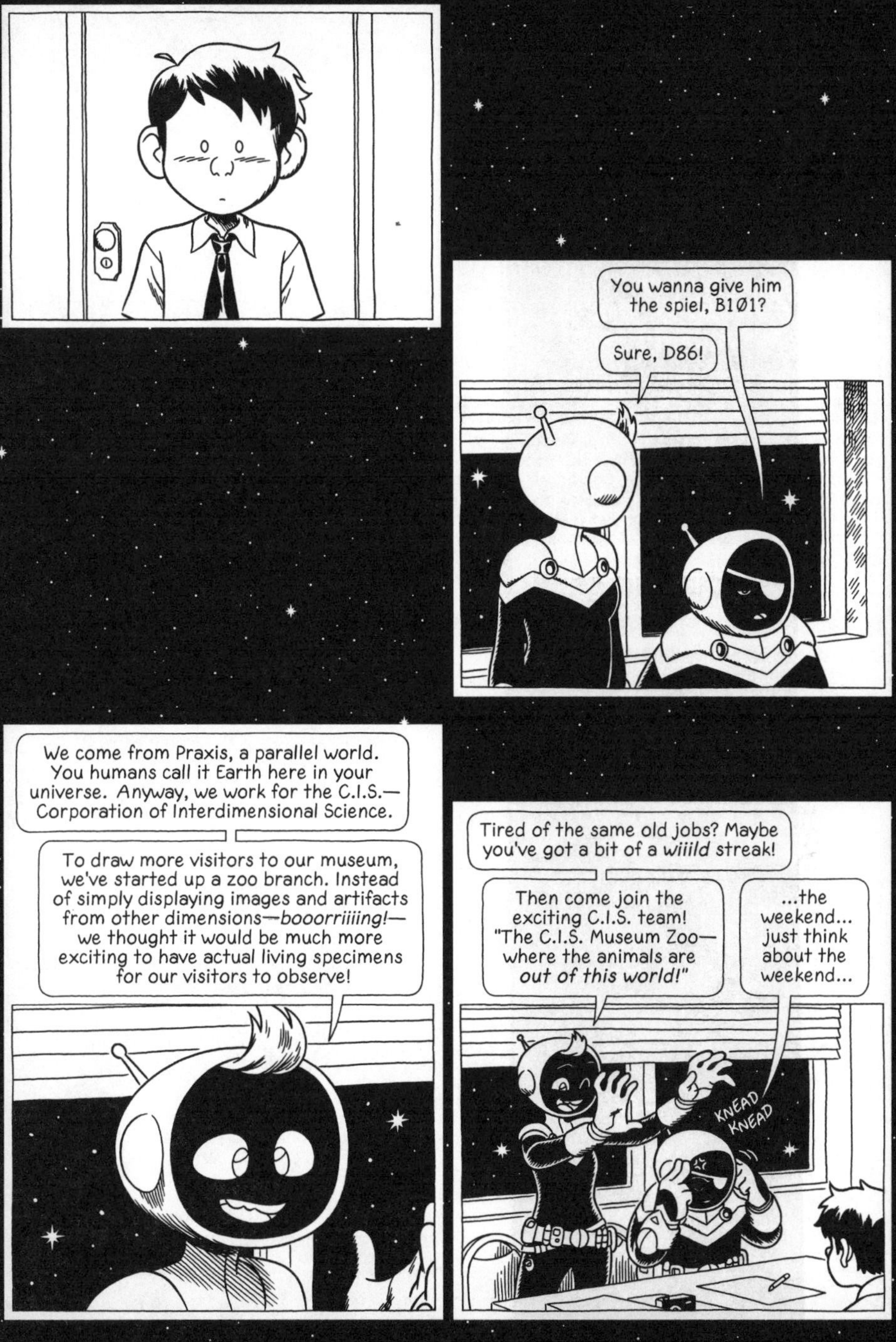
You wanna give him the spiel, B1Ø1?
Sure, D86!
We come from Praxis, a parallel world. You humans call it Earth here in your universe. Anyway, we work for the C.I.S.— Corporation of Interdimensional Science.
To draw more visitors to our museum, we've started up a zoo branch. Instead of simply displaying images and artifacts from other dimensions—*booorriiiing!*— we thought it would be much more exciting to have actual living specimens for our visitors to observe!
Tired of the same old jobs? Maybe you've got a bit of a *wiiild* streak!
Then come join the exciting C.I.S. team! "The C.I.S. Museum Zoo— where the animals are *out of this world!*"
...the weekend... just think about the weekend...
KNEAD KNEAD

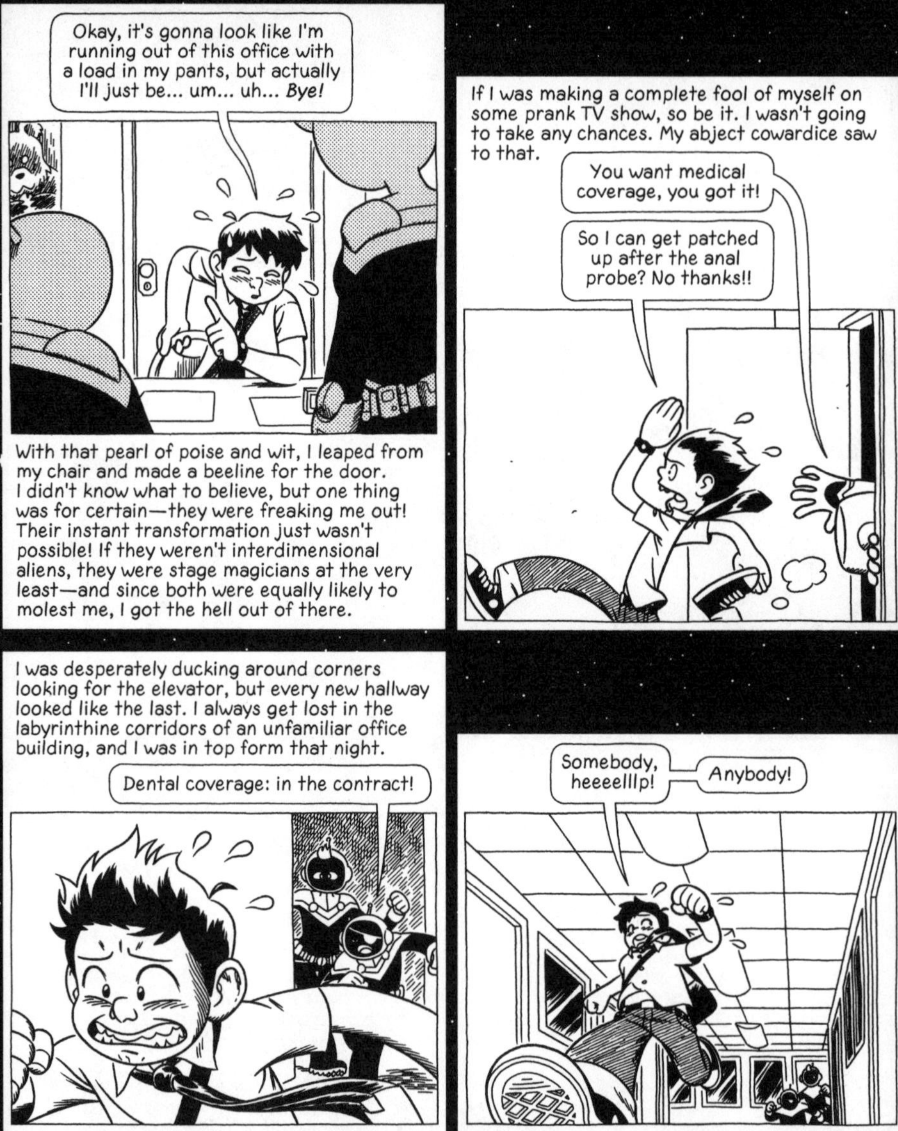
Okay, it's gonna look like I'm running out of this office with a load in my pants, but actually I'll just be... um... uh... *Bye!*
With that pearl of poise and wit, I leaped from my chair and made a beeline for the door. I didn't know what to believe, but one thing was for certain—they were freaking me out! Their instant transformation just wasn't possible! If they weren't interdimensional aliens, they were stage magicians at the very least—and since both were equally likely to molest me, I got the hell out of there.
If I was making a complete fool of myself on some prank TV show, so be it. I wasn't going to take any chances. My abject cowardice saw to that.
You want medical coverage, you got it!
So I can get patched up after the anal probe? No thanks!!
I was desperately ducking around corners looking for the elevator, but every new hallway looked like the last. I always get lost in the labyrinthine corridors of an unfamiliar office building, and I was in top form that night.
Dental coverage: in the contract!
And try as I might, I couldn't lose my 2 recruiters from hell. The scary stocky one kept throwing benefits at me, and I have to say, between my bouts of panic, the job was starting to sound pretty good. But not nearly good enough to overthrow the fight-or-flight response. Or in my case, the flee-or-flight response.
Somebody, heeeelllp!
Anybody!
I kept peering into cubicles and office windows to see if anyone else was in the building. But it was nearing 8 pm and everyone seemed to have gotten off work already. I should have known something was fishy when I found out these "recruiters" were seeing applicants so late.

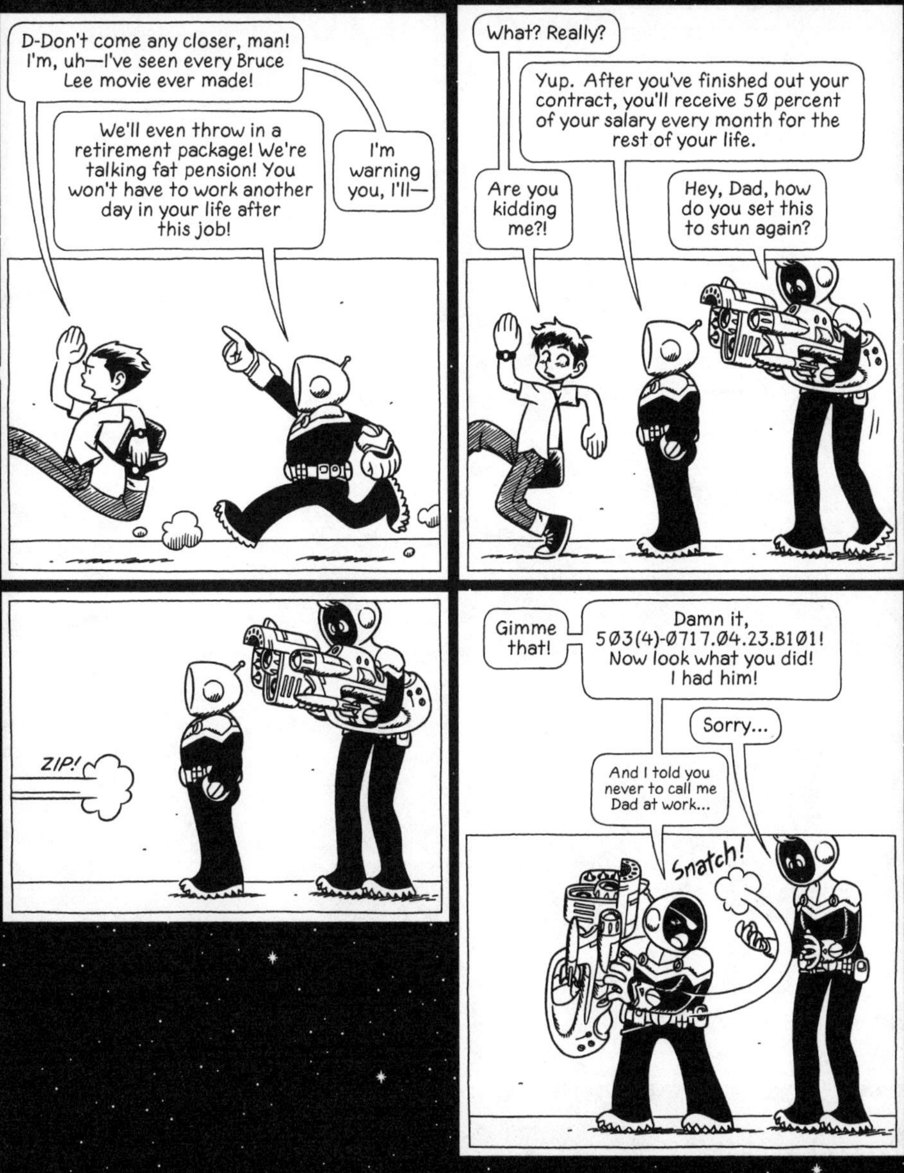
D-Don't come any closer, man! I'm, uh—I've seen every Bruce Lee movie ever made!
We'll even throw in a retirement package! We're talking fat pension! You won't have to work another day in your life after this job!
I'm warning you, I'll—
What? Really?
Yup. After you've finished out your contract, you'll receive 5Ø percent of your salary every month for the rest of your life.
Are you kidding me?!
Hey, Dad, how do you set this to stun again?
ZIP!
Gimme that!
Damn it, 5Ø3(4)-Ø717.Ø4.23.B1Ø1! Now look what you did! I had him!
Sorry...
And I told you never to call me Dad at work...
Snatch!

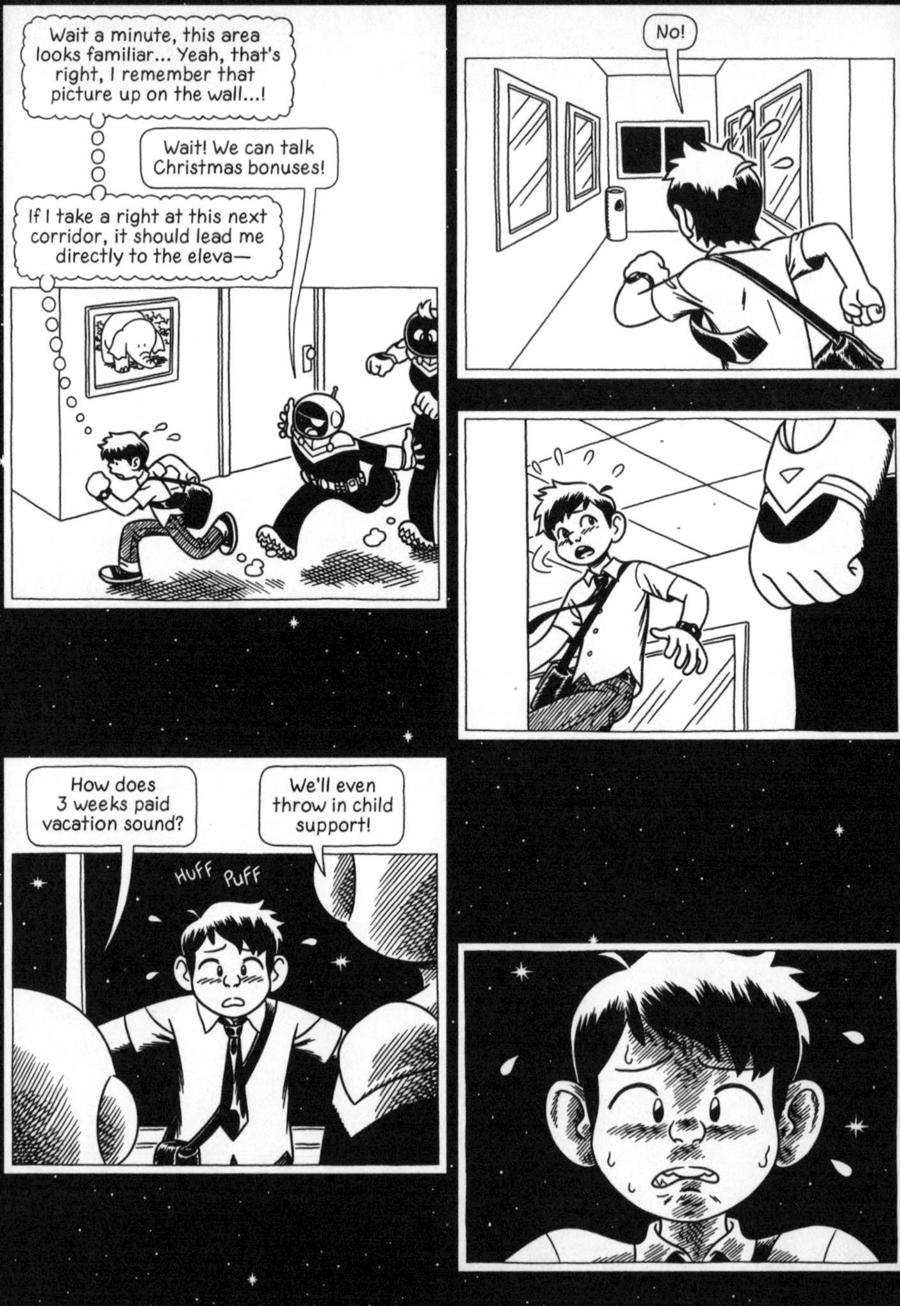
Wait a minute, this area looks familiar... Yeah, that's right, I remember that picture up on the wall...!
Wait! We can talk Christmas bonuses!
If I take a right at this next corridor, it should lead me directly to the eleva—
No!
How does 3 weeks paid vacation sound?
We'll even throw in child support!
HUFF PUFF

CHAPTER
09

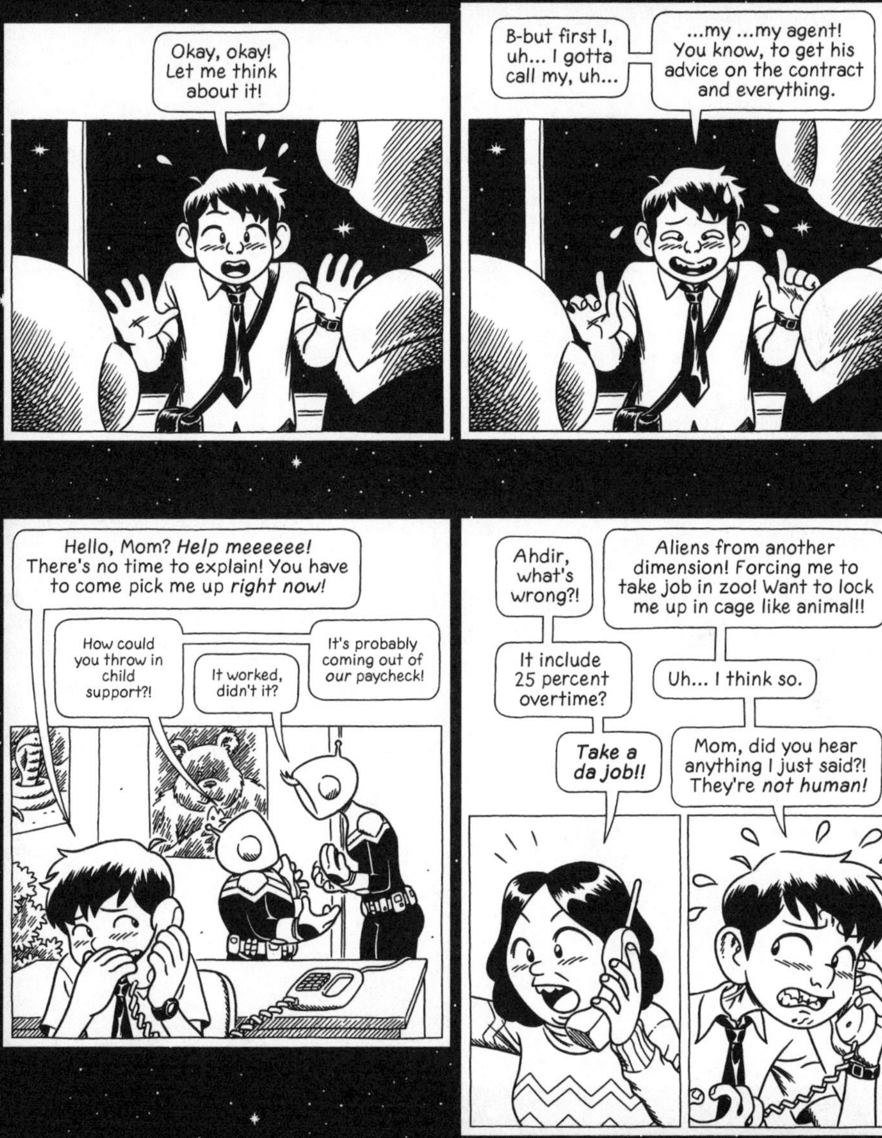
Okay, okay! Let me think about it!
B-but first I, uh... I gotta call my, uh...
...my ...my agent! You know, to get his advice on the contract and everything.
Hello, Mom? *Help meeeeee!* There's no time to explain! You have to come pick me up *right now!*
How could you throw in child support?!
It's probably coming out of *our* paycheck!
It worked, didn't it?
Ahdir, what's wrong?!
Aliens from another dimension! Forcing me to take job in zoo! Want to lock me up in cage like animal!!
It include 25 percent overtime?
Uh... I think so.
Take a da job!!
Mom, did you hear anything I just said?! They're *not human!*

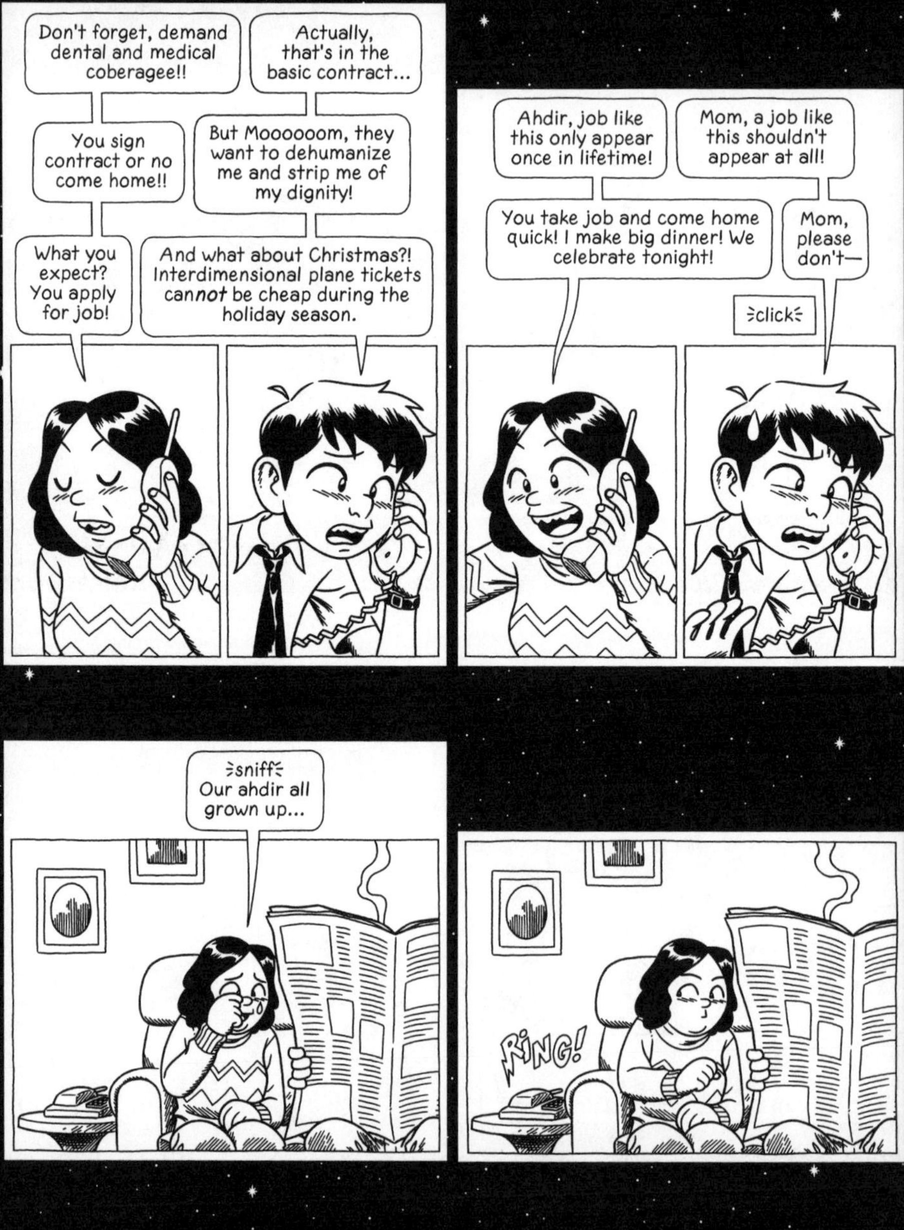
Don't forget, demand dental and medical coberagee!!
Actually, that's in the basic contract...
You sign contract or no come home!!
But Moooooom, they want to dehumanize me and strip me of my dignity!
What you expect? You apply for job!
And what about Christmas?! Interdimensional plane tickets can*not* be cheap during the holiday season.
Ahdir, job like this only appear once in lifetime!
Mom, a job like this shouldn't appear at all!
You take job and come home quick! I make big dinner! We celebrate tonight!
Mom, please don't—
click
sniff
Our ahdir all grown up...
RING!

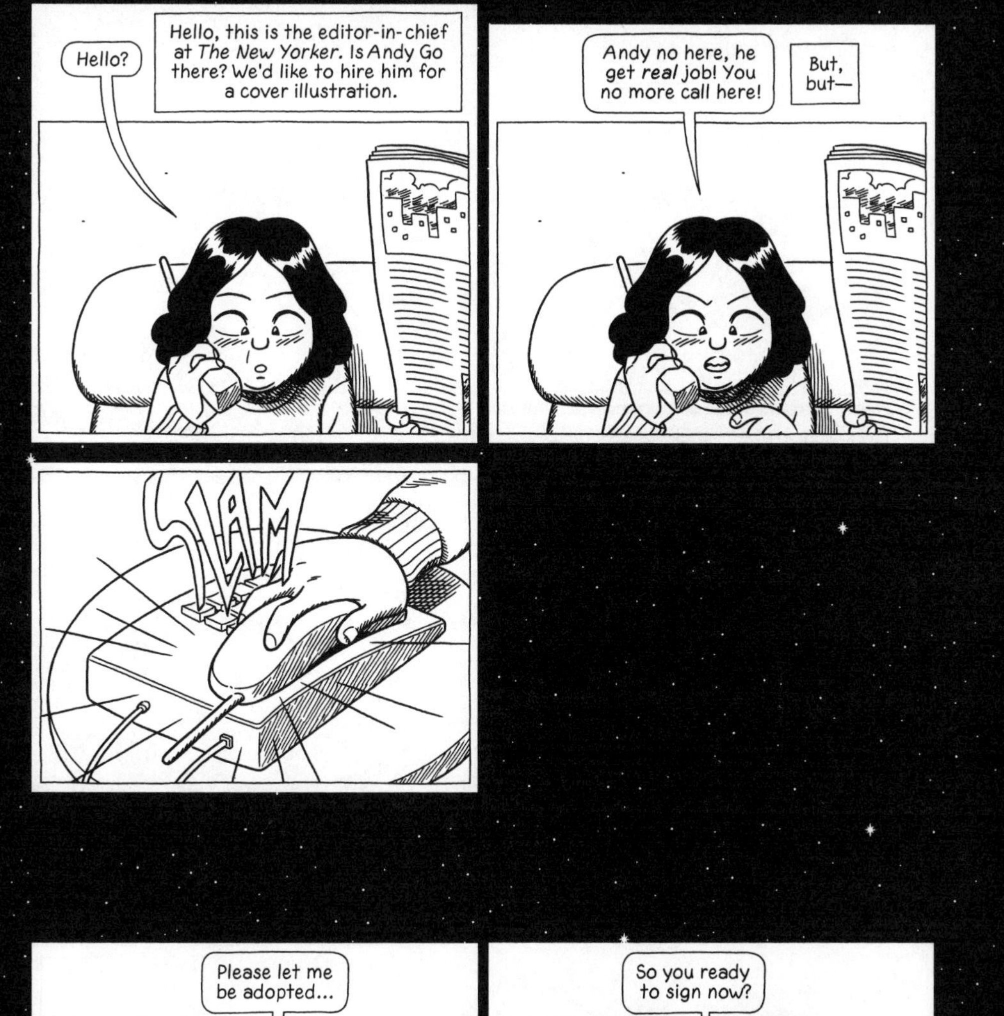
Hello?
Hello, this is the editor-in-chief at *The New Yorker.* Is Andy Go there? We'd like to hire him for a cover illustration.
Andy no here, he get *real* job! You no more call here!
But, but—
SLAM

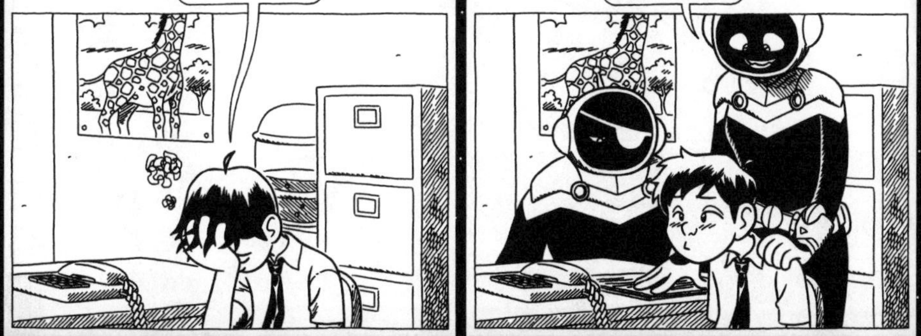
Please let me be adopted...
So you ready to sign now?

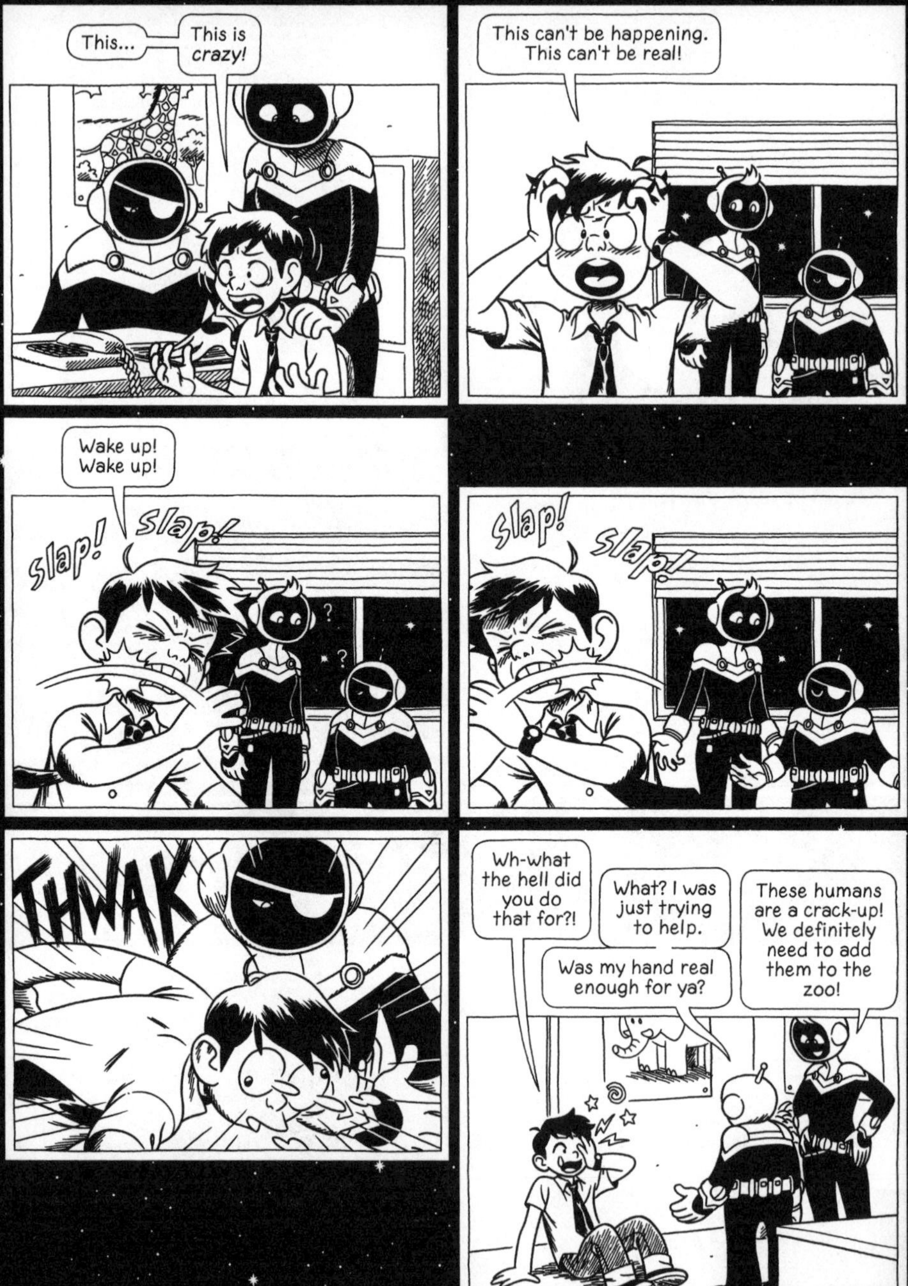
This...
This is *crazy!*
This can't be happening. This can't be real!
Wake up! Wake up!
slap! Slap!
?
?
slap! Slap!
THWAK
Wh-what the hell did you do that for?!
What? I was just trying to help.
Was my hand real enough for ya?
These humans are a crack-up! We definitely need to add them to the zoo!

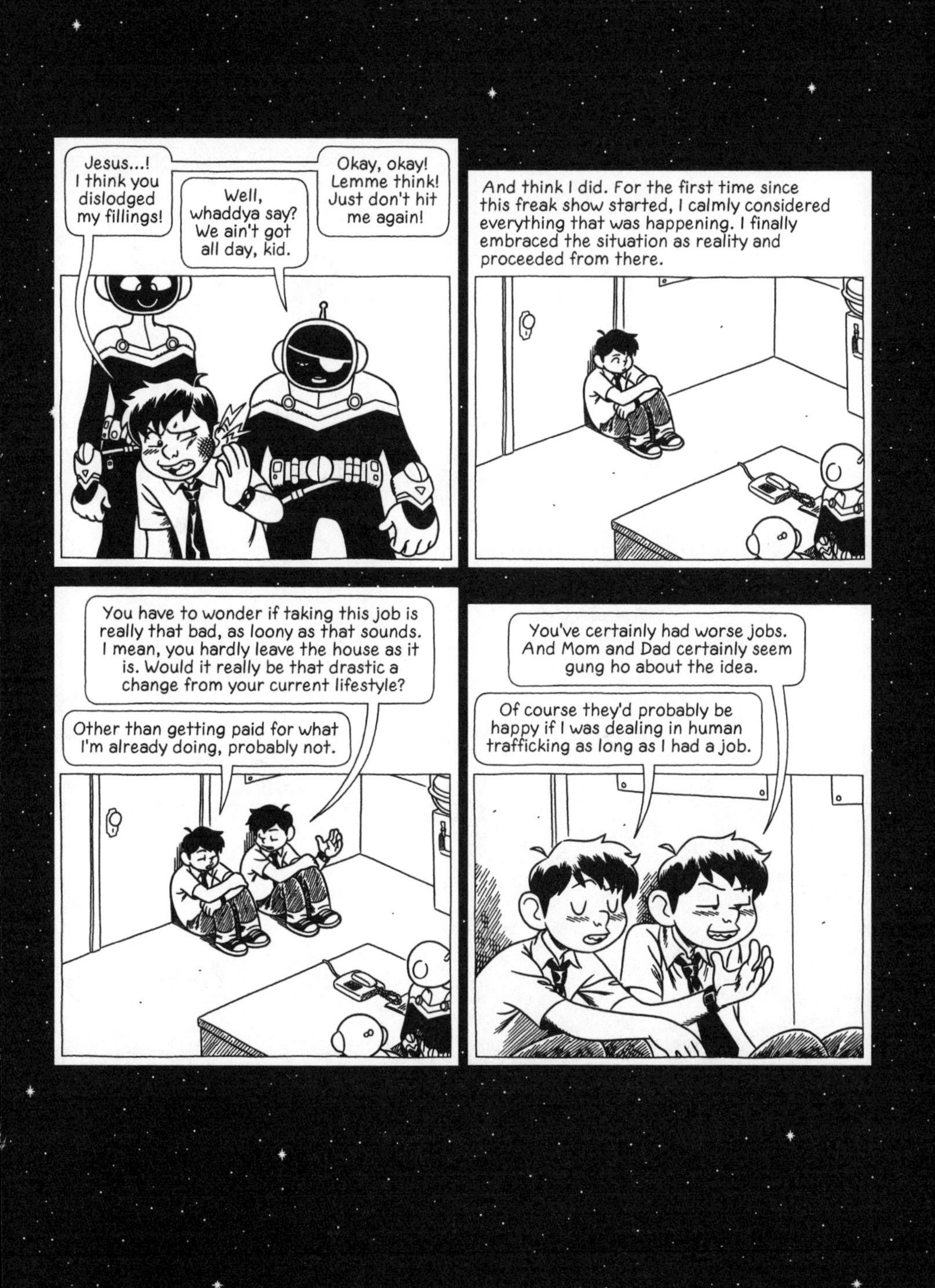
Jesus...! I think you dislodged my fillings!
Okay, okay! Lemme think! Just don't hit me again!
Well, whaddya say? We ain't got all day, kid.
And think I did. For the first time since this freak show started, I calmly considered everything that was happening. I finally embraced the situation as reality and proceeded from there.
You have to wonder if taking this job is really that bad, as loony as that sounds. I mean, you hardly leave the house as it is. Would it really be that drastic a change from your current lifestyle?
Other than getting paid for what I'm already doing, probably not.
You've certainly had worse jobs. And Mom and Dad certainly seem gung ho about the idea.
Of course they'd probably be happy if I was dealing in human trafficking as long as I had a job.

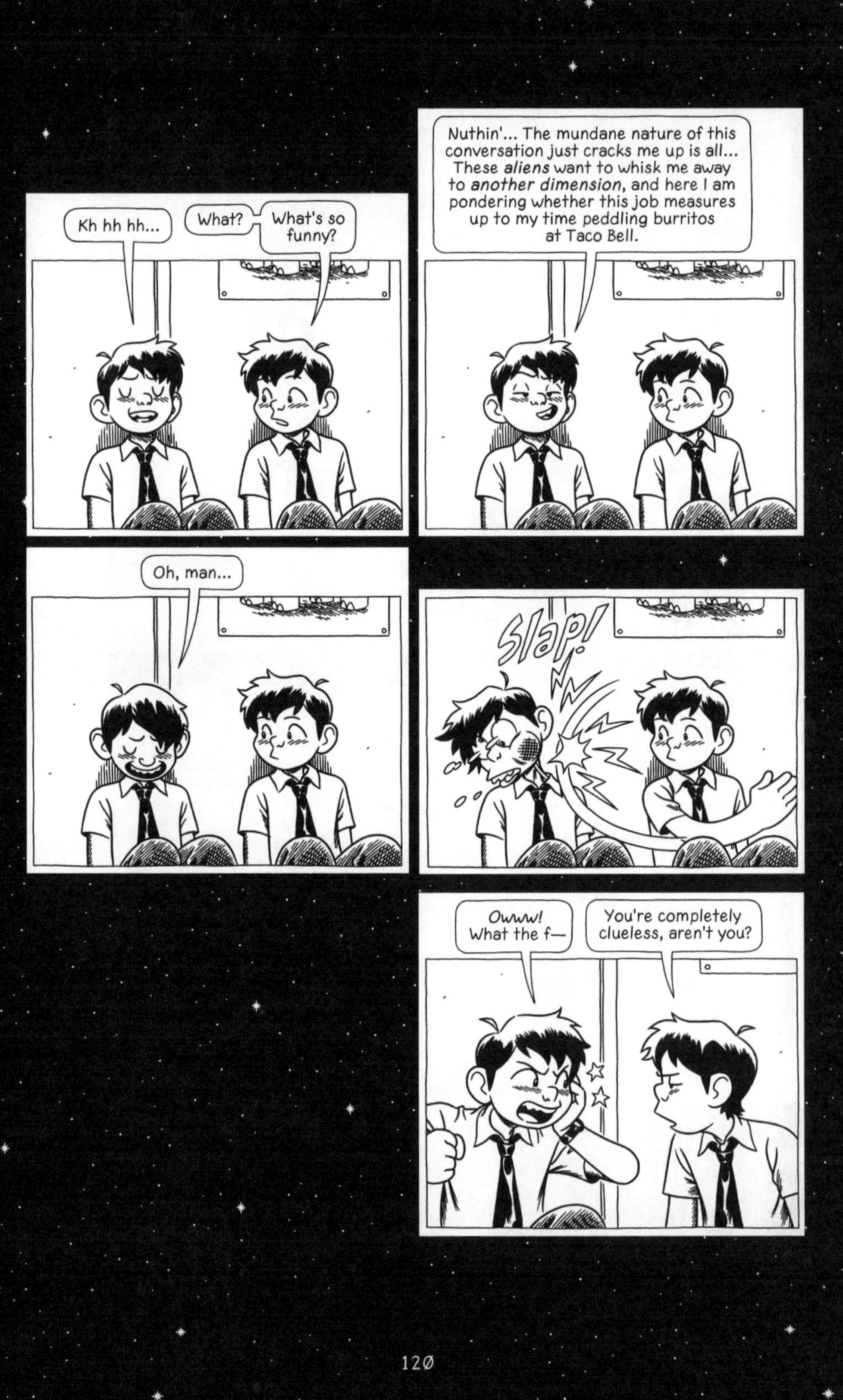

Kh hh hh...
What?
What's so funny?
Nuthin'... The mundane nature of this conversation just cracks me up is all... These *aliens* want to whisk me away to *another dimension*, and here I am pondering whether this job measures up to my time peddling burritos at Taco Bell.
Oh, man...
Slap!
Owww! What the f—
You're completely clueless, aren't you?

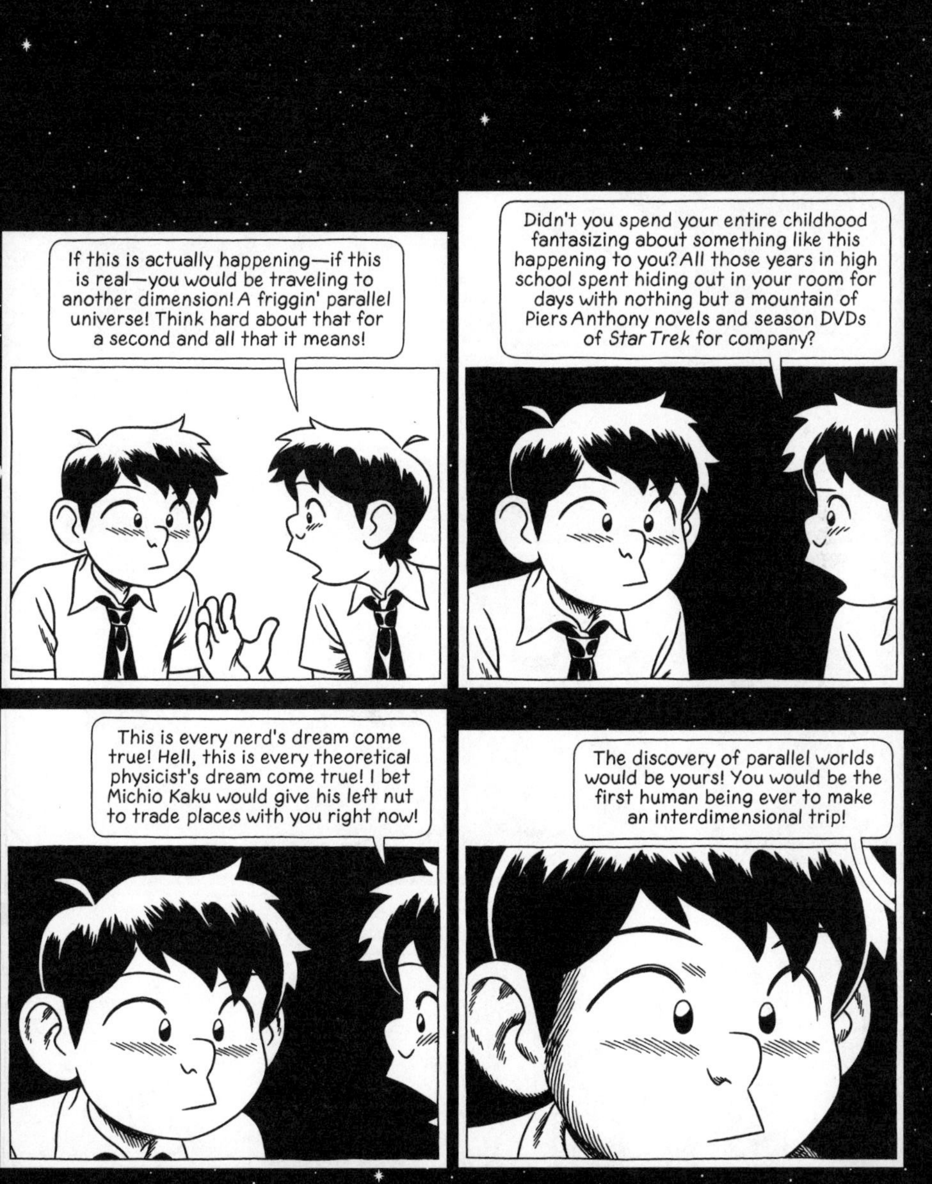
If this is actually happening—if this is real—you would be traveling to another dimension! A friggin' parallel universe! Think hard about that for a second and all that it means!
Didn't you spend your entire childhood fantasizing about something like this happening to you? All those years in high school spent hiding out in your room for days with nothing but a mountain of Piers Anthony novels and season DVDs of *Star Trek* for company?
This is every nerd's dream come true! Hell, this is every theoretical physicist's dream come true! I bet Michio Kaku would give his left nut to trade places with you right now!
The discovery of parallel worlds would be yours! You would be the first human being ever to make an interdimensional trip!

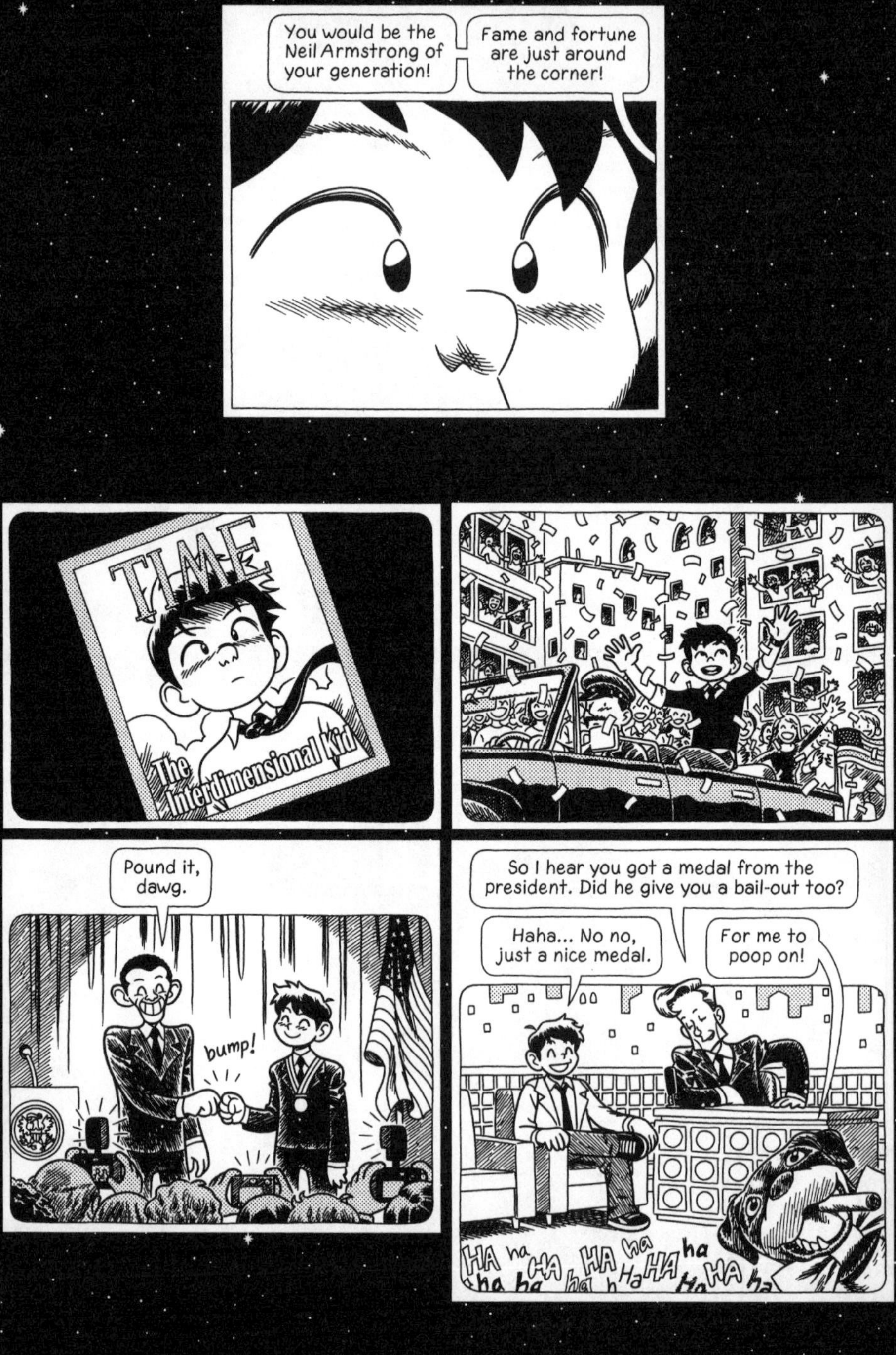

You would be the Neil Armstrong of your generation!
Fame and fortune are just around the corner!
TIME
The Interdimensional Kid
Pound it, dawg.
bump!
So I hear you got a medal from the president. Did he give you a bail-out too?
Haha... No no, just a nice medal.
For me to poop on!
HA ha ha ha HA HA ha ha h ha Ha HA ha Ha HA ha

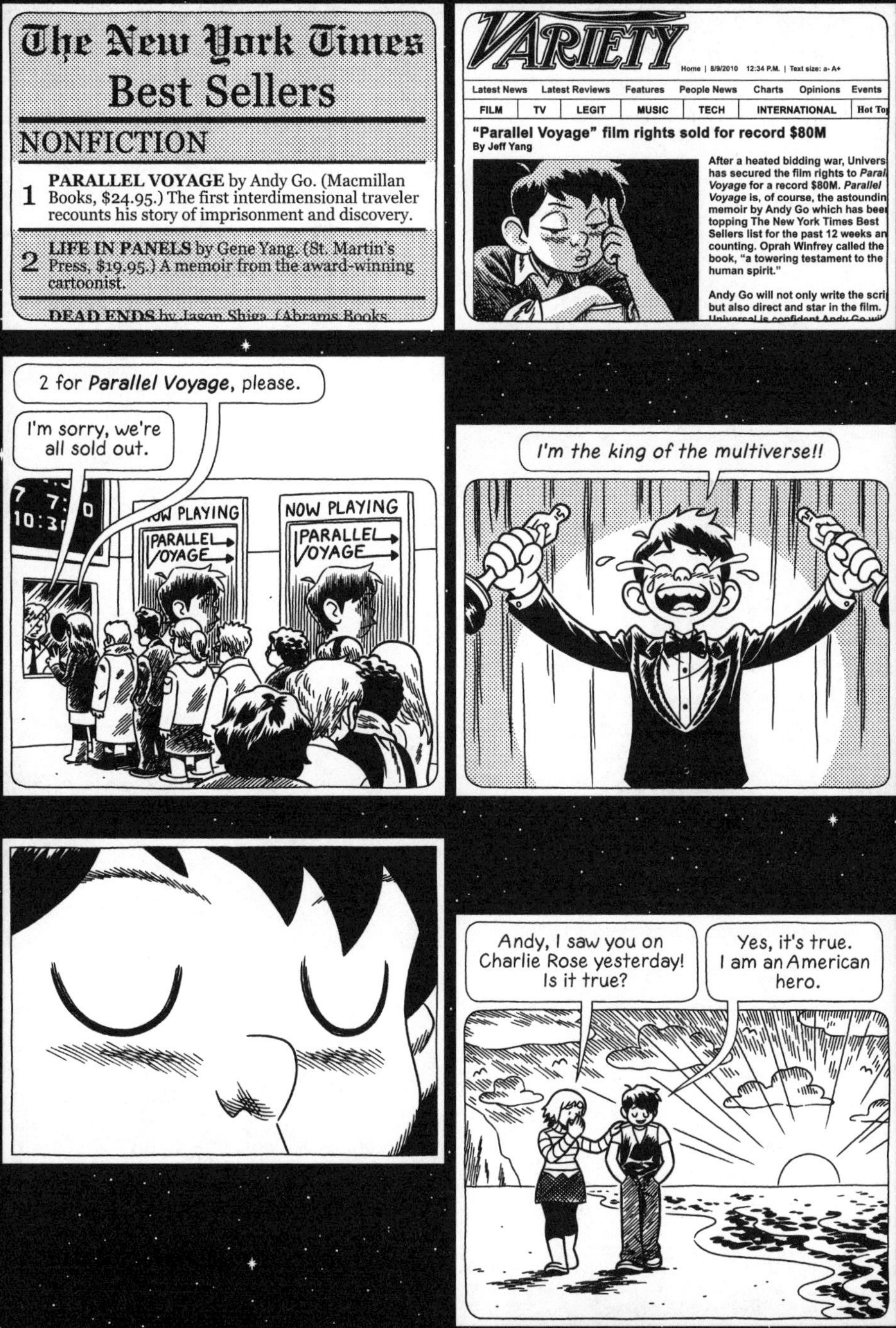
The New York Times
Best Sellers
NONFICTION
1 PARALLEL VOYAGE by Andy Go. (Macmillan Books, $24.95.) The first interdimensional traveler recounts his story of imprisonment and discovery.
2 LIFE IN PANELS by Gene Yang. (St. Martin's Press, $19.95.) A memoir from the award-winning cartoonist.
VARIETY
Home | 8/9/2010 12:34 P.M. | Text size: a- A+
Latest News Latest Reviews Features People News Charts Opinions Events
FILM TV LEGIT MUSIC TECH INTERNATIONAL
"Parallel Voyage" film rights sold for record $80M
By Jeff Yang
After a heated bidding war, Univers
has secured the film rights to Paral
Voyage for a record $80M. Parallel
Voyage is, of course, the astoundin
memoir by Andy Go which has bee
topping The New York Times Best
Sellers list for the past 12 weeks an
counting. Oprah Winfrey called the
book, "a towering testament to the
human spirit."
Andy Go will not only write the scri
but also direct and star in the film.
2 for Parallel Voyage, please.
I'm sorry, we're all sold out.
NOW PLAYING PARALLEL VOYAGE
NOW PLAYING PARALLEL VOYAGE
I'm the king of the multiverse!!
Andy, I saw you on Charlie Rose yesterday! Is it true?
Yes, it's true. I am an American hero.

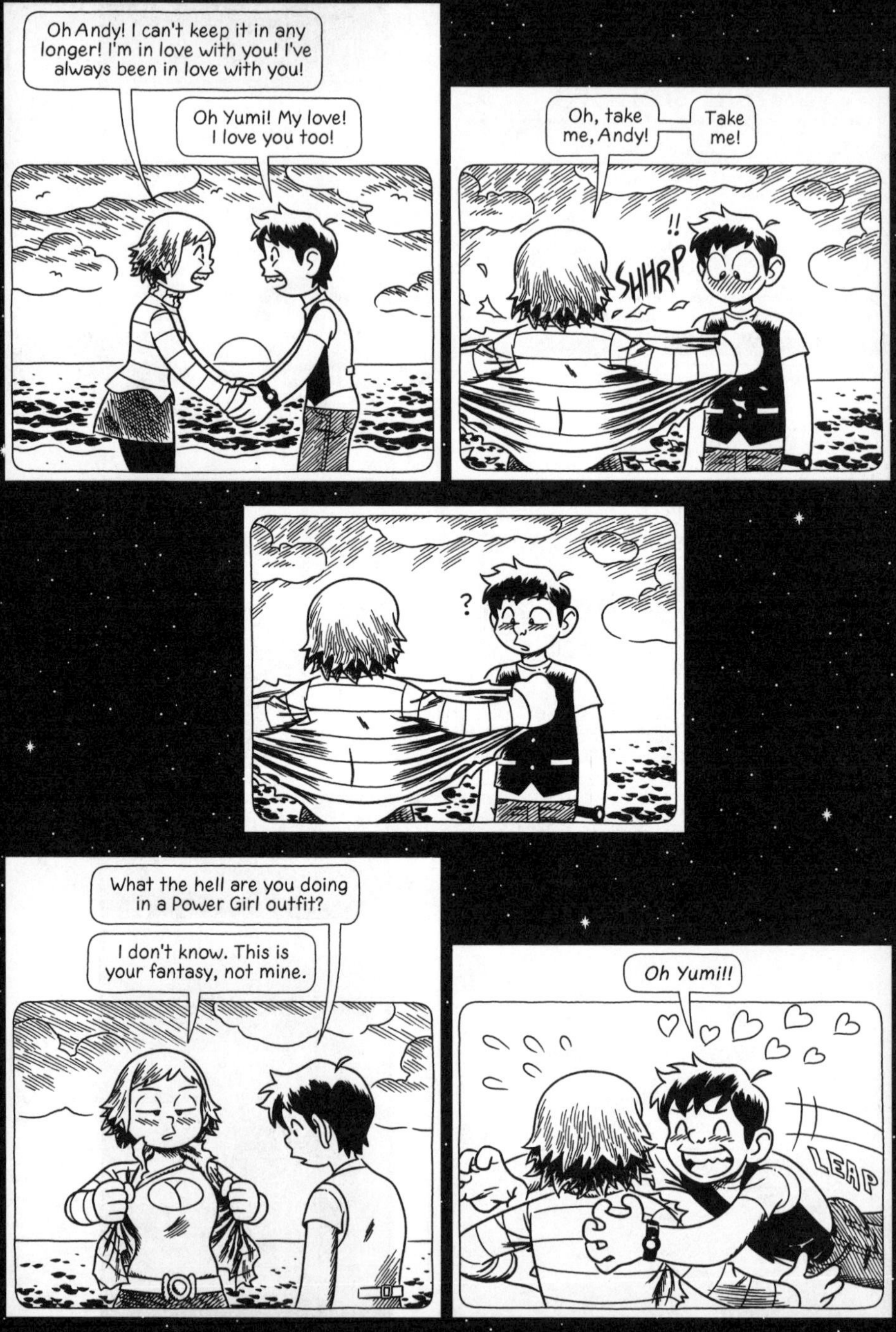
Oh Andy! I can't keep it in any longer! I'm in love with you! I've always been in love with you!
Oh Yumi! My love! I love you too!
Oh, take me, Andy!
Take me!
!!
SHHRP
?
What the hell are you doing in a Power Girl outfit?
I don't know. This is your fantasy, not mine.
Oh Yumi!!
LEAP

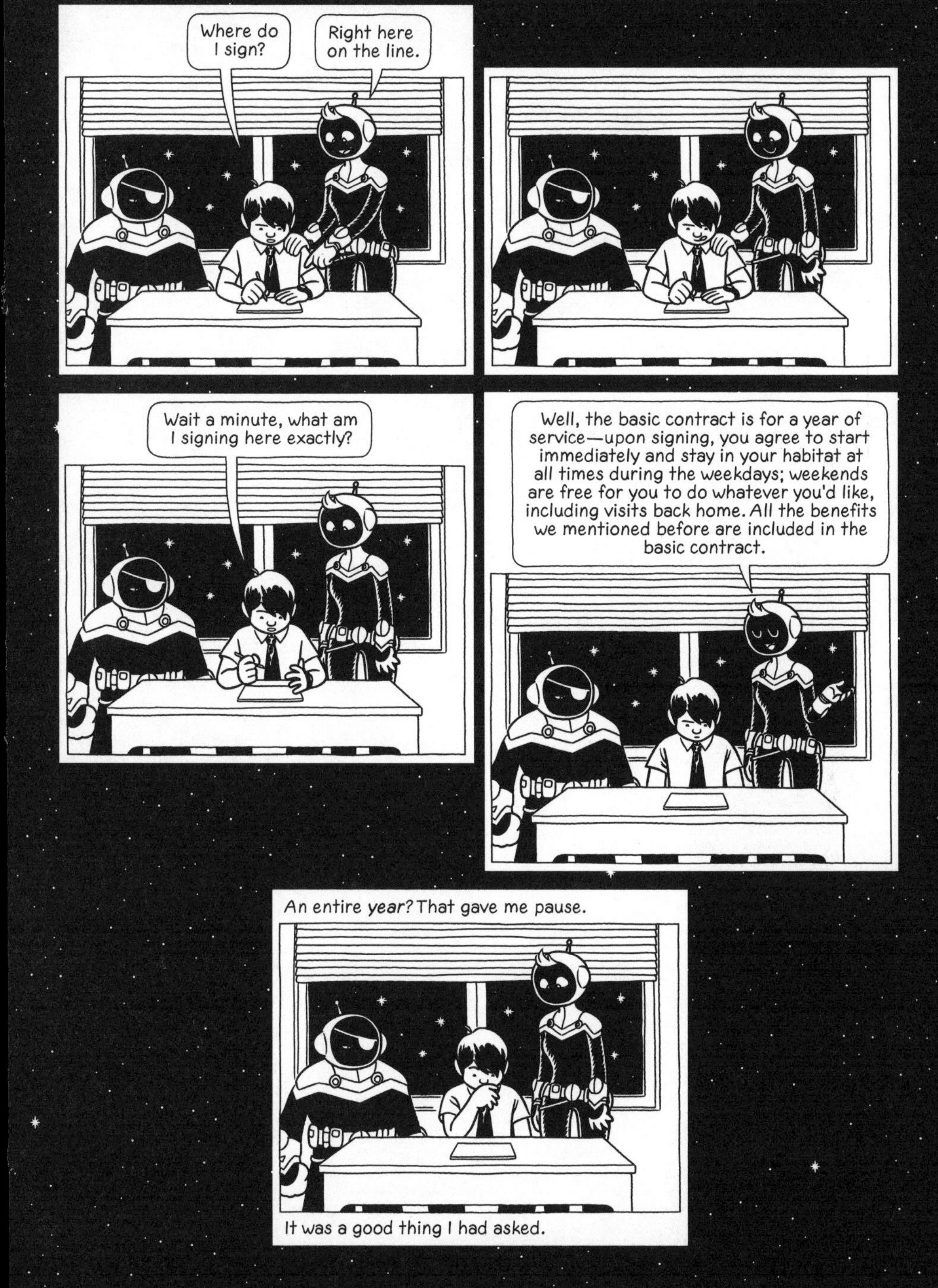
Where do I sign?
Right here on the line.
Wait a minute, what am I signing here exactly?
Well, the basic contract is for a year of service—upon signing, you agree to start immediately and stay in your habitat at all times during the weekdays; weekends are free for you to do whatever you'd like, including visits back home. All the benefits we mentioned before are included in the basic contract.
An entire *year*? That gave me pause.
It was a good thing I had asked.

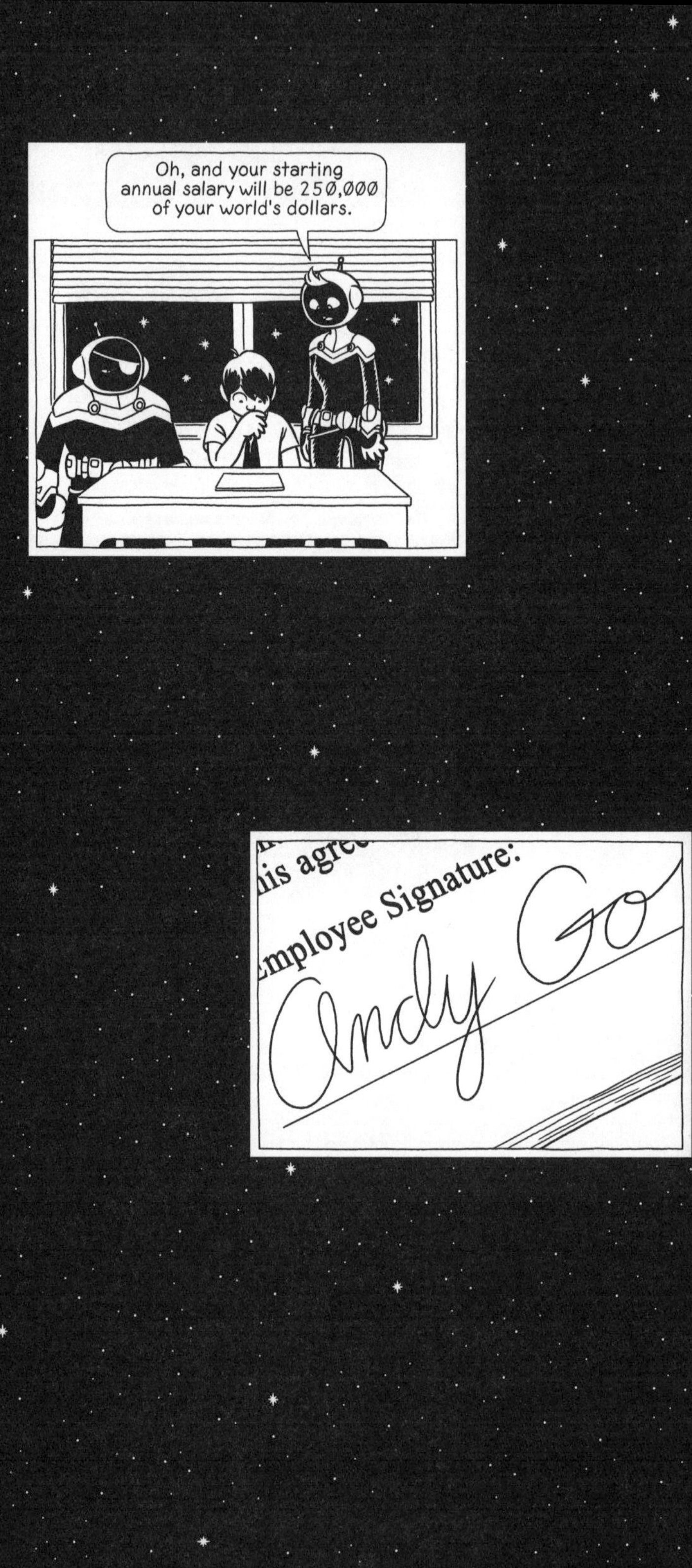
Oh, and your starting annual salary will be 25Ø,ØØØ of your world's dollars.
Employee Signature:
Andy Go

CHAPTER
10

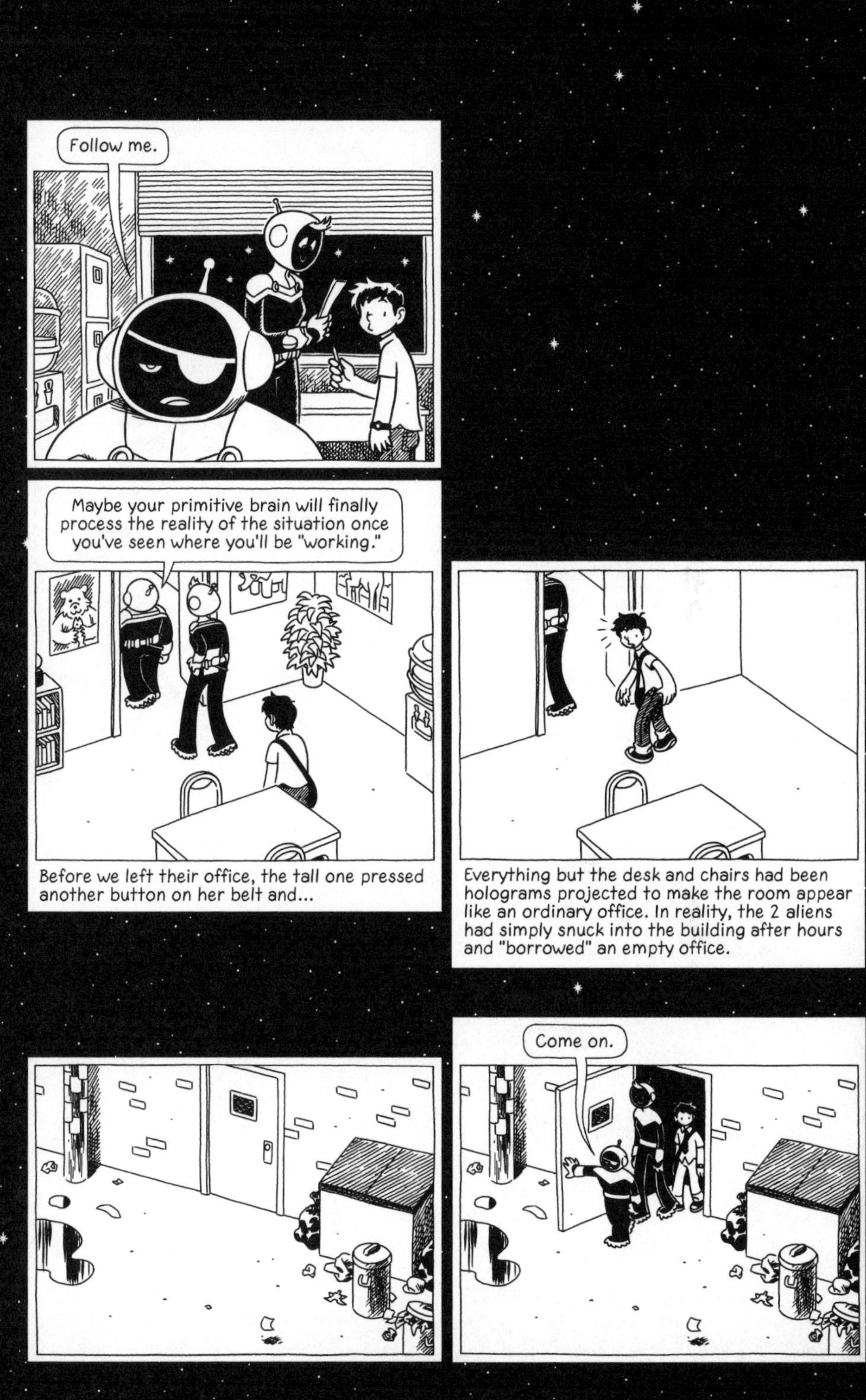

Follow me.
Maybe your primitive brain will finally process the reality of the situation once you've seen where you'll be "working."
Before we left their office, the tall one pressed another button on her belt and...
Everything but the desk and chairs had been holograms projected to make the room appear like an ordinary office. In reality, the 2 aliens had simply snuck into the building after hours and "borrowed" an empty office.
Come on.

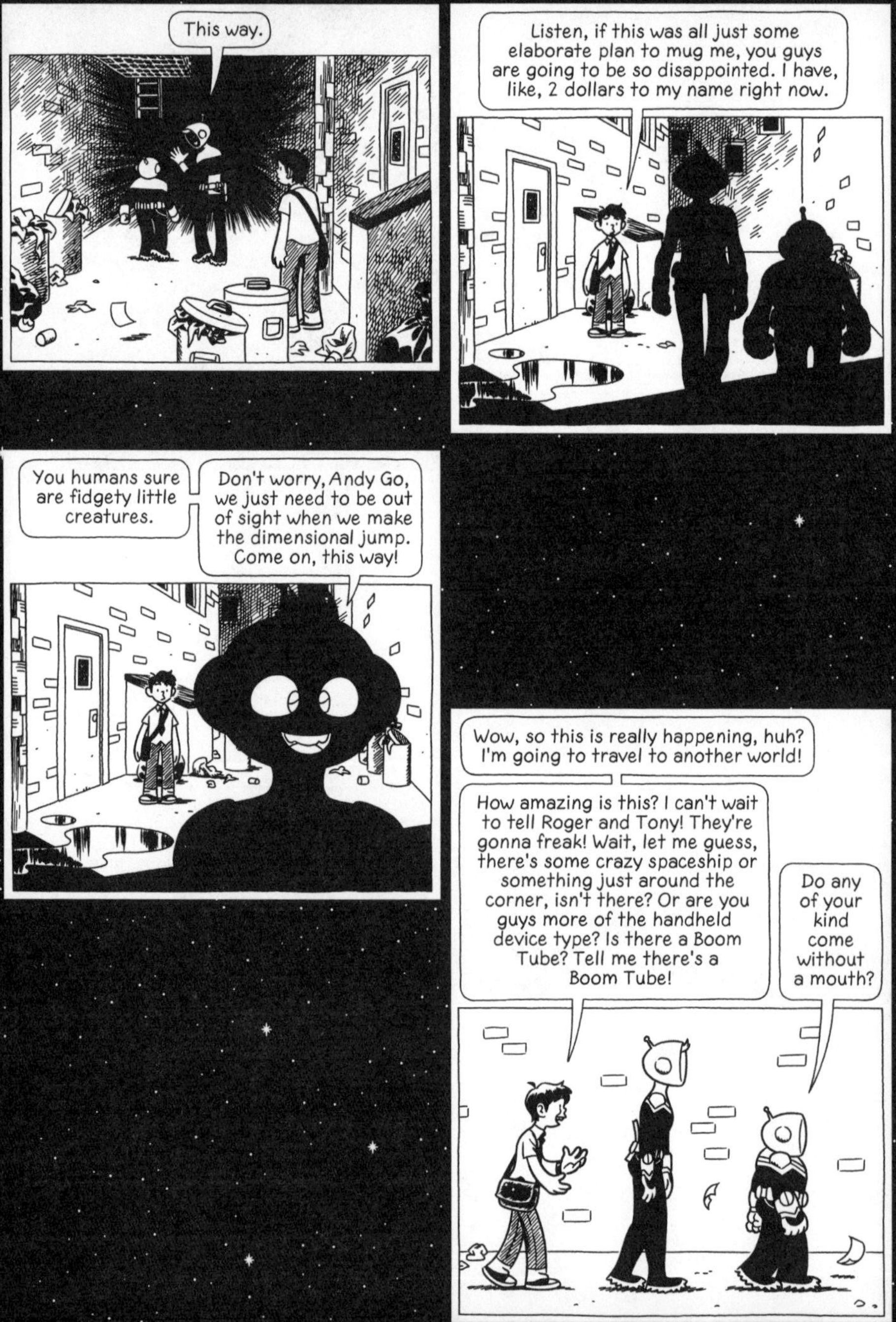

This way.
Listen, if this was all just some elaborate plan to mug me, you guys are going to be so disappointed. I have, like, 2 dollars to my name right now.
You humans sure are fidgety little creatures.
Don't worry, Andy Go, we just need to be out of sight when we make the dimensional jump. Come on, this way!
Wow, so this is really happening, huh? I'm going to travel to another world!
How amazing is this? I can't wait to tell Roger and Tony! They're gonna freak! Wait, let me guess, there's some crazy spaceship or something just around the corner, isn't there? Or are you guys more of the handheld device type? Is there a Boom Tube? Tell me there's a Boom Tube!
Do any of your kind come without a mouth?

Look, you don't know how thrilling this is for me! Back in high school, I spent most of my time dreaming—praying!—that I'd be whisked off to another world. To some fantastical realm—anywhere but where I was. But I never thought it would actually happen!
Believe it or not, you guys are actually fulfilling a childhood dream of mine.
What's "high school"?
Do you know what "hell" is?
Anyway, I don't know what it's like in your dimension, but in our world, we haven't even found alien bacteria yet, let alone intelligent beings that can travel to other universes! Wait till NASA hears about you guys! They're gonna flip out!
Okay, shut up. This is it. You ready?

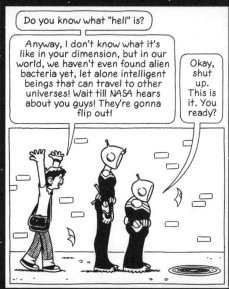

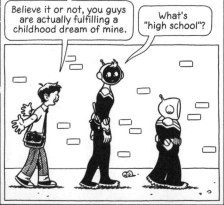

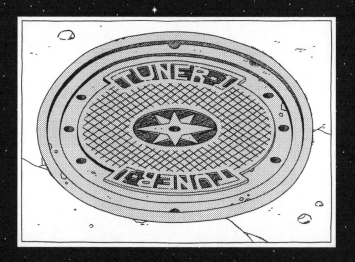

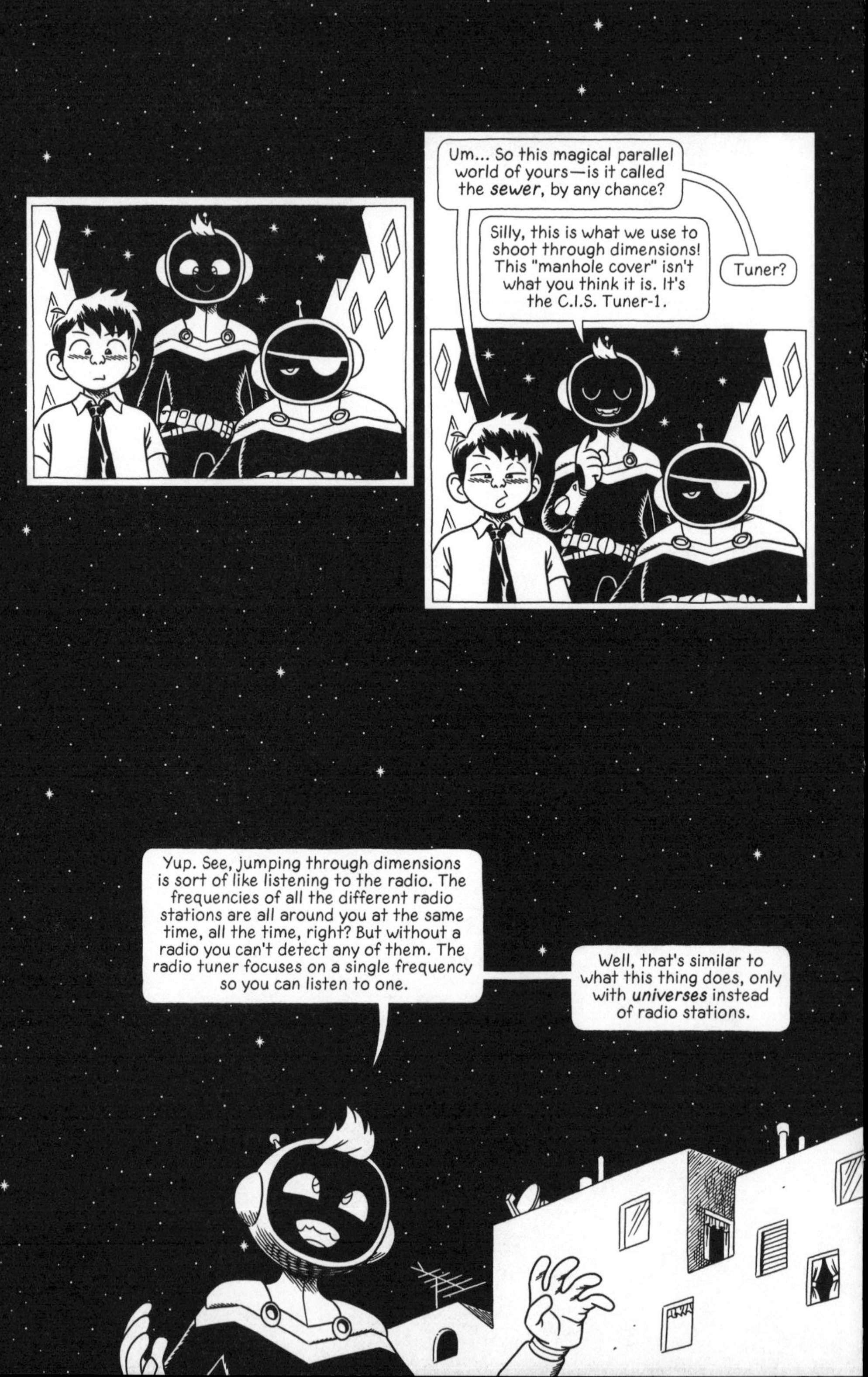

Um... So this magical parallel world of yours—is it called the *sewer*, by any chance?
Silly, this is what we use to shoot through dimensions! This "manhole cover" isn't what you think it is. It's the C.I.S. Tuner-1.
Tuner?
Yup. See, jumping through dimensions is sort of like listening to the radio. The frequencies of all the different radio stations are all around you at the same time, all the time, right? But without a radio you can't detect any of them. The radio tuner focuses on a single frequency so you can listen to one.
Well, that's similar to what this thing does, only with *universes* instead of radio stations.

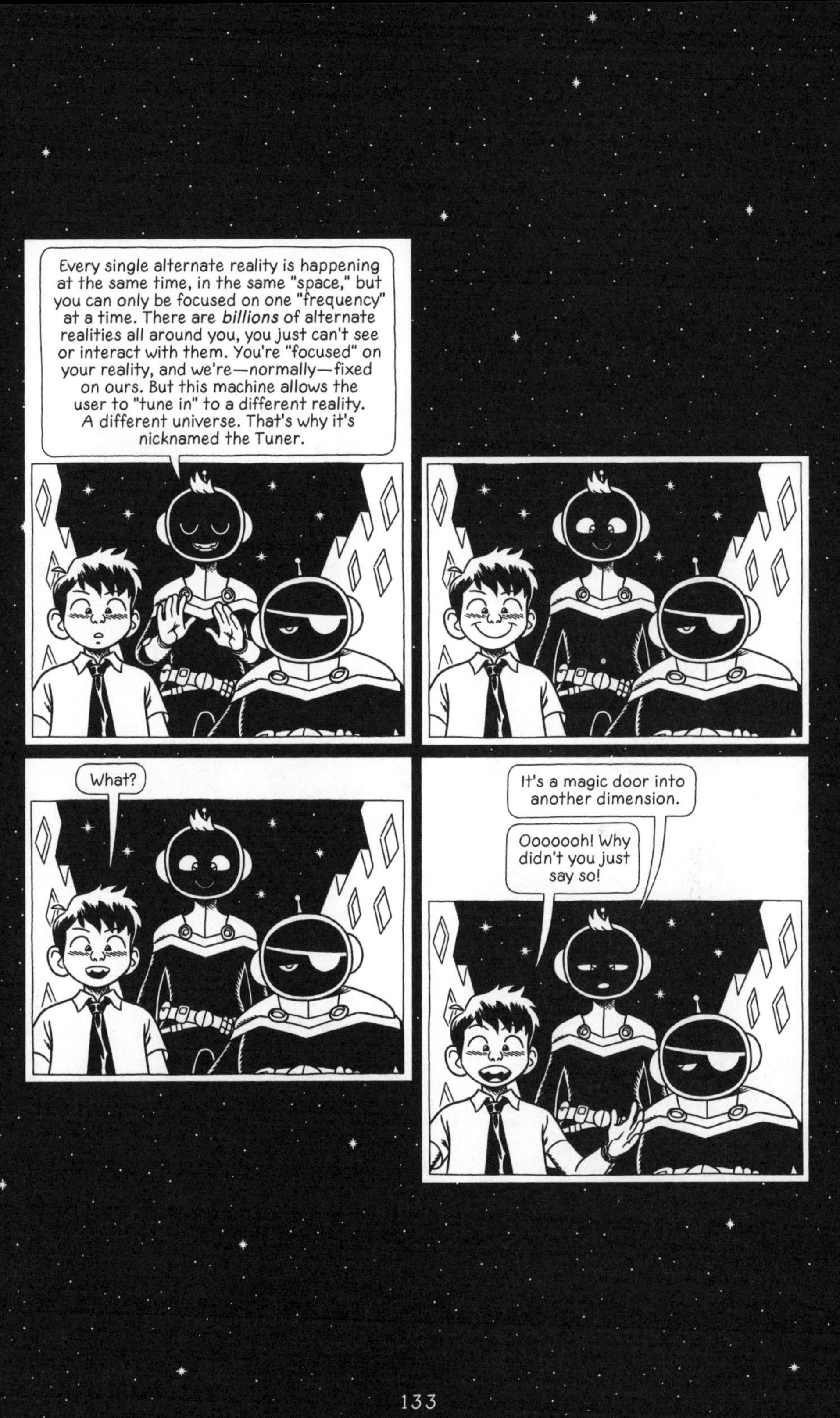

Every single alternate reality is happening at the same time, in the same "space," but you can only be focused on one "frequency" at a time. There are *billions* of alternate realities all around you, you just can't see or interact with them. You're "focused" on your reality, and we're—normally—fixed on ours. But this machine allows the user to "tune in" to a different reality. A different universe. That's why it's nicknamed the Tuner.
What?
It's a magic door into another dimension.
Ooooooh! Why didn't you just say so!

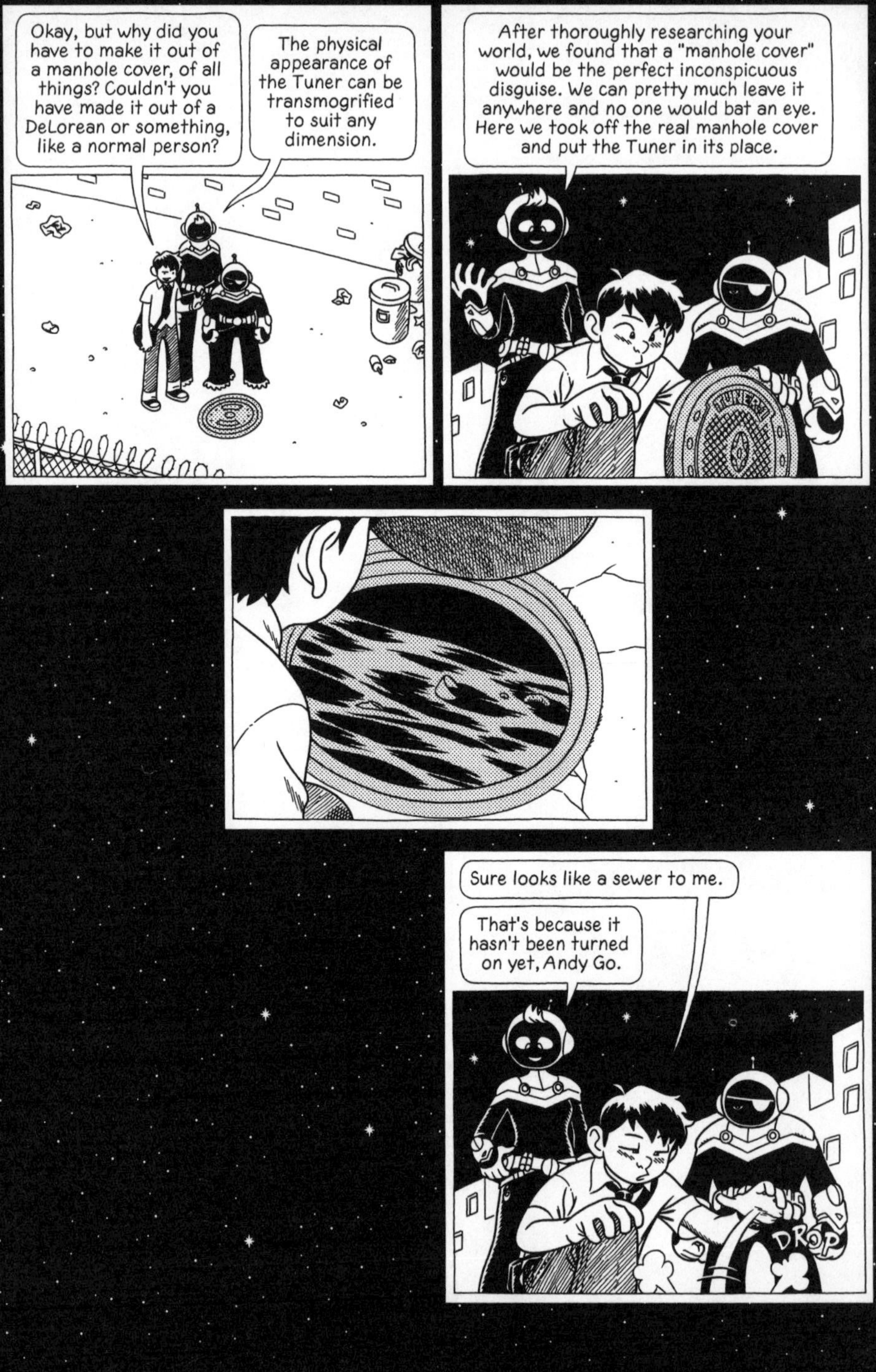
Okay, but why did you have to make it out of a manhole cover, of all things? Couldn't you have made it out of a DeLorean or something, like a normal person?
The physical appearance of the Tuner can be transmogrified to suit any dimension.
After thoroughly researching your world, we found that a "manhole cover" would be the perfect inconspicuous disguise. We can pretty much leave it anywhere and no one would bat an eye. Here we took off the real manhole cover and put the Tuner in its place.
TUNER
Sure looks like a sewer to me.
That's because it hasn't been turned on yet, Andy Go.
DROP

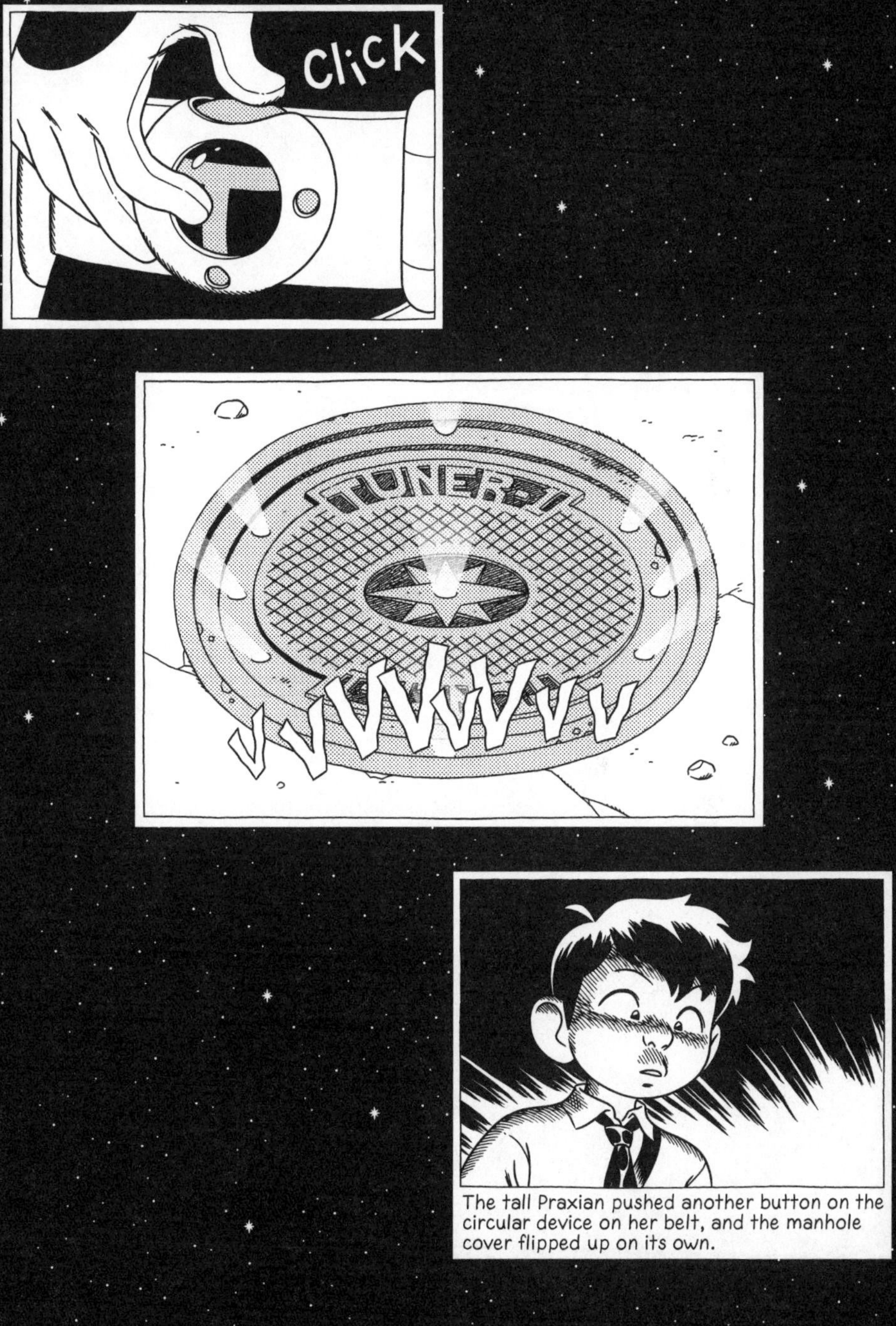
Click
The tall Praxian pushed another button on the circular device on her belt, and the manhole cover flipped up on its own.

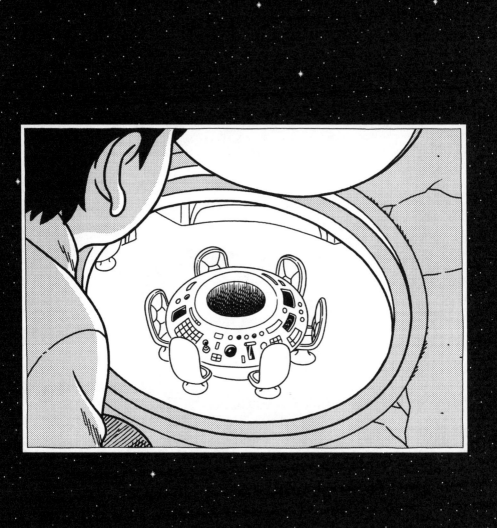

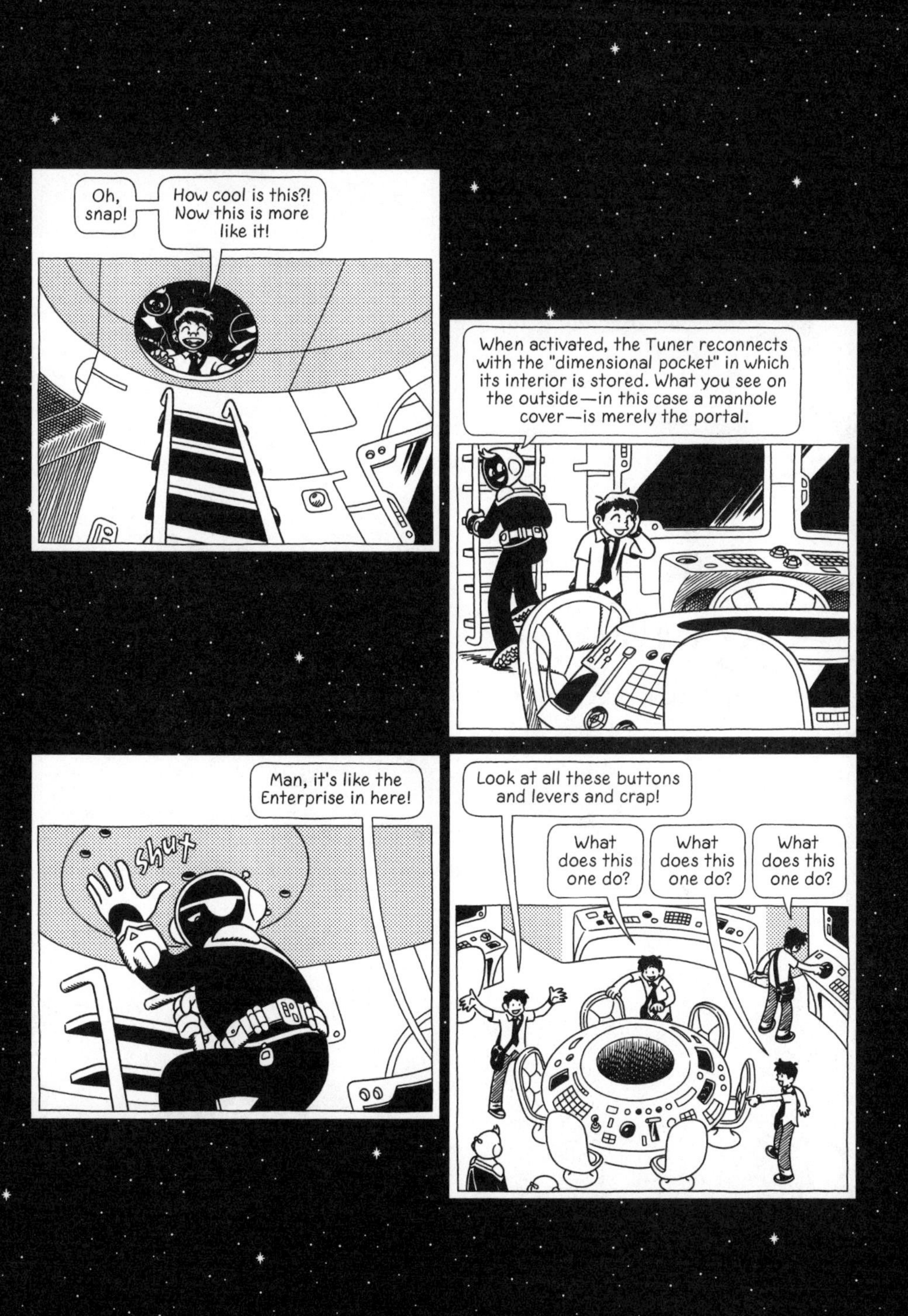
Oh, snap!
How cool is this?! Now this is more like it!
When activated, the Tuner reconnects with the "dimensional pocket" in which its interior is stored. What you see on the outside—in this case a manhole cover—is merely the portal.
Man, it's like the Enterprise in here!
shut
Look at all these buttons and levers and crap!
What does this one do?
What does this one do?
What does this one do?

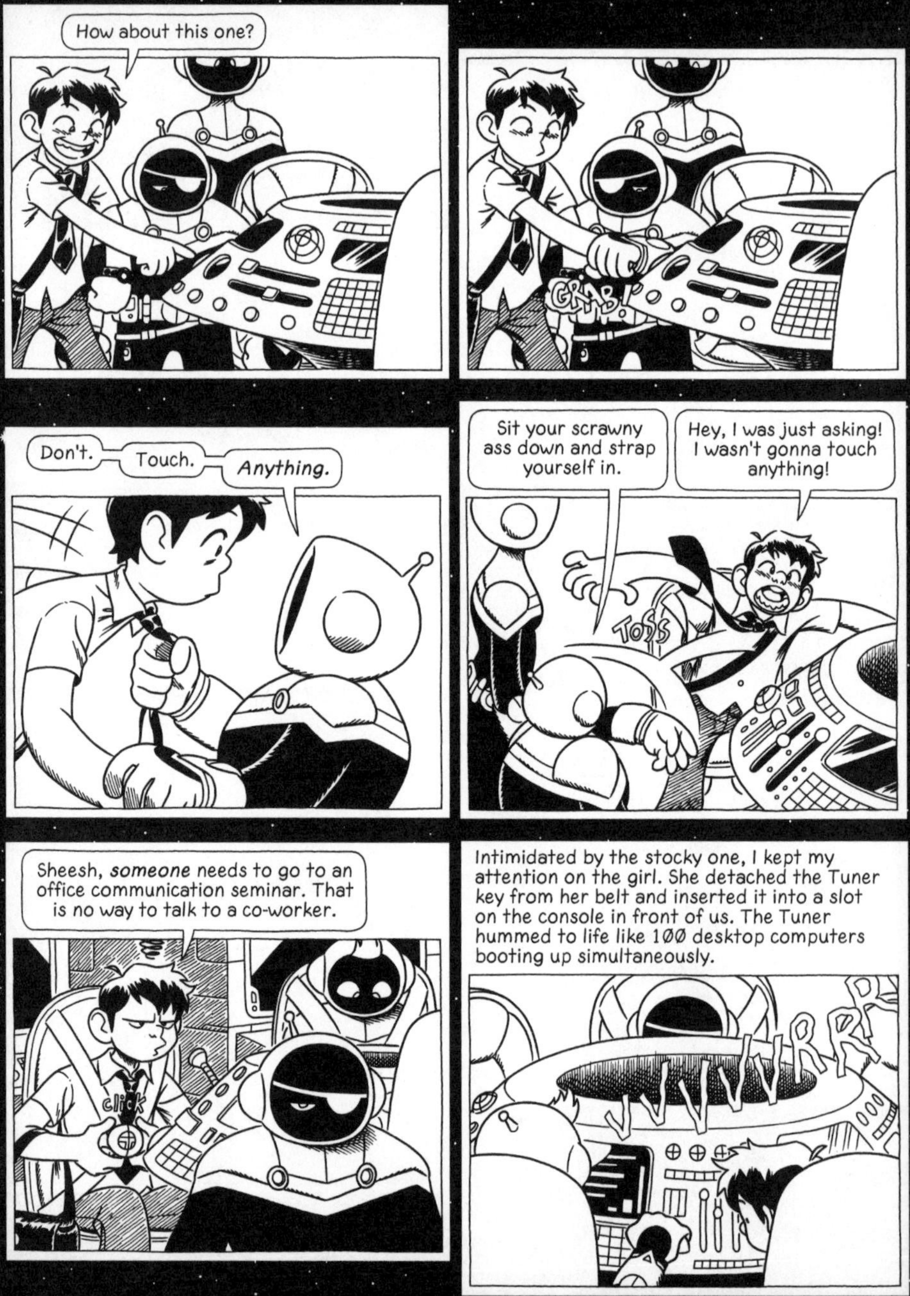
How about this one?
GRAB!
Don't. Touch. Anything.
Sit your scrawny ass down and strap yourself in.
Hey, I was just asking! I wasn't gonna touch anything!
TOSS
Sheesh, *someone* needs to go to an office communication seminar. That is no way to talk to a co-worker.
click
Intimidated by the stocky one, I kept my attention on the girl. She detached the Tuner key from her belt and inserted it into a slot on the console in front of us. The Tuner hummed to life like 100 desktop computers booting up simultaneously.
VVVVVRRR

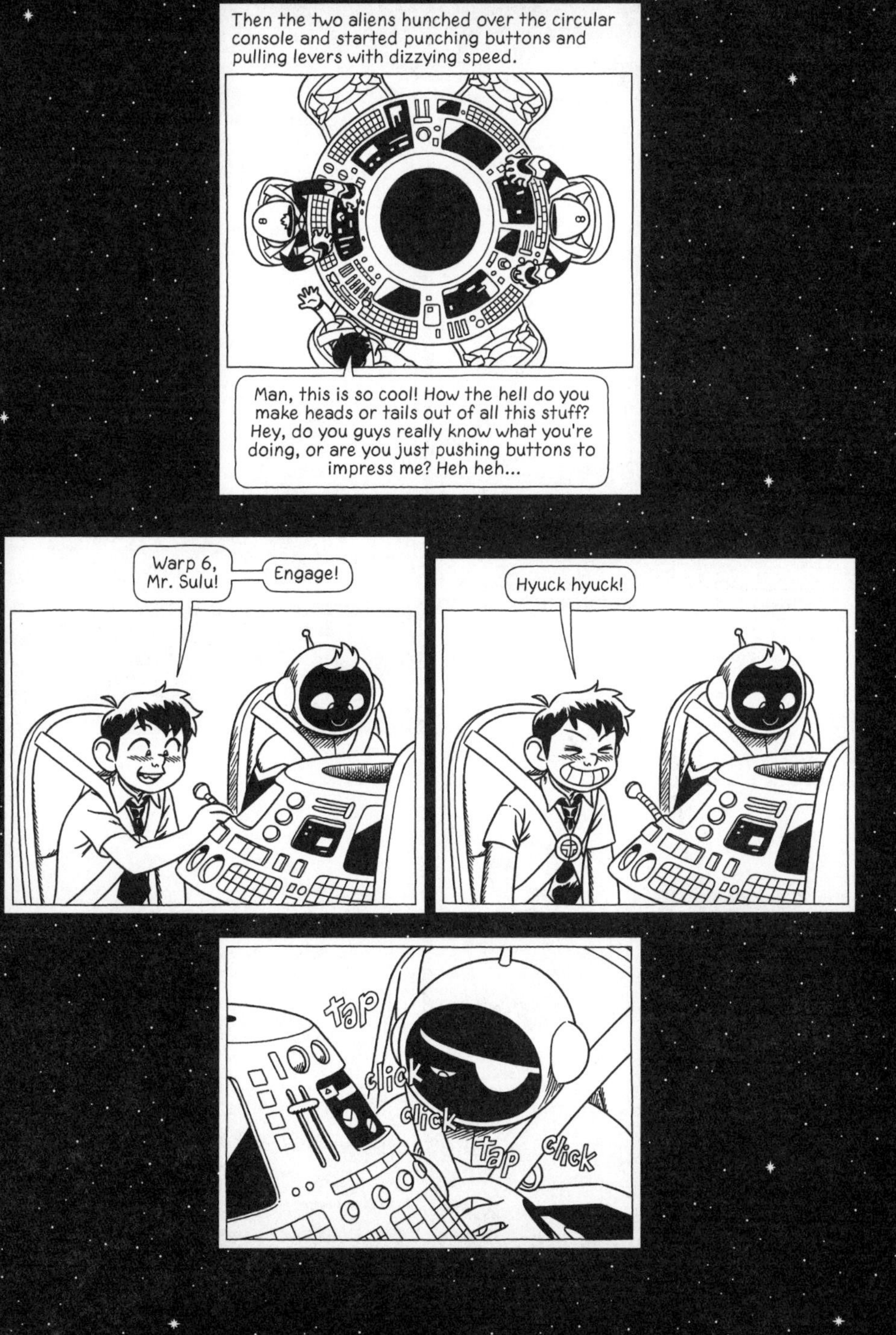
Then the two aliens hunched over the circular console and started punching buttons and pulling levers with dizzying speed.
Man, this is so cool! How the hell do you make heads or tails out of all this stuff? Hey, do you guys really know what you're doing, or are you just pushing buttons to impress me? Heh heh...
Warp 6, Mr. Sulu!
Engage!
Hyuck hyuck!
tap
click
click
tap
click

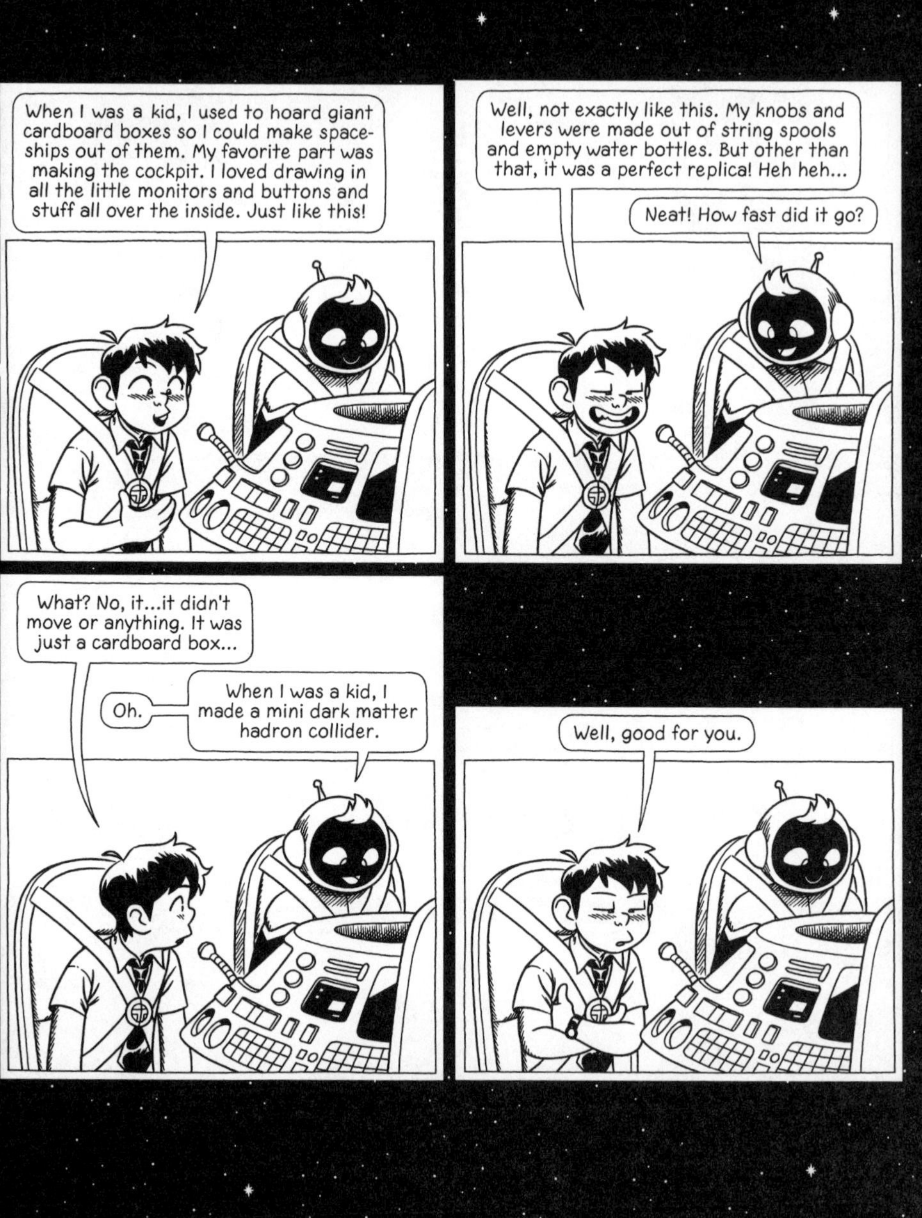
When I was a kid, I used to hoard giant cardboard boxes so I could make spaceships out of them. My favorite part was making the cockpit. I loved drawing in all the little monitors and buttons and stuff all over the inside. Just like this!
Well, not exactly like this. My knobs and levers were made out of string spools and empty water bottles. But other than that, it was a perfect replica! Heh heh...
Neat! How fast did it go?
What? No, it...it didn't move or anything. It was just a cardboard box...
Oh.
When I was a kid, I made a mini dark matter hadron collider.
Well, good for you.

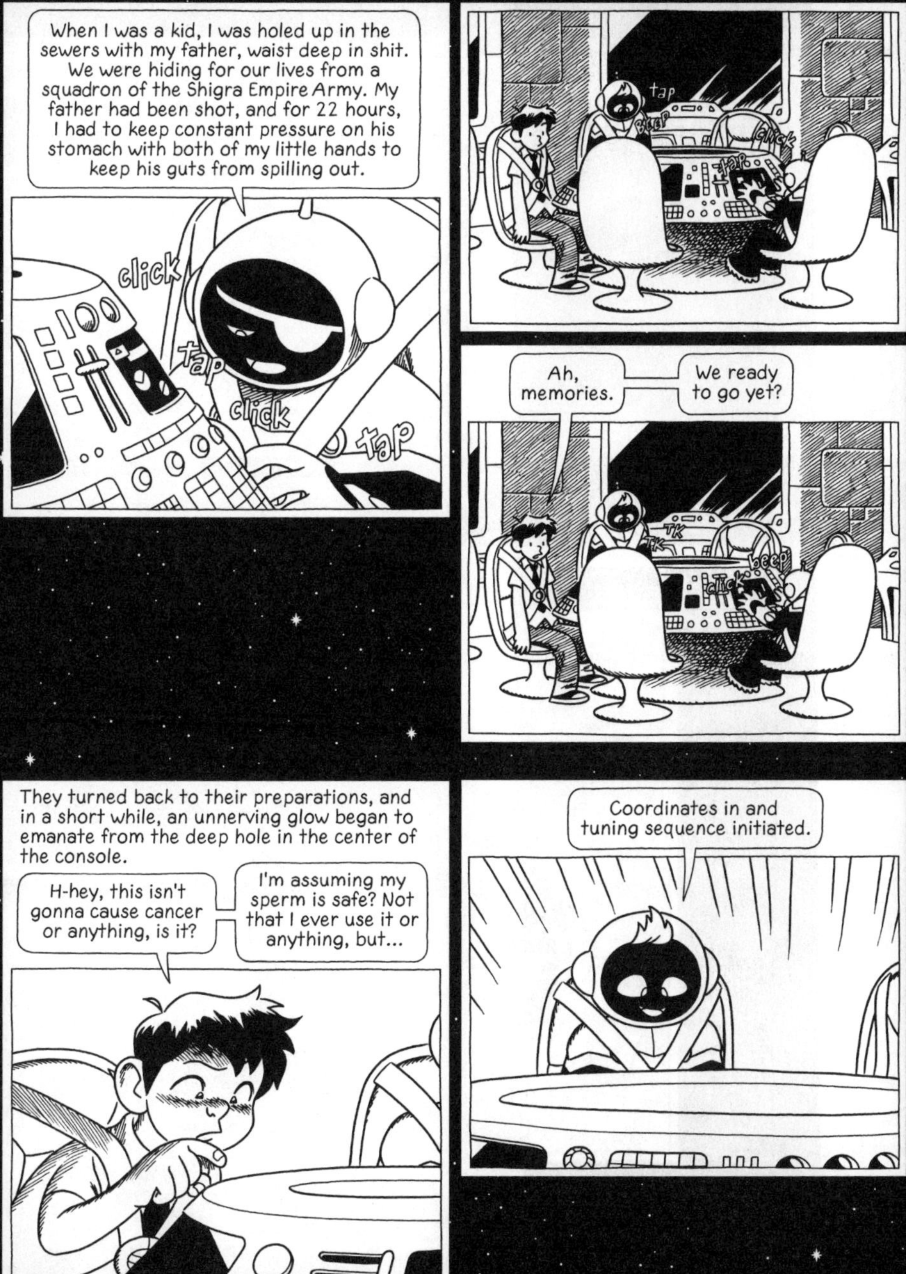
When I was a kid, I was holed up in the sewers with my father, waist deep in shit. We were hiding for our lives from a squadron of the Shigra Empire Army. My father had been shot, and for 22 hours, I had to keep constant pressure on his stomach with both of my little hands to keep his guts from spilling out.
click
tap
click
tap
tap
beep
click
tap
Ah, memories.
We ready to go yet?
TK
TK
click
beep
They turned back to their preparations, and in a short while, an unnerving glow began to emanate from the deep hole in the center of the console.
H-hey, this isn't gonna cause cancer or anything, is it?
I'm assuming my sperm is safe? Not that I ever use it or anything, but...
Coordinates in and tuning sequence initiated.

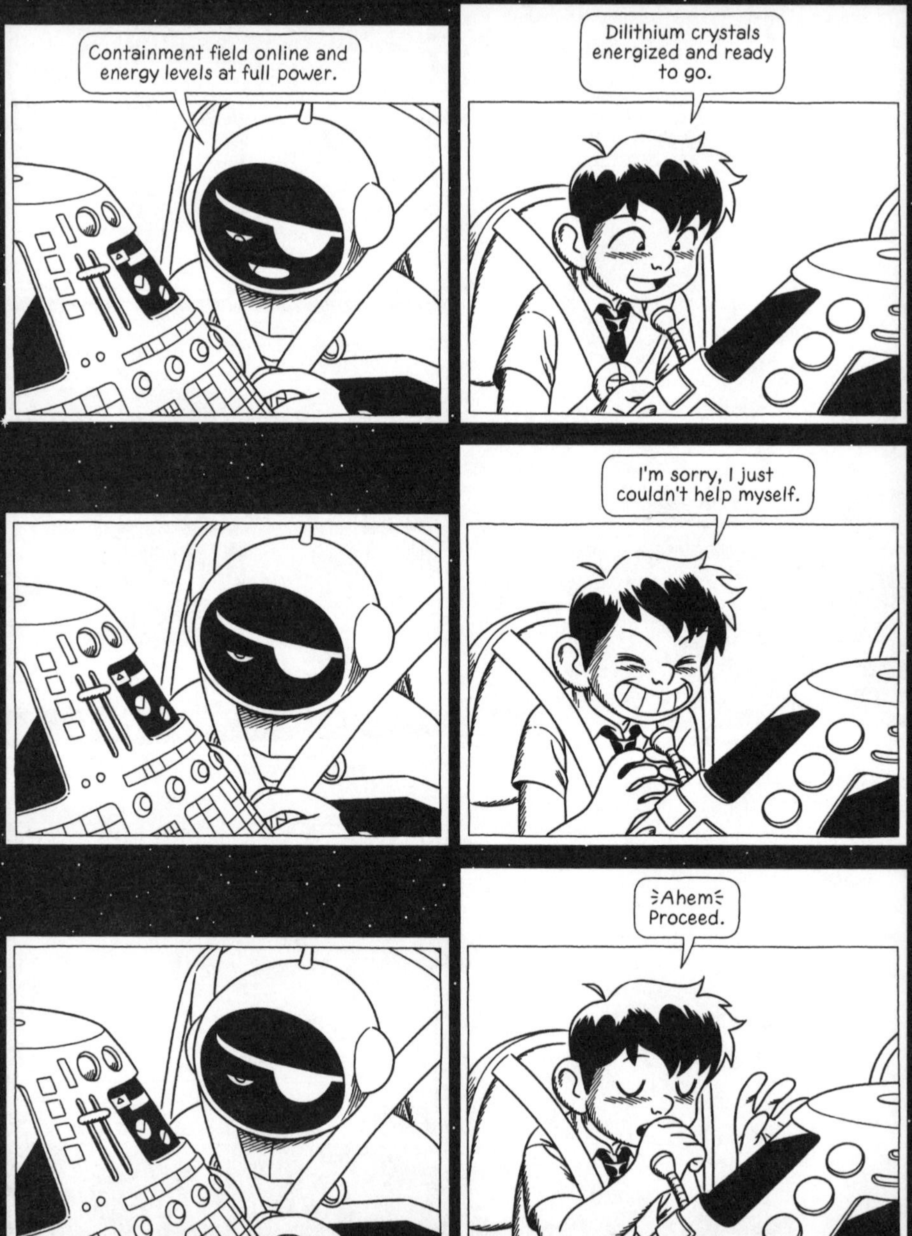
Containment field online and energy levels at full power.
Dilithium crystals energized and ready to go.
I'm sorry, I just couldn't help myself.
Ahem
Proceed.

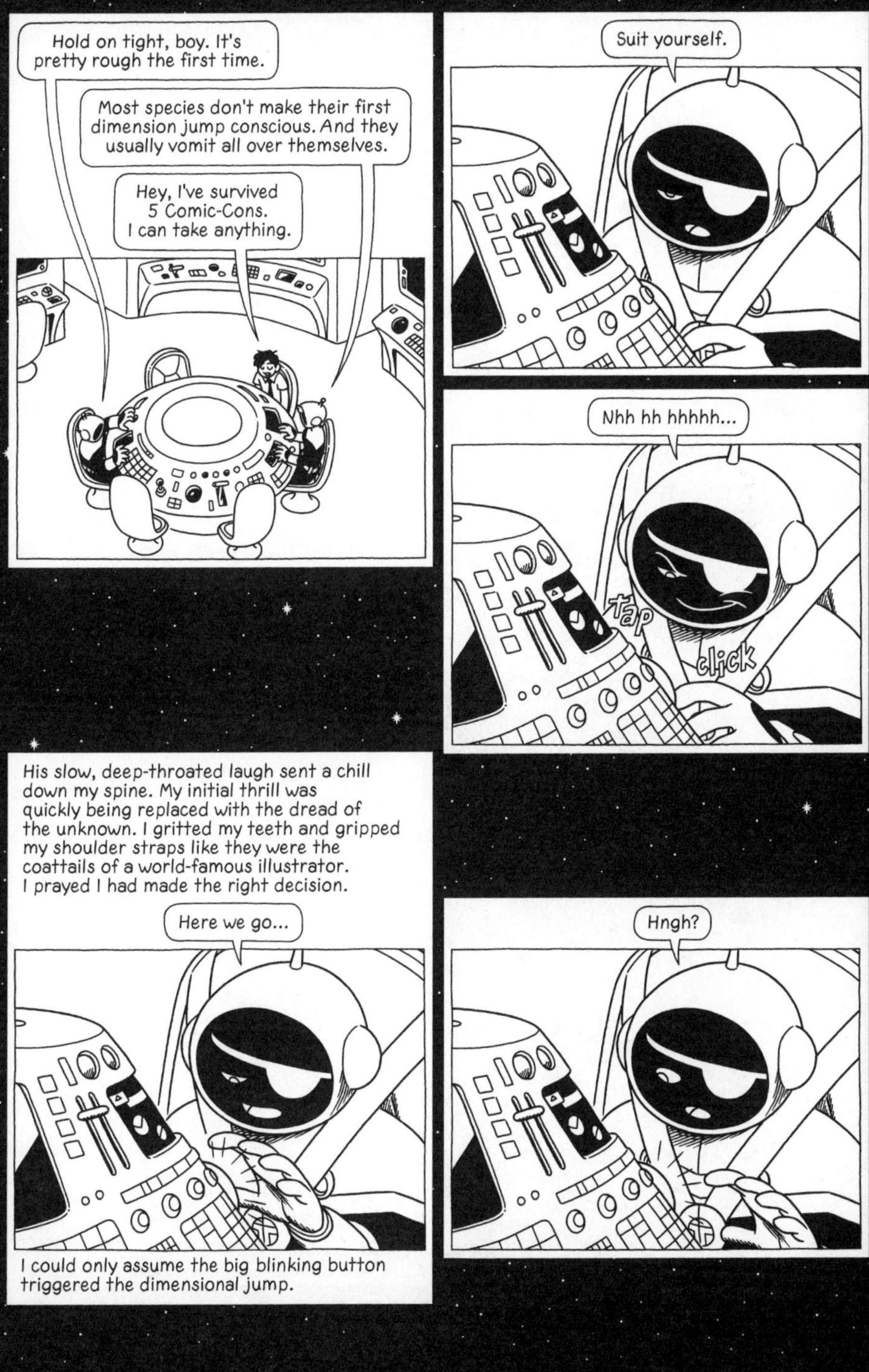

Hold on tight, boy. It's pretty rough the first time.
Most species don't make their first dimension jump conscious. And they usually vomit all over themselves.
Hey, I've survived 5 Comic-Cons. I can take anything.
Suit yourself.
Nhh hh hhhhh...
tap
click
His slow, deep-throated laugh sent a chill down my spine. My initial thrill was quickly being replaced with the dread of the unknown. I gritted my teeth and gripped my shoulder straps like they were the coattails of a world-famous illustrator. I prayed I had made the right decision.
Here we go...
I could only assume the big blinking button triggered the dimensional jump.
Hngh?

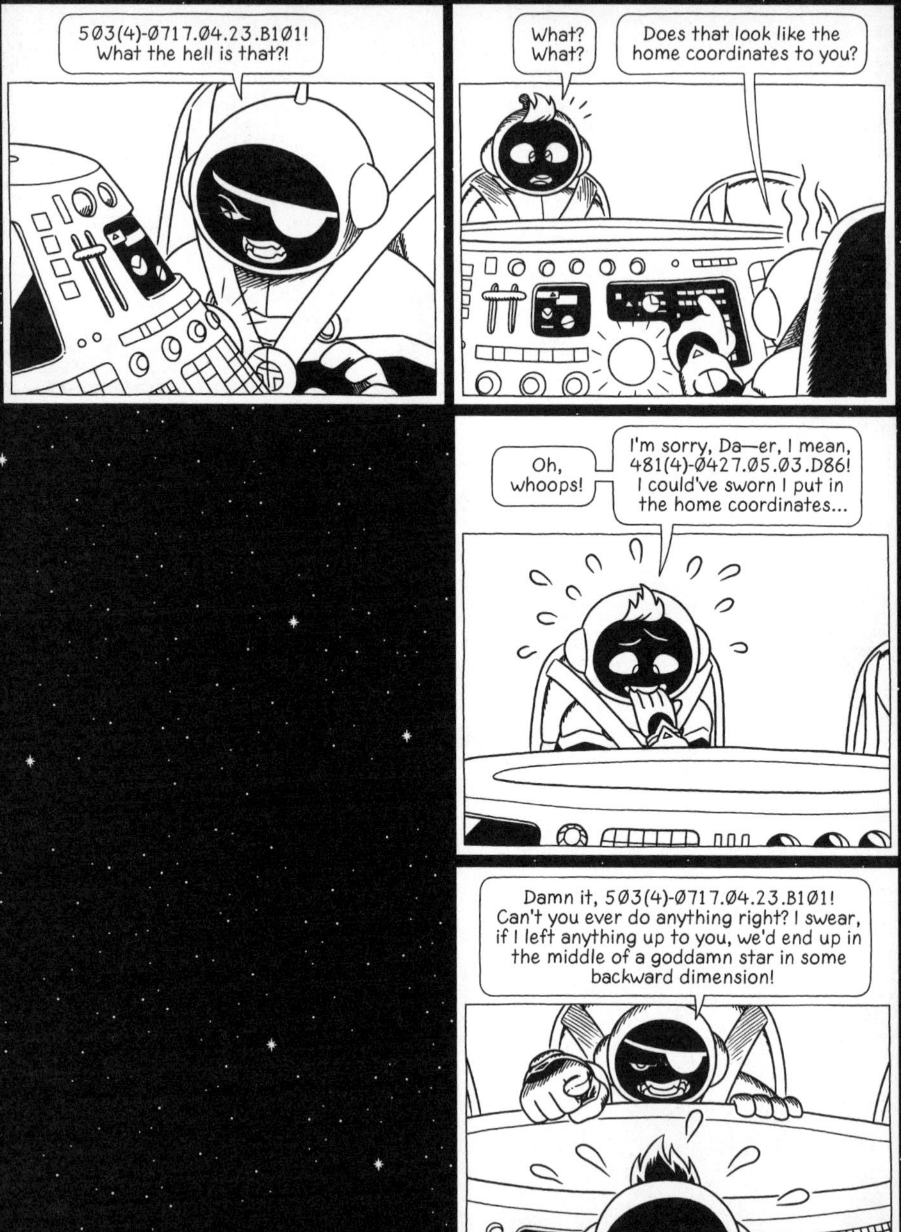

5Ø3(4)-Ø717.Ø4.23.B1Ø1! What the hell is that?!
What? What?
Does that look like the home coordinates to you?
Oh, whoops!
I'm sorry, Da—er, I mean, 481(4)-Ø427.Ø5.Ø3.D86! I could've sworn I put in the home coordinates...
Damn it, 5Ø3(4)-Ø717.Ø4.23.B1Ø1! Can't you ever do anything right? I swear, if I left anything up to you, we'd end up in the middle of a goddamn star in some backward dimension!

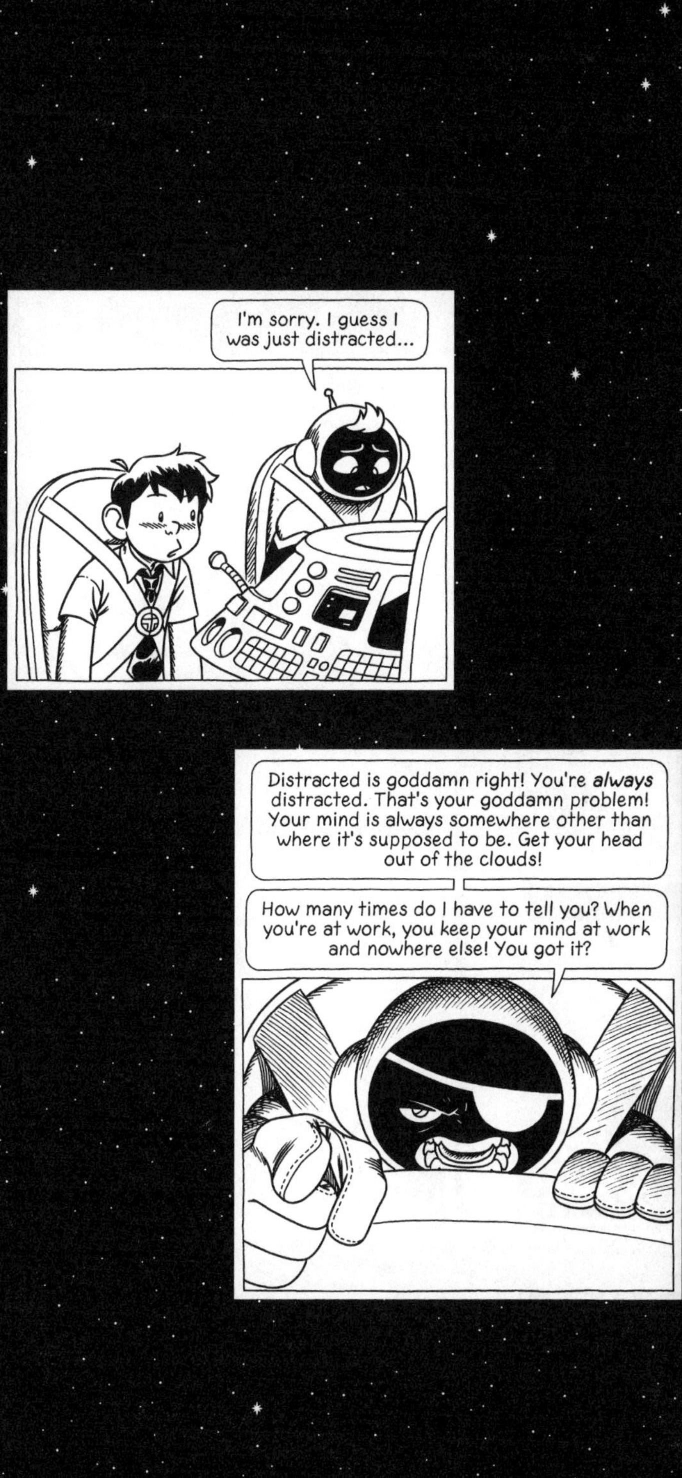

I'm sorry. I guess I was just distracted...
Distracted is goddamn right! You're *always* distracted. That's your goddamn problem! Your mind is always somewhere other than where it's supposed to be. Get your head out of the clouds!
How many times do I have to tell you? When you're at work, you keep your mind at work and nowhere else! You got it?

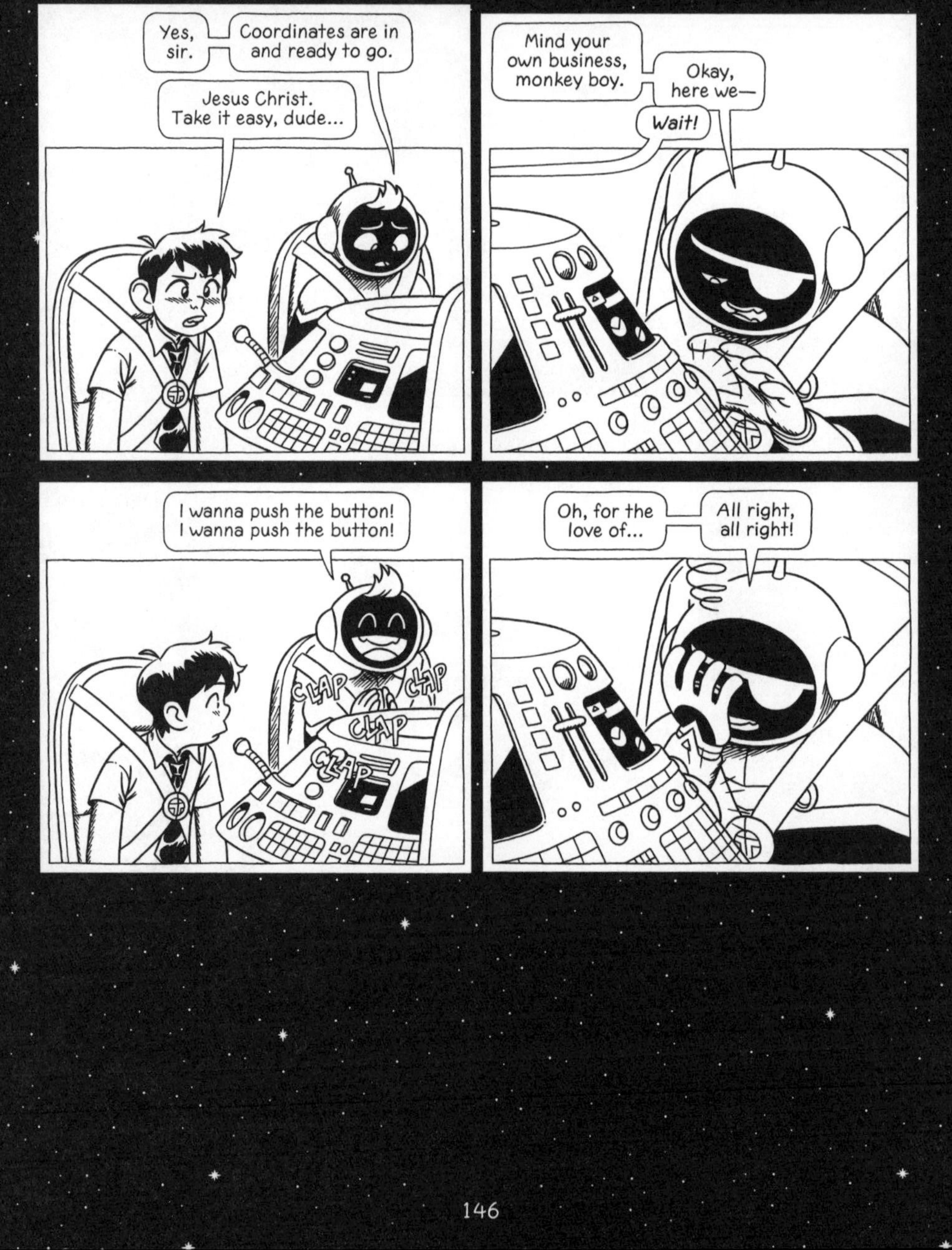
Yes, sir.
Coordinates are in and ready to go.
Jesus Christ. Take it easy, dude...
Mind your own business, monkey boy.
Okay, here we—
Wait!
I wanna push the button! I wanna push the button!
CLAP CLAP CLAP CLAP
Oh, for the love of...
All right, all right!

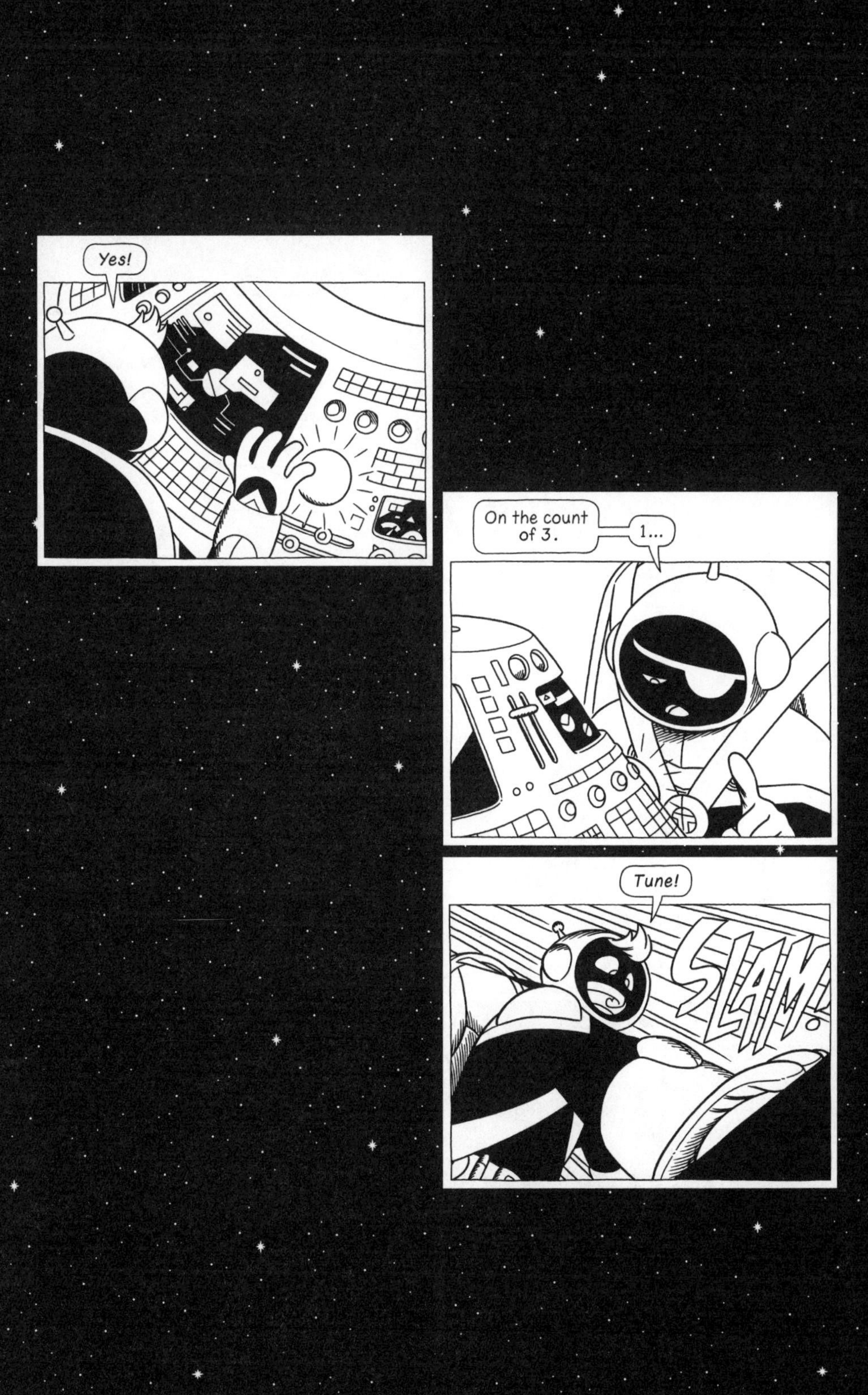
Yes!
On the count of 3.
1...
Tune!
SLAM!

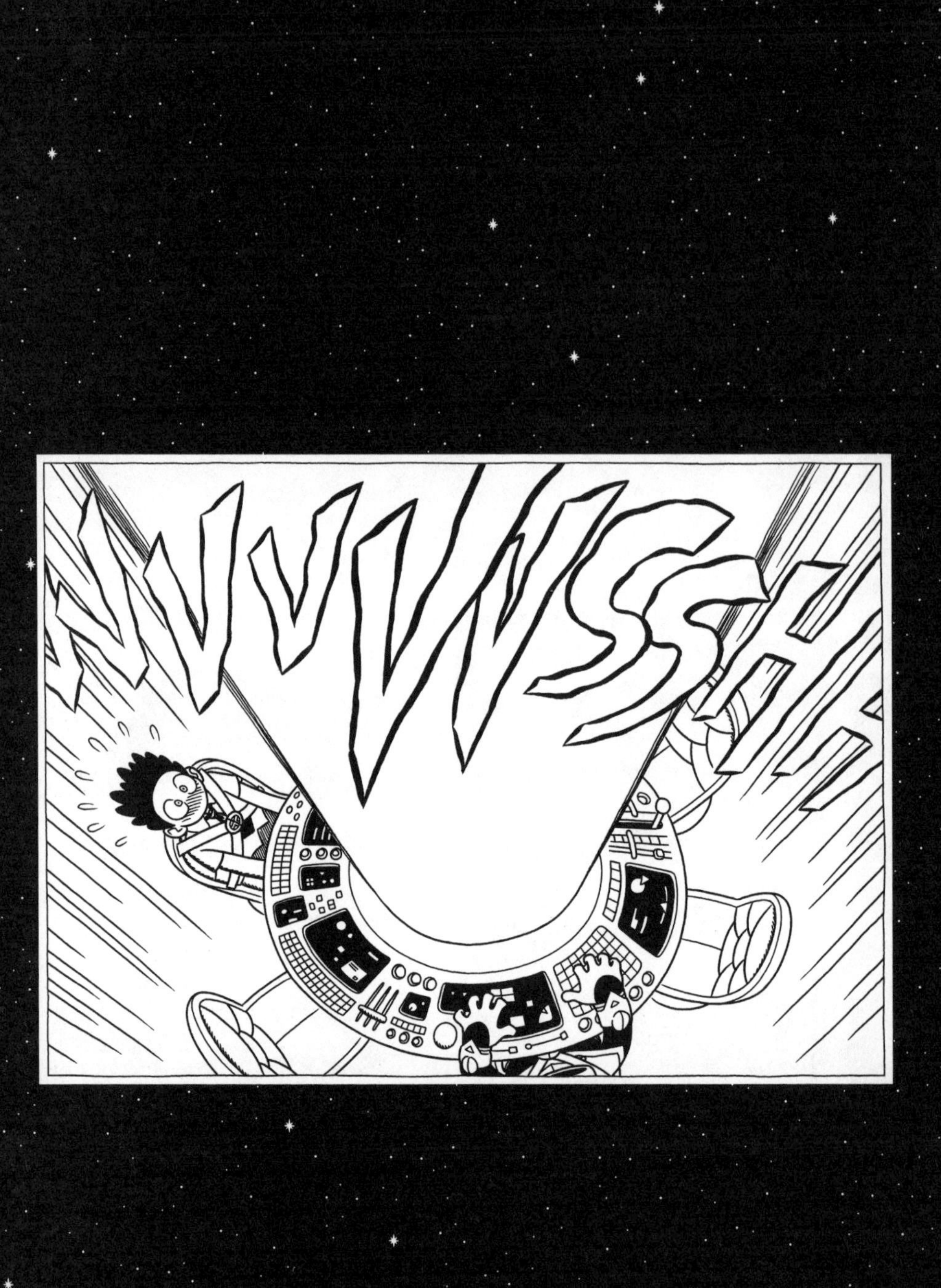

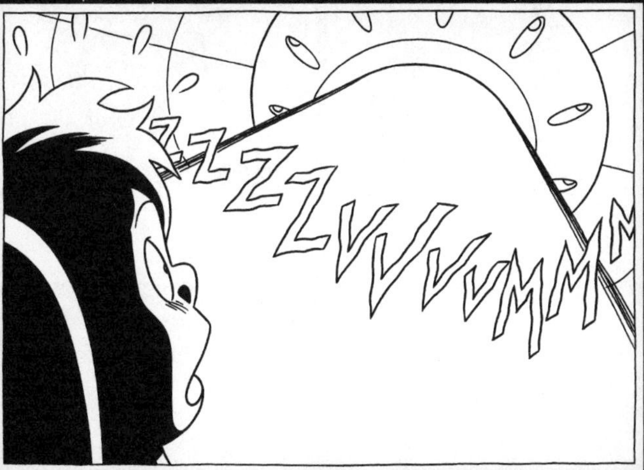
ZZZZVVVVMMM

I nearly had a heart attack, and, for a second, I thought I might be fried. But the pylon of energy didn't radiate any heat, only a pulsating, purplish-white light and a deep drone that smothered all other sounds.

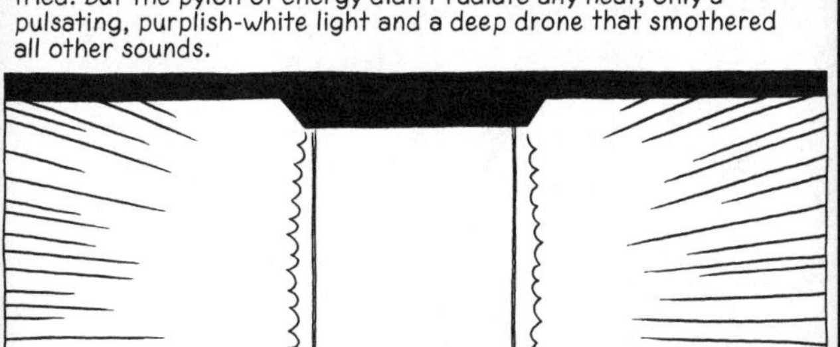

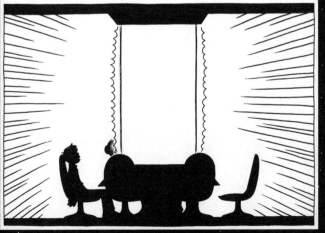

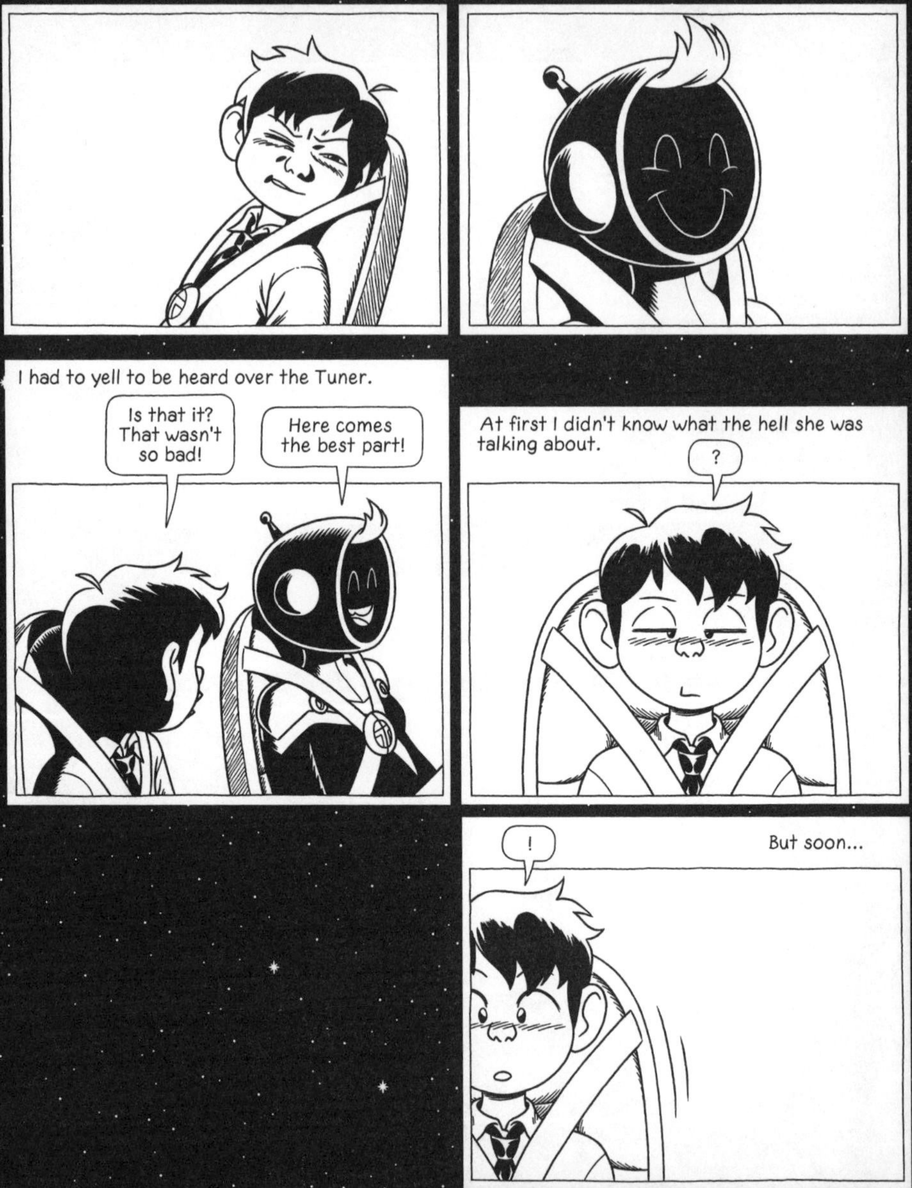
I had to yell to be heard over the Tuner.
Is that it? That wasn't so bad!
Here comes the best part!
At first I didn't know what the hell she was talking about.
?
!
But soon...

...I realized everything was slowly moving in a big circle.

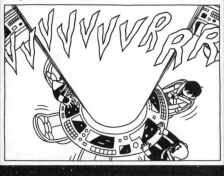

The column of energy was an axis on which the entire room was spinning!

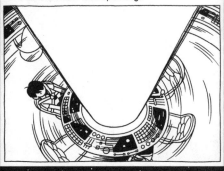

The momentum was building exponentially, and soon we were spinning alarmingly fast.

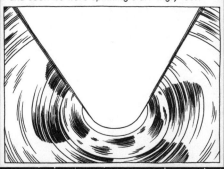

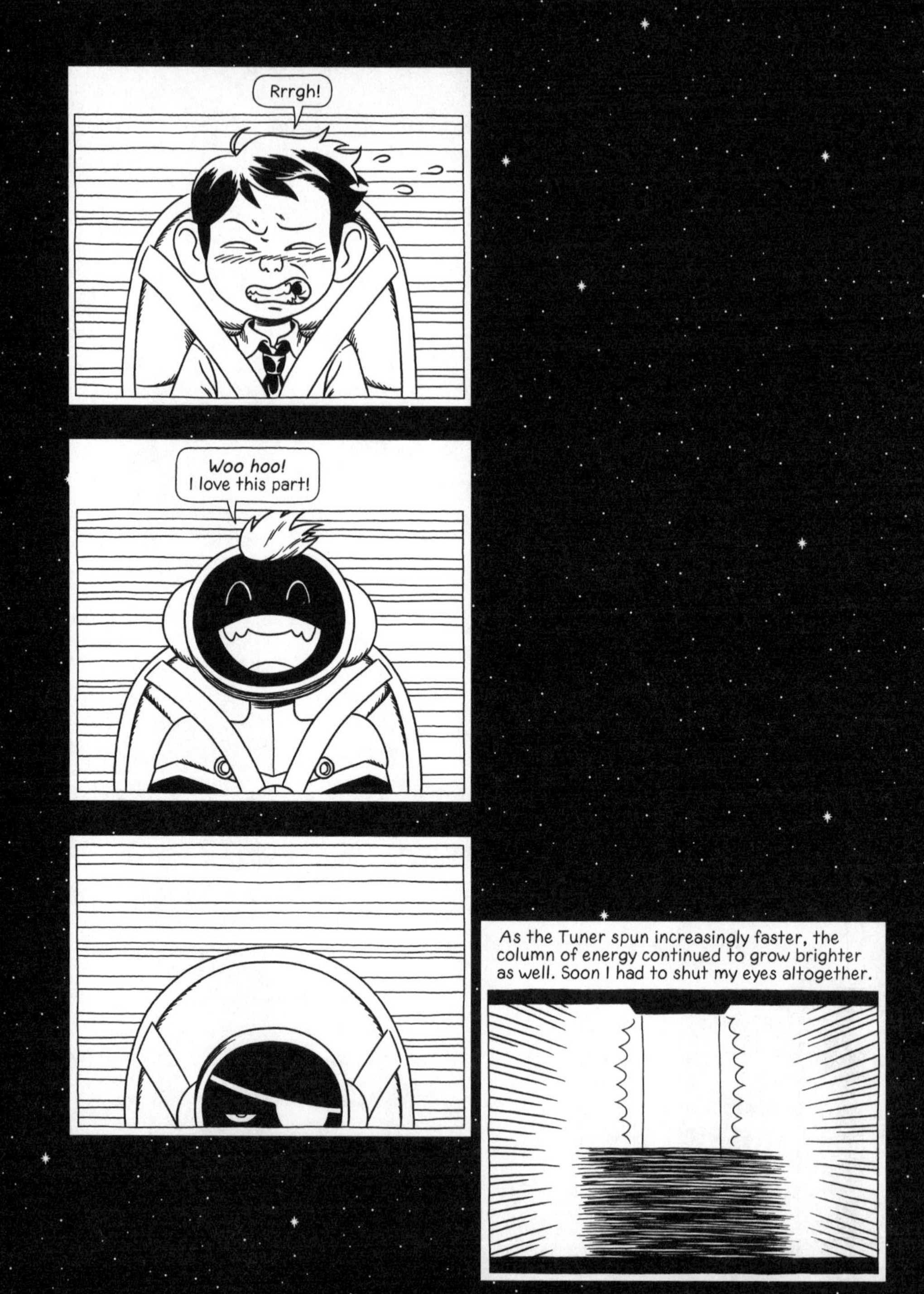
Rrrgh!
Woo hoo! I love this part!
As the Tuner spun increasingly faster, the column of energy continued to grow brighter as well. Soon I had to shut my eyes altogether.

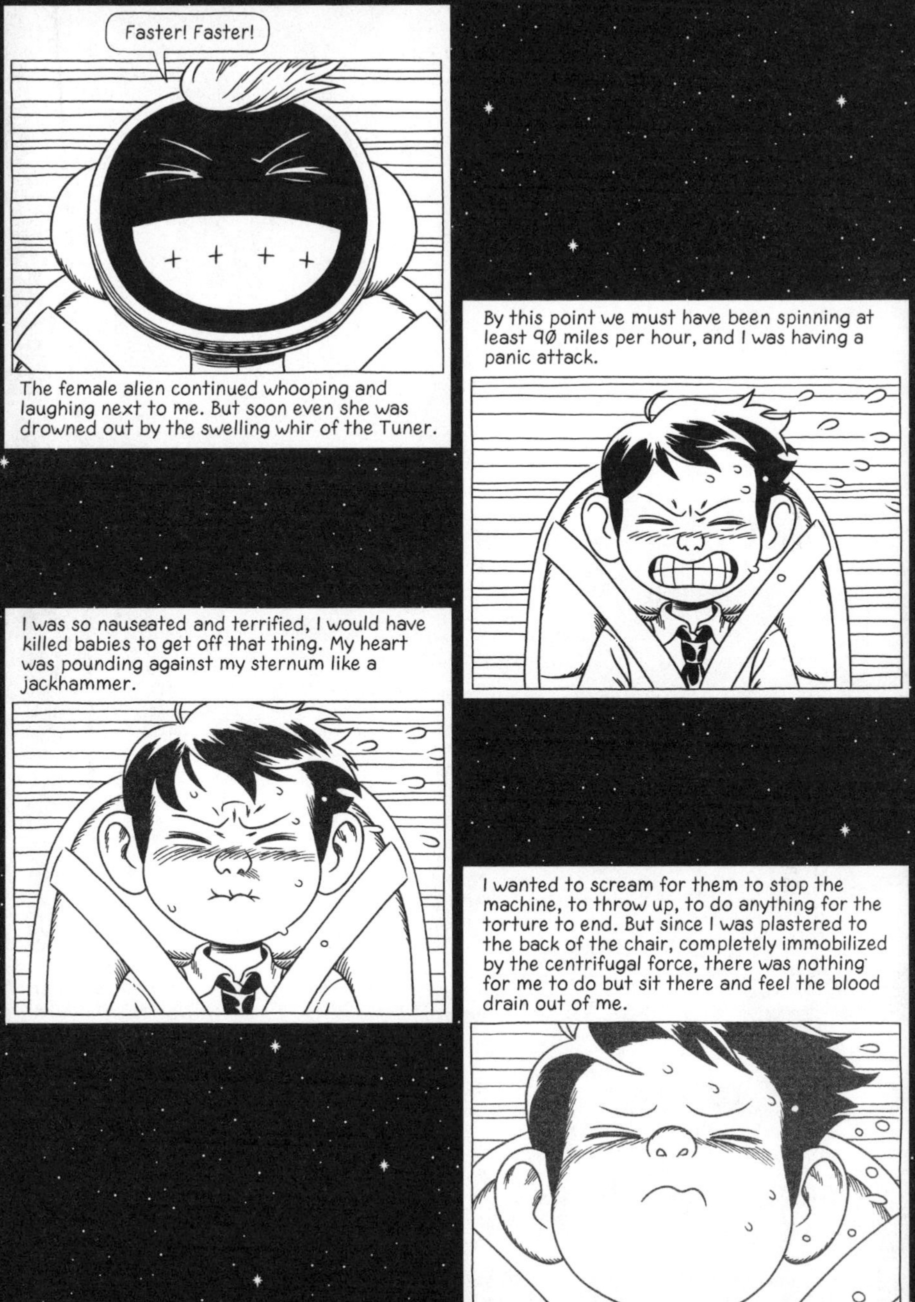
Faster! Faster!
The female alien continued whooping and laughing next to me. But soon even she was drowned out by the swelling whir of the Tuner.
By this point we must have been spinning at least 90 miles per hour, and I was having a panic attack.
I was so nauseated and terrified, I would have killed babies to get off that thing. My heart was pounding against my sternum like a jackhammer.
I wanted to scream for them to stop the machine, to throw up, to do anything for the torture to end. But since I was plastered to the back of the chair, completely immobilized by the centrifugal force, there was nothing for me to do but sit there and feel the blood drain out of me.

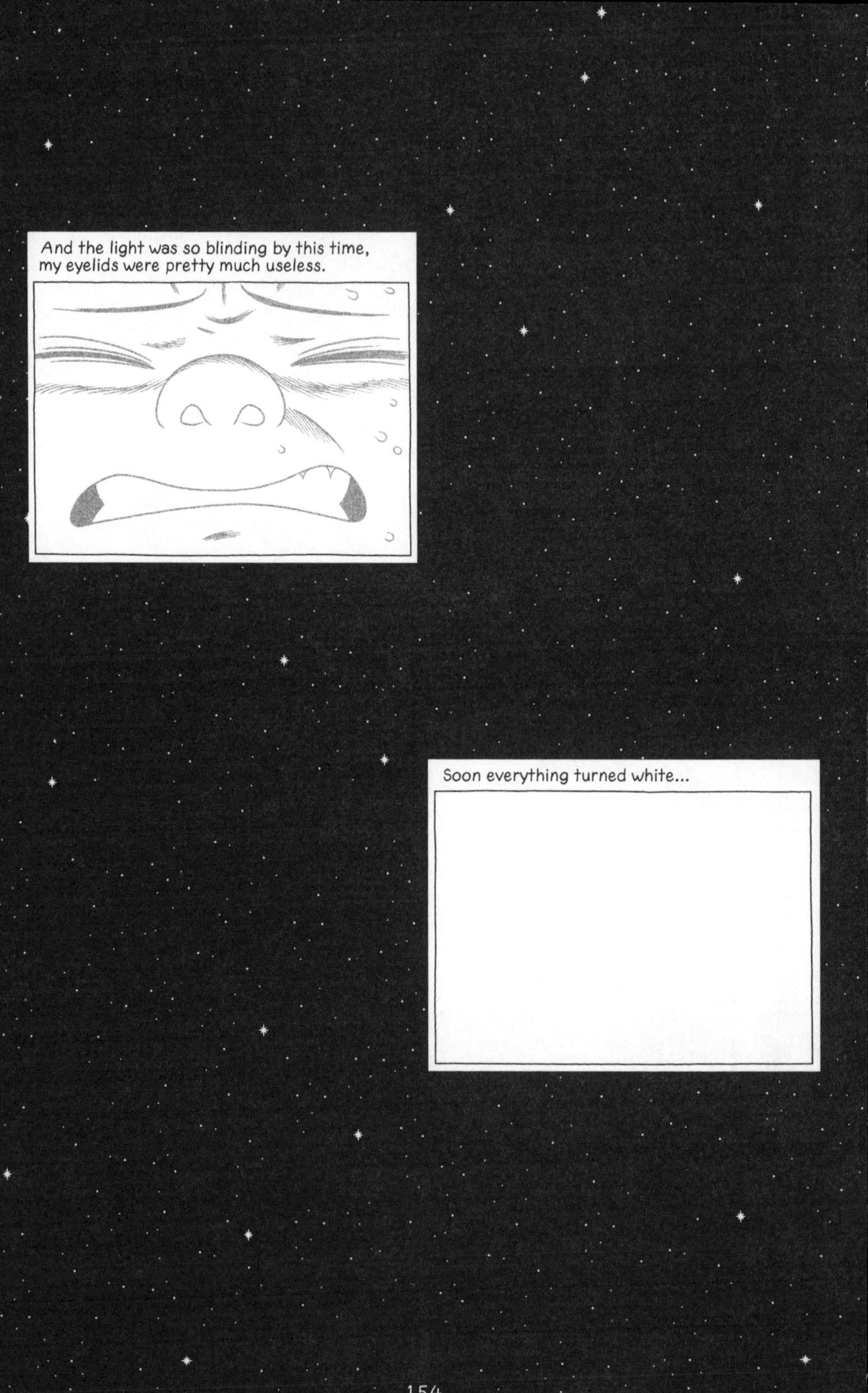
And the light was so blinding by this time, my eyelids were pretty much useless.
Soon everything turned white...

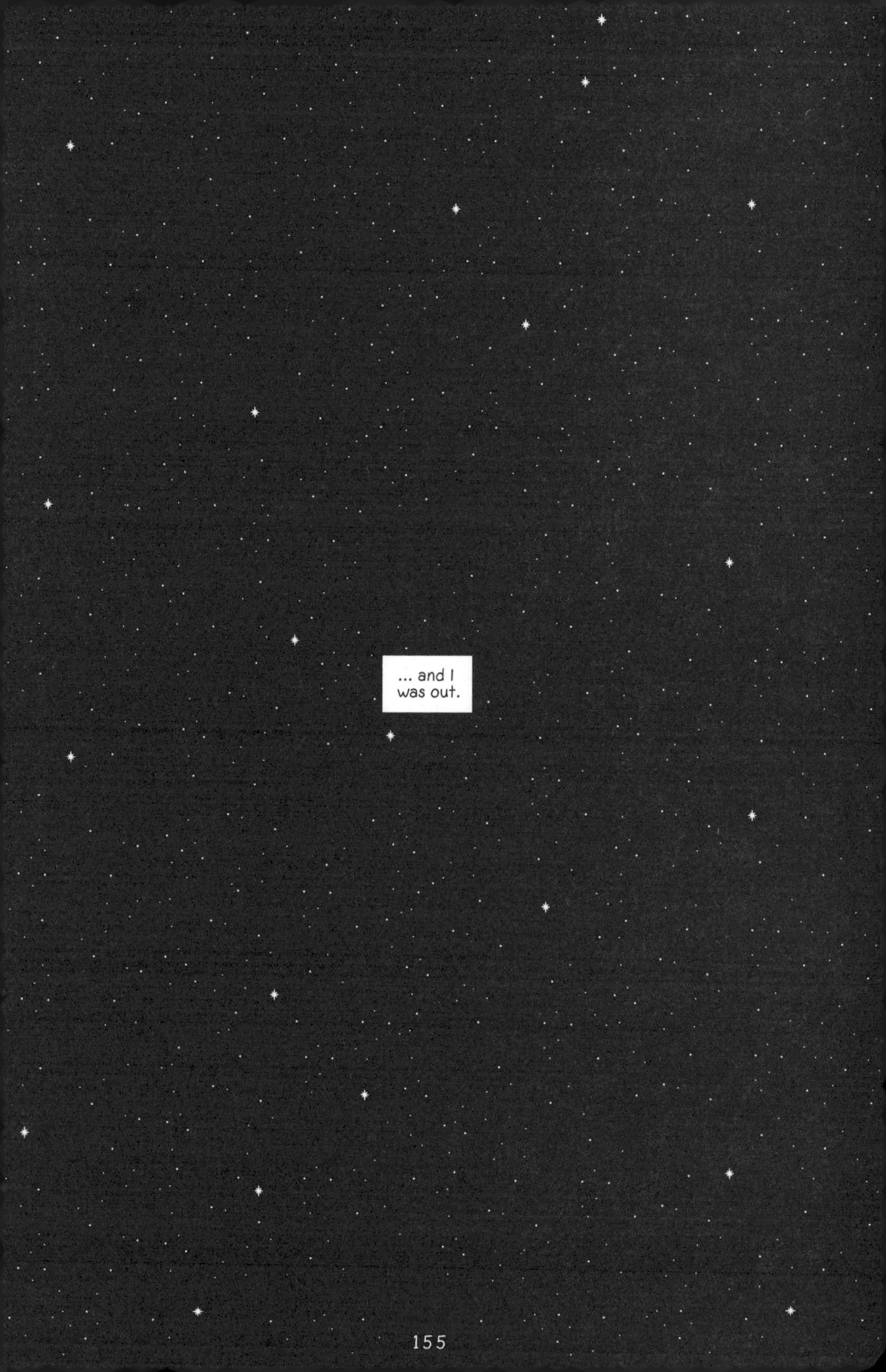
... and I was out.

TO be continued...

www.tunecomic.com